...ewmarket.

...ce (1st load).

@ Newmarket.

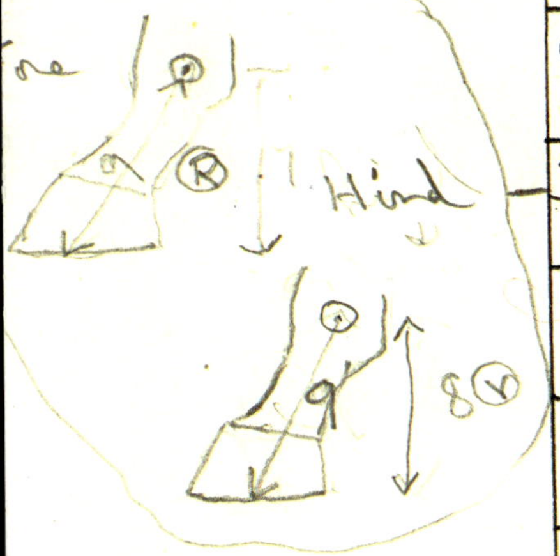

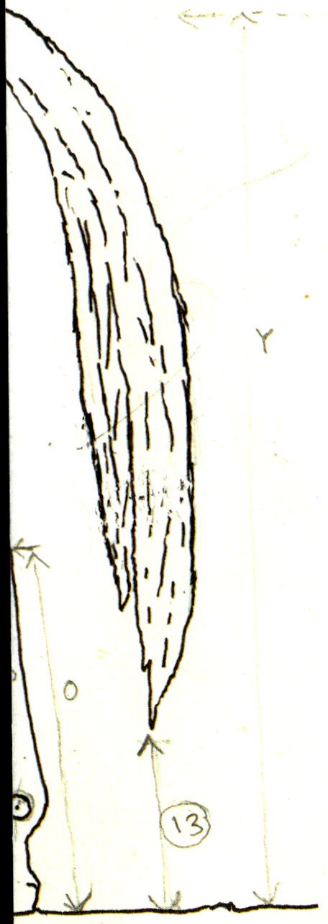

A Length of head 24"+ 25 1/4"	T E...
B Eye to muzzle	U (...
C Depth of head 11 (at jaw)	V Metacarpal to ground 7/9
D Poll to ground (standing up)	W Length of fore hoof
E Carpal (back pt of knee to ground) 19 1/4	X Depth of ~~throat~~ 13
F Elbow to ground 36	Y Tail root to ground 58 1/2
G Depth of neck (widest) 21 1/2	Z Poll to withers 32
H Length of torso 60" 1·60 63	(1) Poll to shoulder pt 37
i Depth of withers → chest 29	(2) Pt of shoulder to ground 42" ✓
J Withers to ground 63" 62 1/4"	(3) Shoulder to elbow 13 1/2
K Quarters to ground 61 1/2" 59 1·50	(4) Depth of shoulder 22 +
L Quarters to stifle 23 1/2	(5) Hip to ground 55 1/2
M Stifle to ground " (patella)	(6) Hip to shoulder 40
N Stifle to hock joint 22 3/4	(7) Hip to ~~tail root~~ arse bone 21-?
O Hock pt to ground ~~24 1/4~~ 23	8 1/2 Width of eyes 8 1/2 " of jaw
P Hock joint to metacarpal 17 1/2	18- " of shoulders " " hips 20
Q Length of hoof (see picture)	" " chest
R Metacarpal to ground 8/9	(8) Elbow to stifle 34
	(9) Hip to ribs (horizontally) 5 1/2
S Chest to penis	
(11) Length of tail to metacarpal	(10) Length of ear 7

1/2"

1/2 (round it)

1/2 metacarpal)

8 1/4 29"

) 21 1/2

...band

3 - (standing length at ...)

Boy with a Dolphin

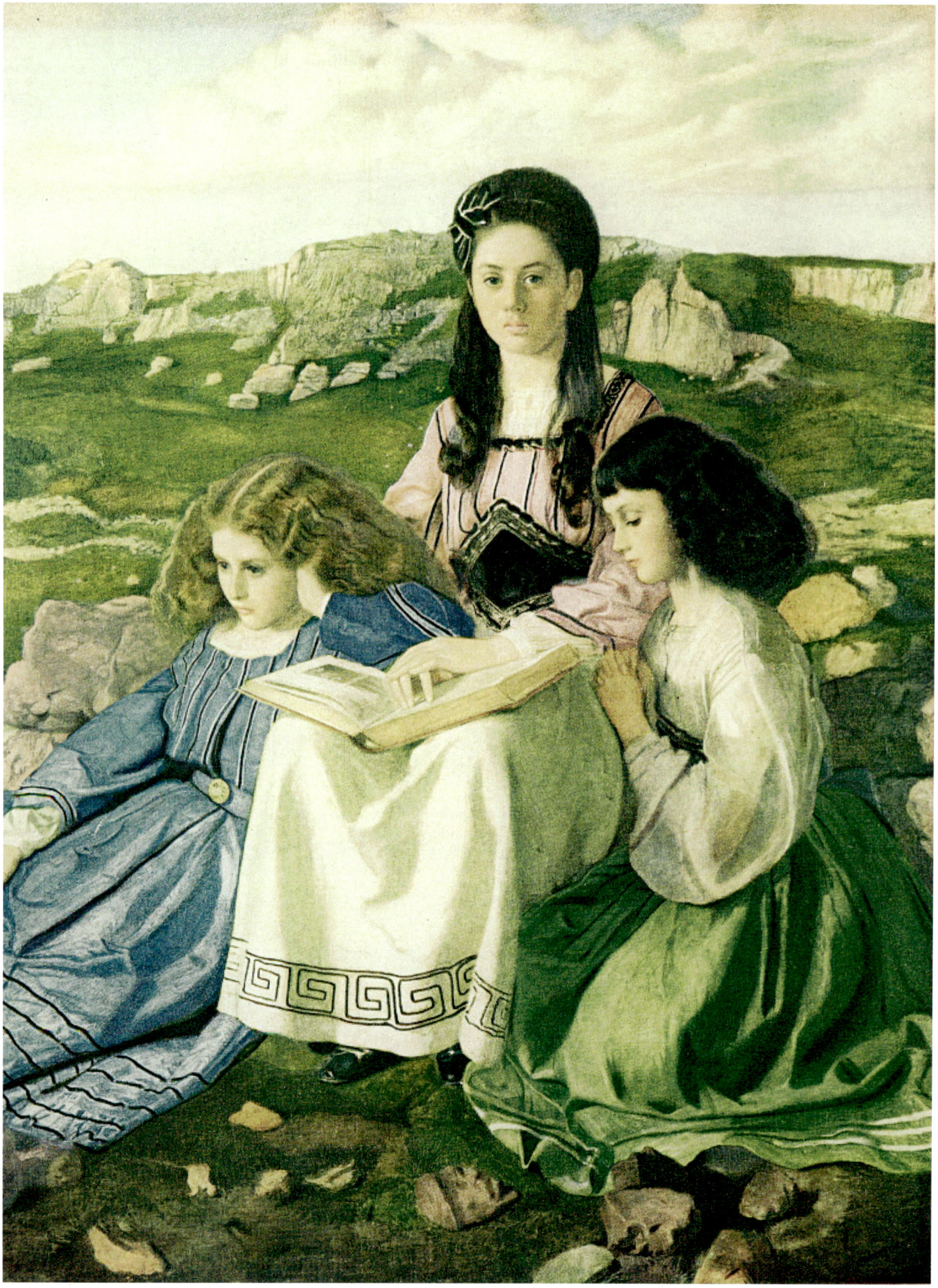

Alice of Wonderland and her sisters. *The Three Daughters of Dean Liddell* by Sir William Blake Richmond, RA

Boy with a Dolphin

The Life and Work of David Wynne

DAVID ELLIOTT

QUARTET

First published in 2010 by Quartet Books Limited
A member of the Namara Group
27 Goodge Street, London W1T 2LD

A catalogue record for this book is available from the British Library

ISBN 978 0 7043 7185 9

Typeset in Great Britain by Antony Gray
Printed and bound in Spain by Estudios Gráficos ZURE

Credits and Acknowledgements

Sue Hide: the illustration on page 2, *Alice and her Sisters*;
Iain MacMillan; the illustrations on pages 23, 26, 27, 31, 33, 34, 40, 43, 44, 52 and 53:
Derek Saville: the illustration on page 49; Thomas Picton: the illustration on page 54:
S. D. Colhoun: the illustration on page 56;
The illustration on page 77: courtesy of the Goldsmiths' Company;
Clive Barda: the illustrations on pages 84, 92, 95, 96, 97, 99 and 116 (left);
Jerry Harpur: the illustration on page 105; Victor Shack: the illustration on page 122;
Peter Tebitt: the illustrations on pages 135, 136, 137, 138, 139 and 140;
Ian Hessenberg: the illustration on page 150;
Alice Rosenbaum: the illustrations on the jacket, pages, 68, 80, 82, 156 and 158.

Every effort has been made to establish the accuracy of the above
credits and the publishers apologise for any errors of omission.
All other illustrations are from David Wynne's archive.

We are not human beings having a spiritual experience;
We are spiritual beings having a human experience.

TEILHARD DE CHARDIN

All my life I have been helped by other people who loved me:

Karim Aga Khan (racehorse owner)
Sally Aga Khan
Heidi Almendinger (Botswana)
Bill Amer (plasterer)
Andy Andrews (stable head lad)
Susan Autgarten (brain surgeon)
Jonathan William Bennett (stepson)
Nicola Josephine Bennett (stepdaughter)
Perin Berry (doctor)
Geraldine Beyts (aunt)
Jock Black (sailor)
Rosie Blake (model)
Bill Cadogon (patron)
Primrose Cadogon
Patrick Caiger-Smith
Robin Caiger-Smith (best friend)
Charles, Prince of Wales
Christina Chapman (model)
Tom Cholmondley (Kenya)
Charlie Edwards (blacksmith and whitesmith)
Jonny Elliot (school friend)
Jacob Epstein (sculptor)

James Fanshaw (racehorse trainer)
My Father
Andrew Gow (Trinity)
Graham Hill (racing driver)
Victor Hill (patron)
Sara Hughs (model)
Charles and Joey Huw-Williams
David Inman (publisher)
Jack James (shepherd)
George Knaggs (best friend)
Kuria (Kenya)
Roger Larson (school friend)
Prince Michael of Kent
My Mother
Harry Murphy (plasterer)
Isabella Norman (model)
Alec Notman (head groom)
Louis Osman (architect)
Wendy Pace (nurse)
John Pisani (marble)
Michael Pugh (patron)
Theo Rossi, Conte di Montelera
Evelyn de Rothschild (banker)
Victoria Salmon (model)
Bill Shand-Kydd (friend)
Hugh & Frances Simpson (Kenya)
Canon F A Simpson (Trinity)
Robert Dorrien Smith (Tresco)
George Springet (sailor)
Ernie Startup (sailor)
Jackie Stewart (racing driver)
Michael Stoute (racehorse trainer)
Patricia Stoute (horsewoman)
George Trevelyan (Master of Trinity)
Robert Livesey Troop (Trinity friend)
Virginia Wade (tennis player)
Bill Waldren (foundryman)
Tony Wallensteiner (Stowe)
Geraldine Watson
Welles Bosworth (architect)
Lloyd & June Willmot (Botswana)
Carl Winter (curator)
Ken Witburn (blacksmith)
Gillian Mary Lesley Wynne (wife)
Roland David Amadeus Wynne (son)
Edward Wynne (son)

1

IF LONDONERS chosen at random were asked to name their favourite among the pieces of public sculpture adorning their city, many would cite the remarkable statue which sits just on the bend of the River Thames by Albert Bridge – David Wynne's work, *Boy with a Dolphin*. South Londoners might recall happy times spent with their children clambering over the huge marble statue *Gorilla* in the park at Crystal Palace, and which tourist has not noticed the startling intricacy and lightness of the coloured Lion and Unicorn centrepiece to the Queen Mother Gates at Hyde Park Corner?

From the small perfection of an eight-inch bronze gazelle to a one-hundred-and-ninety-eight-inch *Teamwork* carved from granite, which for years confronted so many motorists as they meandered their way through the traffic jams at the junction of Western Avenue and Hangar Lane, David Wynne has mastered techniques suited to every material, regardless of subject or size. He is, as Yehudi Menuhin – whose thirty-two-inch bronze portrait Wynne completed in 1963 – declared: 'a born sculptor'. Remarkably, David Wynne has had no formal training.

In a long and very successful career, David has pursued his course, ignoring critics, establishment opinion, commercial agents, the pressure of his peers and the world in general. While still an undergraduate at Cambridge, David met Jacob Epstein to inform the older man of his intention to become a sculptor. Ever since, David has drawn on the collective experience of all those artists who his own aesthetic feeling told him were masters of their craft. There is an element of the Renaissance apprentice in all this, combined with personal conviction of great intensity.

He was taught to appreciate beauty from a very early age by his mother and further encouraged by his teachers at Stowe School. When his wartime naval service took him to the far East at the age of eighteen, he happened to see, when ashore, a huge sandstone Buddha which profoundly impressed him; it seemed to him the figure embodied the very essence of art, communicating emotion without barriers of time, creed, language or any other hindrance; a simple statement of praise. For David, this was an epiphany, as was his trip to Europe, while an undergraduate when he saw the original work of the great artists of the Italian

Renaissance. The figures of Donatello, Michelangelo and others confirmed the young man's growing belief that sculpture could be his way to communicate and celebrate the emotion and feelings of bliss which the world inspired in him.

Safe home from the war and about to return to Cambridge, he was just one of many optimistic young men eager to get on with their lives. All was ahead of him. Yet David possessed the confidence and certainty to embark on what must have seemed to others a life of risk and uncertainty – the life of an artist.

Now over eighty, he can reflect not only on the considerable success of that decision but also on the myriad paths along which his choice has taken him, for David Wynne's life story is indeed a remarkable one. Few eightieth birthday parties could boast live performances from some of the greatest rock musicians of our time, guests ranging from royalty, famous sportsmen, aristocrats and millionaires to artisans and a host of beautiful young women. The birthday boy was dressed in a bright blue and gold rugby shirt and fluorescent trainers and welcomed them all brandishing a harmonica.

This book has two intentions. It will seek to celebrate David's art by providing a pictorial record of his favourite work and an account of each piece's history and evolution, and it will also take the form of a biography, written in close collaboration with the sculptor, looking back on his life and attempting to convey the essence of all those many people and influences that have guided his long and sometimes turbulent career.

As this book was nearing completion, David Wynne recorded, in his own words, his very first memories. It seems appropriate to quote them here, at the start of the reader's journey:

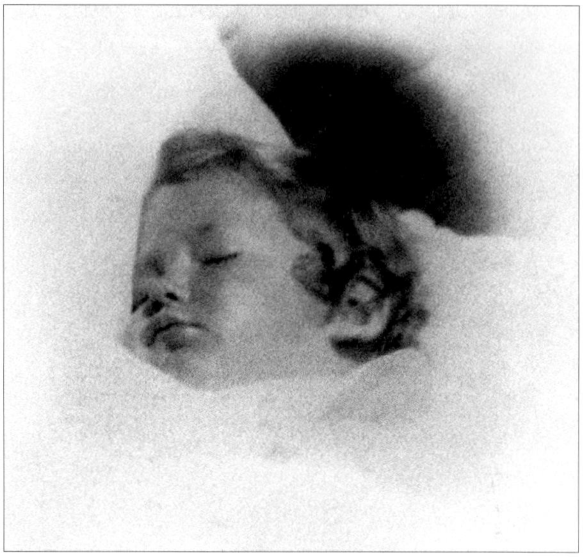

David, as a baby

'I was born on the 25th of May 1926. I remember being born clearly, lying on something very white and smooth. I think there were other shapes around me, and now that I'm older I expect they were people. I was very, very happy. The next thing I remember was when I was one year old. I was in my pram, which smelt good, like a pram should always smell. The pram must have been on a road because I could see telegraph poles going past me, one after another. Then I saw a very big horse, it was reddish and it smelt lovely. My father whom I called 'Dada', was on the horse. I remember being in my mother's arms. She had brown hair with a bun. She was singing. I must have been older, probably two years old. My brother, Gerald, whom I called 'Ger–ger', had golden curly hair. I was being put into a pushchair by someone who must have been my nurse, called 'Didee', whom I

loved very much. My brother was saying that I was too old to be in a pushchair and he didn't want me to be in it. But Didee picked me up anyway and put me in the pushchair and strapped me in across my middle. One Christmas, when I was around three years old, my father was in his chair and I was standing beside him. It was a very big chair, much taller than I was. The arm of the chair was a long way above my head. My father reached down and took the back of my neck between his two fingers, which I liked very much. He said, 'How old are you, rough-'un?' and I said, 'I'm free.' The next thing I remember was probably at the same time, or a day later. I remember a church and I remember holding my mother's hand and looking at a crib which I thought quite good, but not as good as the real Jesus in a real cradle with a real Mary, a real donkey, a real ox and a real Joseph. They were singing 'Once in Royal David's City' and I thought the carol was about me.

'After that, in my memory, I got bigger. I think I was four. My mother talked to me and sang to me about Christmas, about Jesus and poetry and what happened at Bethlehem a long time ago. Next I remember being probably five years old. I knew about Alice in Wonderland. I wanted to be like Alice. I wished I was a girl and not a boy. It was lovely. I was still very, very happy. When I was older, I didn't like to tell anybody that I wanted to be a little girl and not a boy, but nobody who knew me minded – my mother, my father, Didee and Ger–ger. I was still very happy. When I was six, I went to a kindergarten school called Knockmaroon. Ger–ger and I fell in love with a little girl called Mary with golden hair and blue eyes who had a big sister called Helen. After that, I

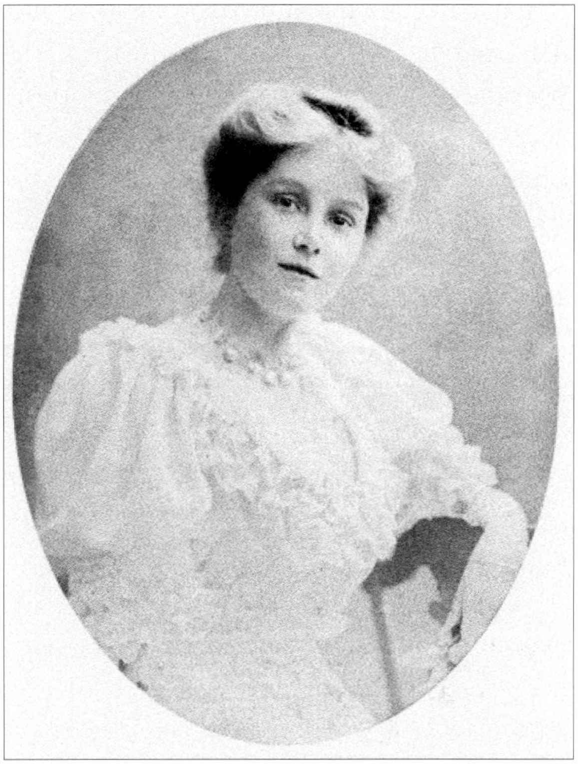

David's mother and father

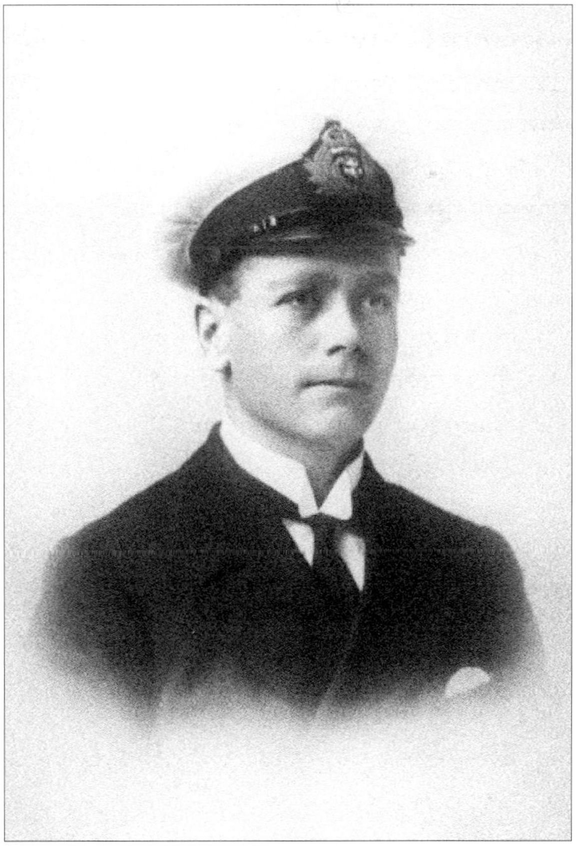

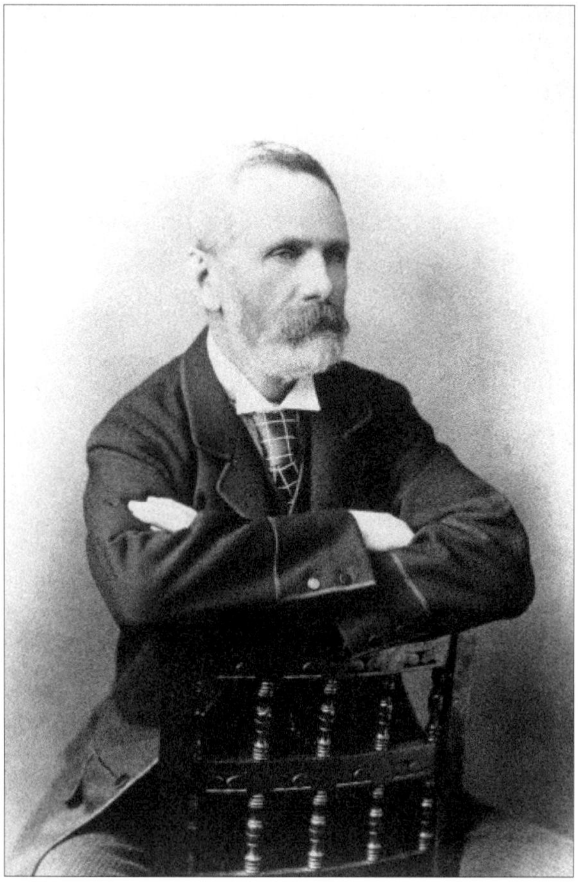

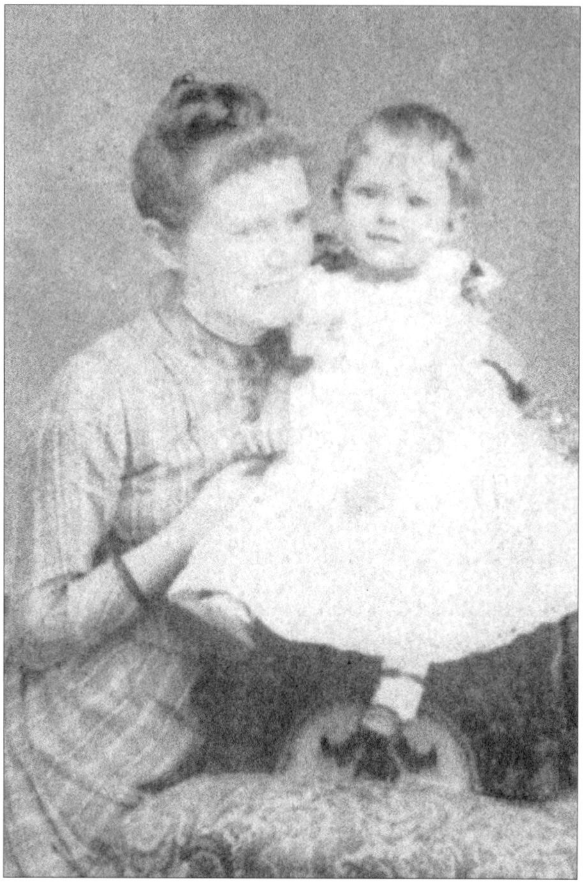

David's paternal grandfather and maternal grandmother with his mother on her knee

was sort of pretending or possibly trying to be bigger and grown up, but I still felt like a girl. But I wasn't ashamed or frightened, just worried. At the prep school we went to when I was seven, I wasn't quite so happy, but Ger–ger was there too, so it was all right. And then I suppose I stopped wanting to be Alice. And after that, I got still bigger.'

David's mother had spent her childhood in Egypt, where her father was a member of the British diplomatic mission. David's father was a sailor who had circumnavigated the world three times under sail while still a young man. David's brother, Gerald, was two years older and the young family lived in modest gentility in the New Forest. His childhood was a loving one. Both parents were encouraging of their offspring, and David's mother instilled in him his life-long love of reading, art and music, and prompted his study of the world's great religions. While other children visited the music-hall or pantomime, the two boys went to the opera. Even in her old age, David's mother taught herself Latin and Greek in order to read the great works of antiquity.

His father was a flamboyant character. He had served in the Egyptian navy and had fought, with the Royal Navy, in both world wars. Sporting a jaunty monocle, always well dressed and attentive to the ladies, he cut a dashing figure to his young sons. David would stay close to his parents throughout their lives. His brother protected him during a somewhat bleak succession of not very good preparatory schools before their grandmother provided the funds to send the young boys to Stowe School.

A love of nature, especially of animals and birds, began at an early age, as did an awareness that some special destiny awaited him. David's sense of his own unique qualities was constantly reinforced by his loving parents' conviction that whatever he chose to do would be successful. However what was perhaps more significant was an almost magical belief he had that whatever he was doing or wherever he was he was intimately connected with the power to make all things possible.

It was David's mother who first aroused his perception of beauty in artistic forms. She was the one who encouraged him and it was in her company that he discovered a philosophical construct that was to remain constant with him for the rest of his life. While still an adolescent, David began going with his mother to meetings, held in a house in South London, conducted by an émigré Russian philosopher, Petyr Demianovich Ouspensky. The effect of his rigorous teachings during the 1930s and 1940s was considerable. James Joyce wrote *Finnegans Wake* under his influence and when he had to leave his native Russia to avoid the wrath of the Bolsheviks, Ouspensky's emigration to England was aided by many of the country's intellectual *élite*.

His most influential work, *A New Model of the Universe*, has remained one of David's most valued texts and David continued to attend Ouspensky's meetings, and those of his successors (Francis Roles, Maurice Nicoll, Jiddu Krishnamurti, Werner Erhard, Sathya Sai Baba and John-Roger), for many years. Ouspensky eschewed a conventional education: he famously dismissed academic discipline, suggesting that professors were killing the university in much the same way priests had killed the church. A disciple, till they parted in mysterious circumstances in the Northern Caucasus, of G. I. Gurdjieff, Ouspensky stayed in England living in comparative obscurity. It has been said that the main characteristic of Ouspensky's esoteric meetings was the extraordinary intensity of them. He demanded the utmost honesty from the group, and also from himself. After a short lecture about his philosophical approach, he invited searching questions, summarily dismissing those he considered irrelevant.

Ouspensky maintained that human beings had one aim – to awake, and that this could only happen when they realised that they were asleep. By observing oneself, and being alive to the external world, one would find everything important verified by one's own experience. The sincerity of suffering afforded a way to personal enlightenment. The experience of grappling each week with often complex, rigorous philosophical and spiritual issues kindled in David a lifelong sense of being in touch with the essential, eternal questions of time, space, nature and, finally, the essence of God.

The German philosopher Heidegger, much influenced by Ouspensky, would declare 'to think eternity requires that we think the moment'. This could be the leitmotif which underlies David Wynne's artistic philosophy.

2

IN 1939, when he was thirteen, David was sent away to Stowe to join his brother Gerald, who had already established a fierce reputation for himself among the school's fraternity as a tough and vigorous defender of his rights. The brothers were united by a strong bond and shared an intense dislike of the preparatory schools to which they had been sent prior to Stowe.

Their childhood had been happy. Their father had owned a livery stable in the New Forest, but financial pressures often required the family to change its living arrangements. David retains a deep affection for his family. He remembers sitting on his father's knee listening to Mozart on the wireless together and of his mother singing him to sleep. Recollections of his early education are less glowing. His first two schools were often terrifying to the young boy. He was bullied and homesick; without the protecting presence of his brother, his life would have been unbearable.

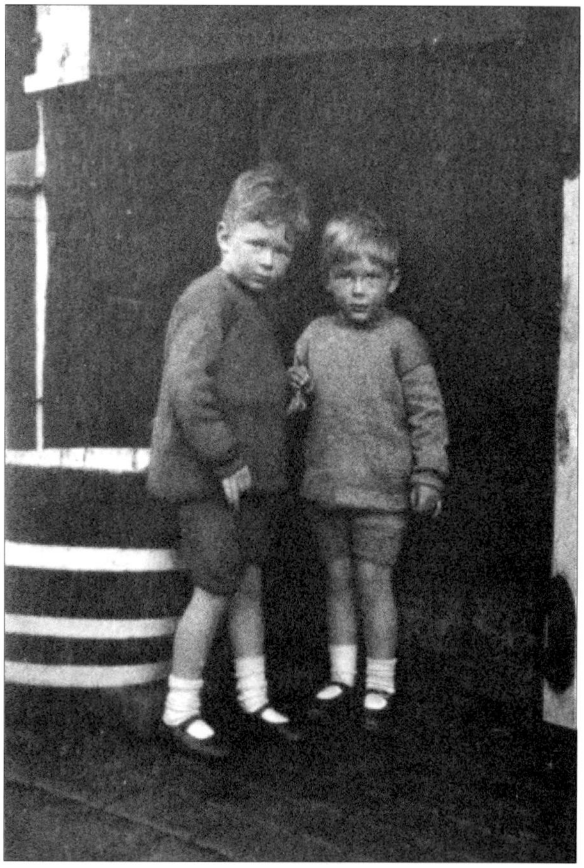

Gerald and David

During the holidays from school at their home in Rottingdean the first flicker of his talent was noticed. The family had rented a house there. The boys were expected to swim every day, and the beautiful blue drawing-room which overlooked the sea was, for him, a magical place. The house felt almost luxurious after the cold, dreary classrooms he endured at preparatory schools. His parents had become friendly with a neighbour, Sir William Watson. Born in 1858, Watson was a Victorian poet. His verses on the death of Tennyson had been well received at the time, though his reputation did not last and he is now best remembered for his verse *April*, which still can be found in the odd poetry anthology. The poet's daughter, Geraldine, encouraged David with his drawing, and gave him lessons. David still has a portrait of himself which she painted.

His love of drawing animals and birds was all-consuming. He remembers constantly observing what he saw around him, seized with a growing conviction that his future life's work would somehow be involved with the natural world. Geraldine Watson clearly saw David's potential. It was not surprising that a child, born in the New Forest and surrounded by natural beauty at a time when motorways did not criss-cross the landscape, should aspire to be a naturalist when he grew up.

The two brothers were inseparable. The misery of school life strengthened the bond between them which sustained him when David entered Stowe. He also discovered the delights of the *Dr Dolittle* books. Hugh Lofting's creation was an eccentric doctor, turned vet, who could communicate with animals, a skill David especially admired. Dolittle's first adventure took him to Africa, where his grateful patients present him with a pushmi-pullyu, a shy animal with a head at each end, one for eating and one for speaking. Perhaps by more than co-incidence, David Wynne would later spend many months in Africa, drawing and sculpting the exotic wild life, often at very close quarters.

Stowe is set in 750 acres of landscape garden and parkland. Founding the school in 1923, with initially ninety-nine pupils, the first headmaster, J. F. Roxburgh, set out to foster in the boys 'a love of scholarship, service and beauty'. Any ex-pupil, he believed, would 'know beauty when he sees it all his life'. The school is housed in the splendour of the former home of the Dukes of Buckingham and Chandos, though by the time of David's arrival sixteen years later, the number of pupils had risen to five hundred. Designed by some of the greatest

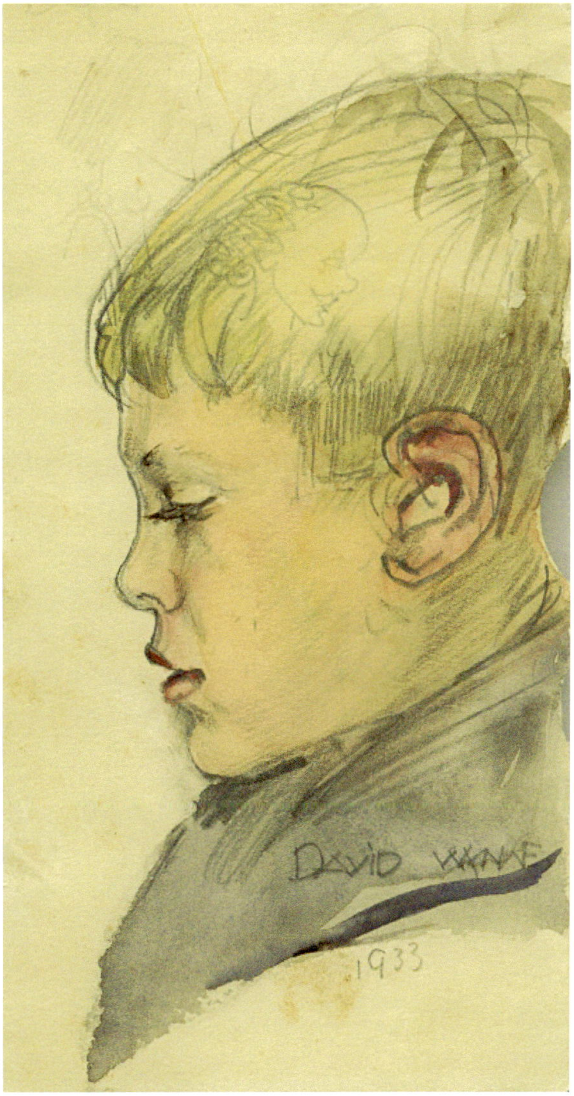

David, age seven, by Geraldine Watson

English architects and landscape gardeners, including Sir John Vanbrugh and 'Capability' Brown, the magnificent main house and park present a sweeping panorama of great beauty. The grounds, now owned by the National Trust, were rich with wildlife and designed, with spectacular use of Palladian detail (classical statues, grottos, bridges, temples), to highlight startling vistas and intimate retreats.

The day David Wynne arrived, in 1939, the school was preparing itself for war, which had been declared that same month. Black-out blinds were being put up at the windows in accordance with air-raid precautions. Though the war would impinge little on school life, younger masters were required to fight and David would be taught by much older men, whose age prevented them from joining the armed services.

Stowe's rarefied atmosphere suited David, and though his academic work was not exceptional, he enjoyed playing French horn with the school orchestra and became proficient in the school's fencing team. David enjoyed the rustic simplicity and harmonious rhythm of the seasons. One day, hiding under his jersey a baby owl he had found, he sought permission to keep it as a pet. When the restless bird suddenly popped its head out, the headmaster was won over, permission was given and David and the owl remained together.

Protected by his brother, David's interest in the natural world flourished as did his growing appreciation of pictorial and sculptural representation. The masters encouraged him to look through books of paintings and drawings by great artists and he was already developing a keen eye for what he liked and disliked. There can be little doubt that his time at Stowe, surrounded by great architecture and landscape, encouraged by caring masters and steadily developing assurance and confidence, was invaluable to him. His eventual acceptance at Trinity College, Cambridge, would be on the personal recommendation of J. F. Roxburgh – a formative influence on David.

David entered Trinity College to read zoology under the government's scheme whereby undergraduates eligible for military call-up would spend six months at university before joining the armed services. In the early part of 1945, aged nineteen, David was required to enlist. Following in his father's footsteps, he joined the Royal Navy.

He was sent north to Greenock to join a minesweeper, HMS *Blackpool*, whose main task was to patrol the English Channel, just after the D-Day landings. As a young rating, he decided 'to make a go of it' and later was commissioned Midshipman in an aircraft carrier, HMS *Pretoria Castle*. For David, life on the lower deck had been a revelation and he 'learned many lessons about how to behave'. His fellow sailors were mainly working-class Glaswegians, and though 'rough and tough', treated their young messmate with great kindness and he loved it.

Finally alone, without the comforts of his parents' love or his brother's protection, David was thrown back on his own resources. His time in the navy allowed him the space to develop a belief in his own strength of character and a pride in his wartime role. His father had always cut a fine figure in uniform, never without his monocle, and this encouraged his son to emulate him. David loved the navy and began to enjoy the camaraderie of life at

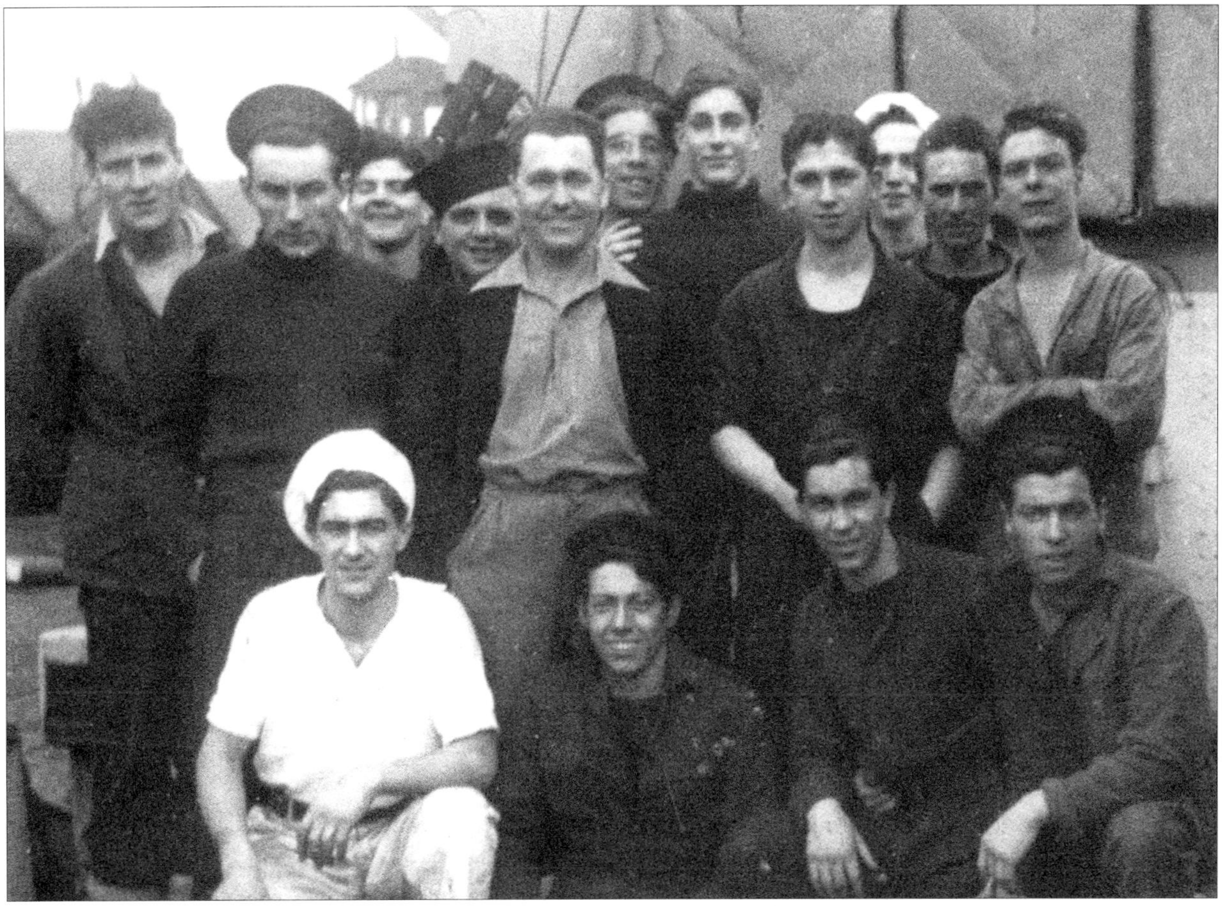

Some of the crew of HMS *Blackpool*. David is standing fifth from right, back row

sea. Although the youngest sailor on board, he began to recognise a skill he would be able to exercise later on; an ability to get on well with people of every sort.

One incident, especially, would give this growing sense of his own worth a huge boost. Among his duties, as midshipman on the *Pretoria Castle*, was to command a launch sent to collect sailors who had been on shore leave – the 'liberty boat'. On one such occasion, at night, a sailor fell overboard and was washed away by the current. David leapt into the rough sea and found and held the man until both were rescued. It was an action not without some risk to his own safety. 'In a tight corner,' he says, 'I discovered I would do the right thing. I got to trust that in a difficult situation, I would behave properly!'

The conviction that after the navy he would become a sculptor was to be reinforced when he found a copy of Jacob Epstein's *Let There Be Sculpture* in the ship's library on HMS *London*, a cruiser bound for the Far East.

A dream he had at sea remains as powerful in its symbolism now as it was then. He dreamed he was an athlete – a runner – in Ancient Greece, who would one day be asked by the gods to take a message. So as to be ready, he practised and practised and practised . . .

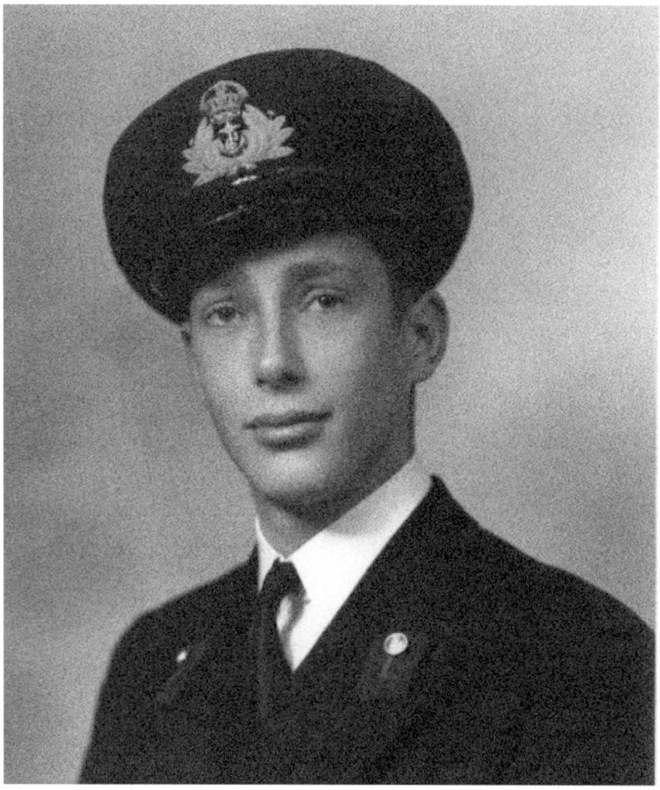

Midshipman Wynne

His time in the Far East allowed David plenty of opportunities to go ashore. As he explored Penang and Ceylon, he visited many temples and ruined buildings, some dating back to antiquity. The statues and carvings he saw would change his life, especially a huge sandstone Buddha. He realised that true sculpture communicated directly, and it was nothing less than a glimpse of the infinite.

Years later, David wrote, 'The object of art is praise. It is to communicate emotion, to remind us of another order, where all is harmony.' As he sailed home in HMS *Indefatigable*, he was certain in which direction his future lay. To make with his hands works to communicate feeling would be his path to fulfilment and grant him a sense of both power and wellbeing.

3

DAVID went back up to Trinity College, Cambridge in 1949. After the navy, it seemed as if he had entered a new and glorious world. He made new friends and with some, like George Knaggs, he would be friends for life. David found new interests, enjoyed countless parties and finally began to sense that life's promise was boundless. He stroked the first Trinity boat in the May Bumps.

Joris Foster-Arnold was another good friend at Trinity. David and he shared the same tutor; when asked why he had chosen them, the tutor replied that they were the only two students who constantly asked to borrow money, so he only had to go to the bank once a week.

After they had left Trinity, Joris appeared at David's Campden Hill studio, driving the first prototype Austin Healey sports car and suggesting they travel around Europe together, David to look at art while he explored good food and wine. They ran out of money in Venice. Joris took their last hundred-lira note and went to the Lido. David was woken later by his friend poking him with a sheaf of thousand-lira notes. The winnings were spent on such an extensive selection of fine wines that David had to ship his suitcase back to England to make room in the car for them all. (Again it was to be a lifelong friendship; Foster-Arnold travelled down from Canada, where he was then living, to celebrate with David at the party thrown by PepsiCo at the unveiling of his Bear sculpture in 1976.)

It was at Cambridge that David finally decided to make sculpting his chosen art. It was, he found, 'easier than painting. You could turn it around in your hands.' He started upon his very first attempt at sculpting a head from life when his college friend Robert Troop agreed to pose for him. Andrew Gow, Professor of Greek at Trinity and Trustee of the National Gallery, came to see the completed bust. His encouragement focused David's energies and led him to discuss all manner of aesthetic and philosophical aspects of sculpture. Carl Winter, the director of the Fitzwilliam Museum, was another influential academic who admired David's work and was extremely supportive.

G. M. Trevelyan, the Master of Trinity, sent David a note saying: 'The Fellows of this College have decided that you will be more use in the world as a sculptor than as a zoologist, therefore you are excused all lectures and will not be required to sit examinations. We hope that you will continue at Trinity for the rest of your time, However, two things must not suffer; the May boat which you are stroking and the May Ball, which you will be asked to bring back to its pre-war splendour.'

A flavour of David's undergraduate life is seen in a recollection of his friendship with the eccentric Fellow of Trinity, F. A. Simpson. In *A Last Eccentric*, published in 1991 by Christian Action, David recalls Trevelyan's instructions to undergraduates 'to make the going with senior members of the college . . . ' From time to time, David would therefore give a dinner party to which he asked both students and dons. He had become as close a friend of Andrew Gow as he was of Simpson. It was odd to be friends with two people who only 'fought and snarled like lion cubs' at each other for these men, back from the war, were very different.

David still remembers a comment from Andrew Gow. When Gow was dying and David was visiting him in Addenbrooke's hospital, he asked if there was anything else he'd like to know about the mystery of sculpture. David, just back from Rome, enthused about the statue of Marcus Aurelius which seemed to him near perfect. Andrew Gow thought for a long time looking as though he was asleep and then said, 'It is possibly lacking in incident.' Years later, when David was working on a sculpture of a young girl, Gow's words came into his mind. The sculpture was virtually finished but David was not yet satisfied. Remembering the professor's criticism, David changed the girl's hands, making the fingers stretch upwards, thus giving the sculpture 'incident'.

David began to feel confident his life now

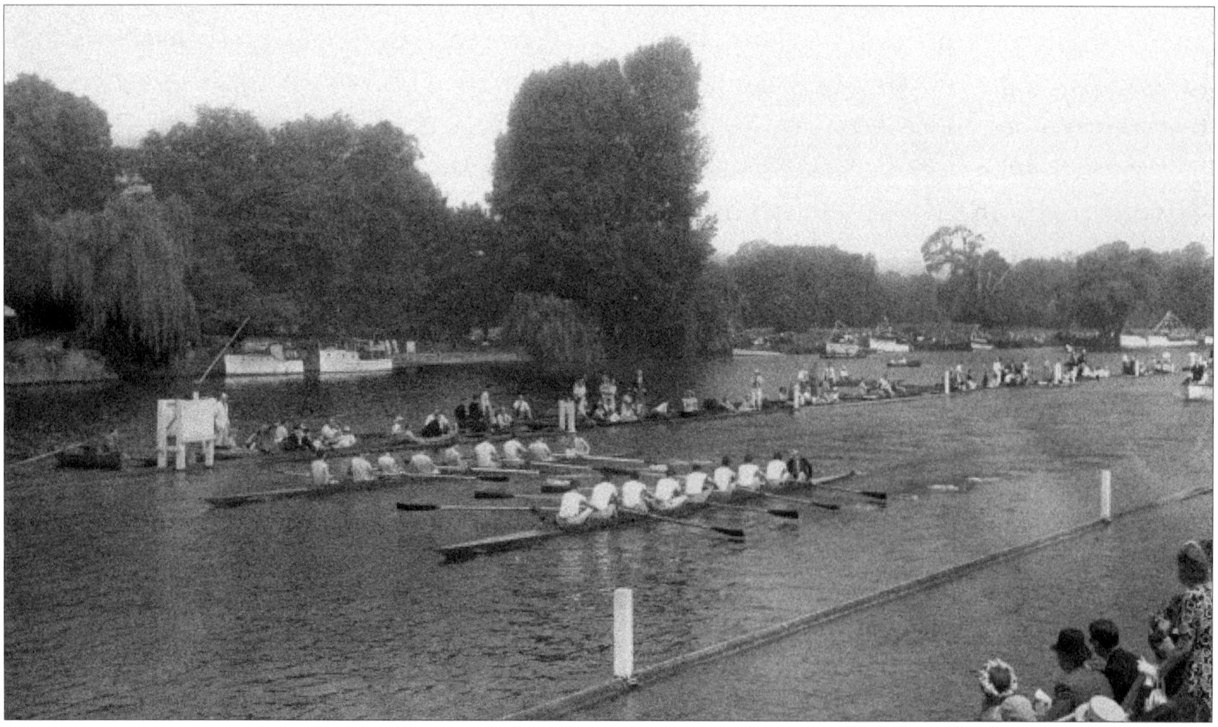

First and Third Trinity beating Christ's College Cambridge in a heat of the Ladies Challenge Cup at Henley

had a true aim. He was focused. He made frequent visits to the Fitzwilliam Museum where he would study and draw the museum's outstanding collection of casts, Greek sculpture and antiquities. He also continued to pursue his passion for English literature. The Master of Trinity took a special interest in David's progress. Famous for his vast study of Garibaldi and his social history of England, Trevelyan was also a passionate advocate of reading literature for pleasure. His Clark Lectures of 1953 endorse his love of Robert Browning, Walter Scott and A. E. Housman. He had little time for professional academics who saw the study of literature as 'a set of intellectual conundrums, to be solved by certain rules. It is joy, joy in our inmost heart.' Here was the perfect mentor for the young, impressionable undergraduate.

David was still rather shy of women when he returned to Cambridge, despite the best attempts of the crew of the *Blackpool* to instruct him in the art of seduction. He fell in love with a girl working in a Cambridge bookshop named Juliet. David would watch her at work whenever he could, but they never spoke. One day, after he had left Cambridge, a friend of his told him he had been at a party where a girl had mentioned David's name. They had been playing forfeits. On her turn she had to say who it was she would most like to have met. She said David Wynne. 'It made me realise,' he recalls, 'it wasn't just a toss-up. If you fell for someone, they probably fell for you as well.' It was an important memory and one that would influence his future relationships.

In 1959 David completed a granite sculpture, *Teamwork*. It had been commissioned by the Taylor Woodrow Building Company. After a talk he gave about the project in the Midlands, the *Dudley Herald* reported:

> A thirty-two-year-old self-taught sculptor, told members of the Dudley Inner Wheel . . . how he carved out of granite the biggest piece of statuary in Europe . . . Artists, he said, were generally considered to be people who struggled a great deal and starved in garrets. In his own case . . . he had received encouragement from his early years . . .

The newspaper was incorrect: *Teamwork* is one of the largest pieces of statuary in Europe, but David's debt to his university was acknowledged.

David made many lasting friends at Trinity. Two of them, Robert Troop and Nicholas Horton-Fawkes went with him to France and Italy during the summer vacation. With just thirty pounds each, the three friends set off in Troop's little car.

A recurring feature of David's life is meeting with people who influence him. David had been given a letter of introduction to the architect William Welles Bosworth in Paris. Rockefeller's favourite architect, the American Welles Bosworth was in charge of the restoration of the cathedral at Chartres and the buildings of the Louvre. Born in 1869 in Philadelphia, Welles Bosworth trained at the architectural school of the MIT in Boston. He had studied painting with the English artist Alma-Tadema and continued his architectural studies at the Ecole des Beaux-Arts. It was here that he fell in love with France and he went on to spend the rest of his long life (he lived to be ninety-seven) in a large house of his own design on the outskirts of Paris. His most famous design, the AT&T Building in New York, reflects his profound knowledge of the classical forms, as do the buildings he created for the campus at MIT. He would often commission works of sculpture to adorn his buildings and the results can still be seen in the public parks of Boston and New York.

Besides enjoying their lengthy talks about art and the difficulties of the creative life, Bosworth was enchanted by David's developing sense of his own talent, while being much impressed by the young man's cavalier attitude to money. The three undergraduates had pooled what little funds they had for the expedition. On being introduced to his daughter by Welles Bosworth, David asked, 'Sir, may I take her out to dinner?' 'Where?' enquired the doting father. 'The Ritz,' answered the younger man, naming the only Parisian restaurant of which he had heard. With total disregard of the cost, the young couple went, and what was left in the kitty was spent with abandon.

David stayed another two nights as the architect's guest before rejoining the others and continuing their travels. Welles Bosworth in due course introduced David to his many friends and associates, enabling him to begin his professional life with an impressive list of connections, but first the trio had to motor down through Western France over the Alps to Italy. For the first time David could see for himself the wonders of Florence – the doors of the Baptistry, Michelangelo's *David*, the works of Donatello and the other great Italian masters. Behind the fun and laughter of being young men abroad, for David there was a more serious purpose. What he saw simply reinforced his commitment, and he returned to England more determined than ever to succeed

David had gone to see Jacob Epstein while still at Cambridge. He admired Epstein who loved and helped David till his death in 1959. It was Epstein who told David that any question formulated about sculpture could be answered by visiting the British Museum. Epstein's great carving, *Ecco Homo*, was exhibited in Blackpool, after his original patron deemed the work obscene. Epstein was a rebel uninterested in politics or religion, yet, like Whistler before him, stood rock solid on his conviction that his work was all that mattered.

David first met Epstein when the great man was modelling the head of the Ethiopian emperor, Haile Selassie. Epstein's somewhat gruff response to David's approach did nothing to diminish the young man's ambition or his audacity. At breakfast with the emperor's daughters, the young sculptor was asked by one of them how often he shaved. 'Once a day,' he replied. 'How often do you?'

David's father asked Epstein whether it was right to give his son money for his first studio. Epstein replied: 'If you can afford it, yes.' The studio was at Campden Hill, and it was at this time David met Georg Ehrlich. Born in 1897, Ehrlich was an Austrian. He was trained in Vienna to become a painter but decided in his mid-twenties that he preferred sculpture. He and his wife, also an artist and a writer of children's books, were Jewish. Forced to leave Austria in 1937, they had settled in London where the sculptor made his mark, doing many portrait heads and developing a love of sculpting animals. Ehrlich's head of his friend Benjamin Britten can be seen in the National Portrait Gallery.

David became friends with the Austrian. Ehrlich introduced David to his model, Gilli. She was to become David's wife.

In 1950, David created *Negro Boy*: 'the first decent sculpture I made'. One day, at Campden Hill, a Bob-a-Job Scout, looking for errands to run, knocked at the door. This lad, whose name was Hector, inspired David's first satisfactory piece. An attempt at a life-size human figure soon followed, when he was commissioned by the architect who was rebuilding the bomb-damaged church of St John the Baptist, Rudmore. David was asked to create a statue for the church in remembrance of a Wykehamist who had drowned. Using his brother Gerald and his friend Robert Troop as models, David set to work. There were difficulties – for instance, an arm fell off across Troop, asleep on a sofa. David realised he knew nothing about armatures. The statue was finally delivered in an old taxi, driven down from London with its roof open.

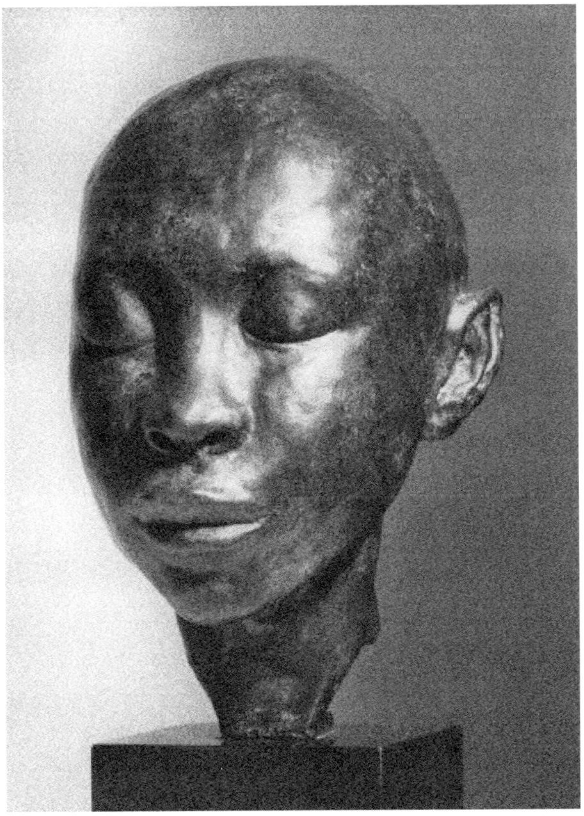

Negro Boy

Since his student days, David had longed to go to Greece. His early success did not necessarily mean affluence. In need of funds, as ever, he signed on as a crew-member on a small merchant ship sailing from Marseilles to Piraeus. Under the Mediterranean stars seeing the glow of Mt. Etna with his shipmates, he watched a dance getting underway on the passenger deck above. Comments were made about a pretty girl. Within minutes, David was up and off. Sneaking through the bowels of the ship wearing his only suit, he made his way up to the first-class section and, to his comrades' glee, danced the young lady around the deck. The captain, however, was not so delighted.

He was interviewed by a Greek journalist in the library of the British Archaeological School at Athens (' . . . a young man under thirty, clever, with a very sympathetic face,' observed the newspaper), David said Greece was ' . . . the most beautiful country in the world for a sculptor, for she has this wonderful sunlight. It is very difficult to evaluate a statue which is in a room . . . ' He was 'dumbfounded' by Delphi:

> . . . Pure sculpture was produced at that time. Now, in our epoch, the sculptor first makes a model and then he casts it in plaster and after that he copies it in marble. It is comparatively easy work, but that was not the method applied in antiquity. They worked directly on the marble. I repeat, Greece has been for me a great revelation . . .

When asked how many works he had finished, David replied, 'Quite a few . . . At this moment I have four of my works in the exhibition at the Royal Academy. Three are studies of deer, and one is a head made out of lead.' He mentioned the St John the Baptist. 'This was my first big work, and it seems it was successful.'

He stayed in Greece for several months, amazed at the sheer splendour, attempting to see everything he possibly could. He also paid his first visit to the Holy Land. His formative education was over. Although his academic record could never be described as distinguished, he had learned perhaps the greatest lesson that his mentor Ouspensky, had taught. The only real knowledge is that which you discover and believe for yourself. He had begun to win commissions, exhibit and meet people of influence and taste. He was finally ready to return home and continue his true profession – that of sculpture.

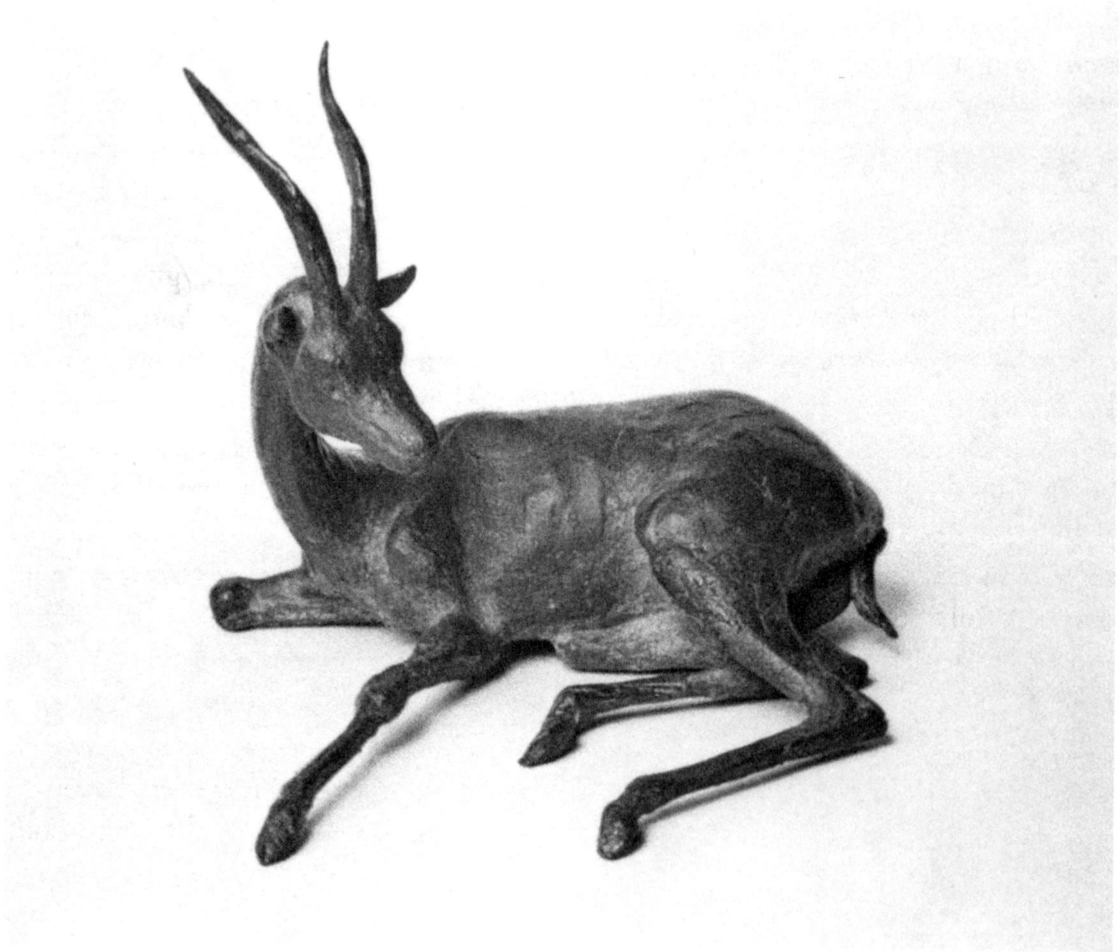

Reclining Antelope

4

IN 1968, less than fifteen years after David's return from Greece and the Holy Land, the first book about his work was published by the London publisher, Michael Joseph. At the back of the book, in the Complete List of Works by David Wynne from 1949–1967, more than two hundred and fifty sculptures were itemised, together with a further twenty-three made but destroyed. As a body of work, it was an astonishing achievement.

Apart from the few lessons with Georg Ehrlich and three months spent as a stonemason in Paris, working for Paul Landowski, David had received no formal training in any aspect of sculptural technique. Though tutored in art history by Andrew Gow in his final year at Trinity, Wynne decided not to pursue the traditional path when he left. He did feel that sculpture was something he could do, but rejected any idea of following the routine courses involving theory which conventional art schools still espoused.

The critical essay which introduces the book was written by T. S. R. Boase, president of Magdalene College, a former director of the Courtauld Institute and the editor of *The Oxford History of English Art*. The essay gives some clue to the mystery of David's success. Writing of Wynne's work in the late 1960s, Boase says:

> Interest in his work is growing. There are now many patrons who have examples of it, and are watching his career, men who have not only, at stages when it was needed, given financial support, but whose knowledge and encouragement have meant, in very different ways, much in his career. He has been outstandingly fortunate since his undergraduate days in the counsels and friendship of older men, and he has always known how to listen to advice, even if by no means always to take it.

Patronage has played a vital role in David's success. At moments in his life a few wealthy collectors and benefactors have bought his work systematically or introduced him to others who could commission, in some instances, sculpture of huge proportions. Moreover, David has never employed an agent or gallery to represent him on any regular basis. He has always maintained a strict control over whom he works for and what he does.

The three years David spent in London

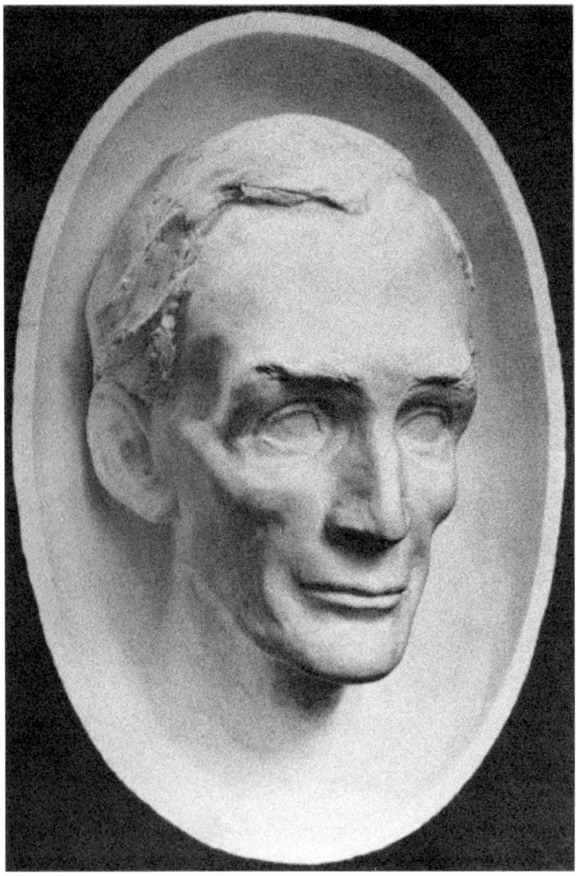

Humphrey Sumner, Warden of All Souls

immediately after Cambridge were productive, if somewhat precarious. Boase noted that 'if his progress as a sculptor were not promising he had it in mind that he would go back to sea'. His life-size bronze of St John the Baptist had been successfully installed in the Church of St John Rudmore. David described the sculpture as being of a zealot, dressed in skins, exhorting the people to repent – 'the voice of one crying in the wilderness'. The saint stands, his left hand outstretched, his left leg bent forward, his mouth open because he is speaking. Interestingly, the face is that of a young, virile man. *La Revue Moderne*, in November 1952, wrote of the statue in glowing terms, comparing it favourably to the work of Rodin, describing David's work as showing 'beaucoup de noblesse'.

Two more commissions followed. A posthumous portrait of Humphrey Sumner, Warden of All Souls, was modelled by David from the death mask and photographs of the great man. It was set in the wall of the antechapel of All Souls, and during its completion David often dined at the High Table there, meeting Isaiah Berlin. Maurice Bowra, John Sparrow, Sir John Simon and G. M. Young. Stunning company for any young man. In June 1954, a bronze memorial panel to the late Bishop of Birmingham, Dr Ernest Barnes, a man considered in his time to be the finest preacher in England, was unveiled in Birmingham Cathedral. The panel is sculpted in low relief except for the Bishop's hands, which are, as the *Birmingham Post* commented shortly after the ceremony, one of the most prominent features and are rendered in full relief. The newspaper report continued: 'When the sculptor was commissioned by the Cathedral Council, he wanted to include the bishop's hands because of their expressiveness.'

From David's Campden Hill Gardens studio came work worthy of selection by the Royal Academy. At the 1952 Summer Exhibition David exhibited a head and three studies of antelopes. One of his animal casts, *Standing Antelope*, was bought by Sir Horace Seymour, who had seen the maquette at the Summer Exhibition. Seymour would later commission figures of the Virgin and the Angel for the Chapel of the Annunciation at Bradford-on-Avon. Part of the old town hall in the centre of the Wiltshire town was to be converted into a Catholic church by the architect Louis Osman, also commissioned

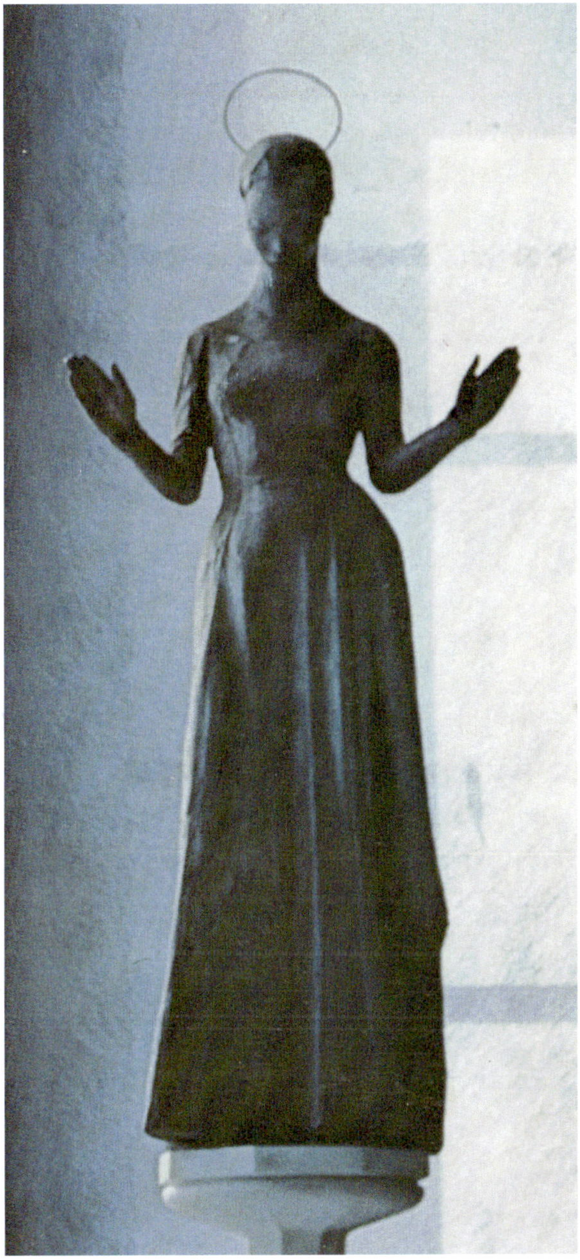 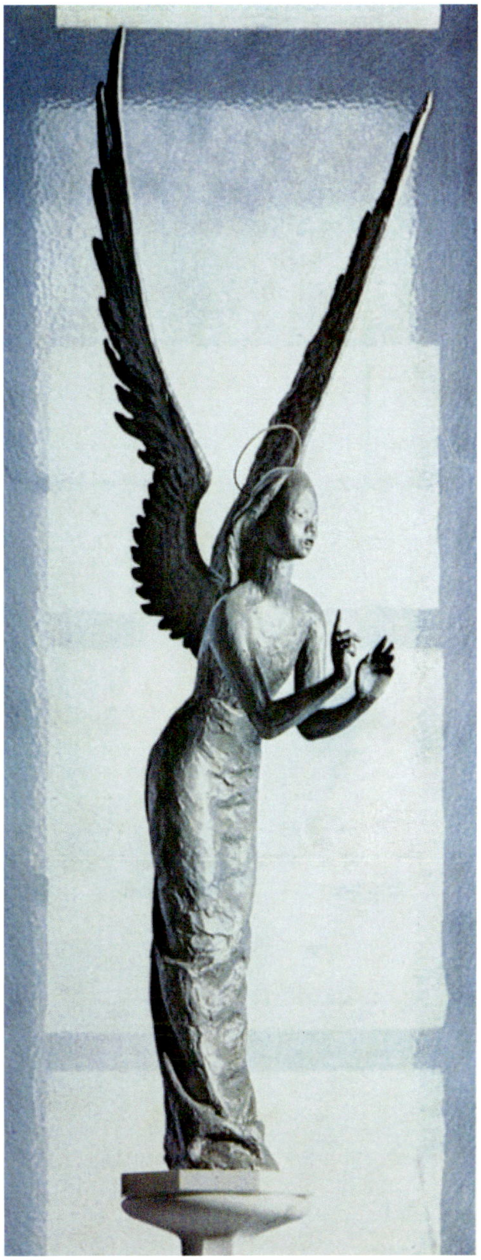

Virgin and the Angel for the Chapel of the Annunciation at Bradford-on-Avon

by Sir Horace to supervise the building's conversion.

Louis Osman would remain of great importance in David's life, bringing him some significant commissions. The heraldic stags which adorn the entrance to Ditchingham Hall in Norfolk, completed in 1954, were a result of David's friendship with the famous architect and were the first of David's commissions to be placed in the grounds of a great private house.

Another example of that critical support to which Boase refers was the commission by Michael Pugh, a London businessman and great sportsman, to sculpt the heads of his two sons. Wynne had made an im-

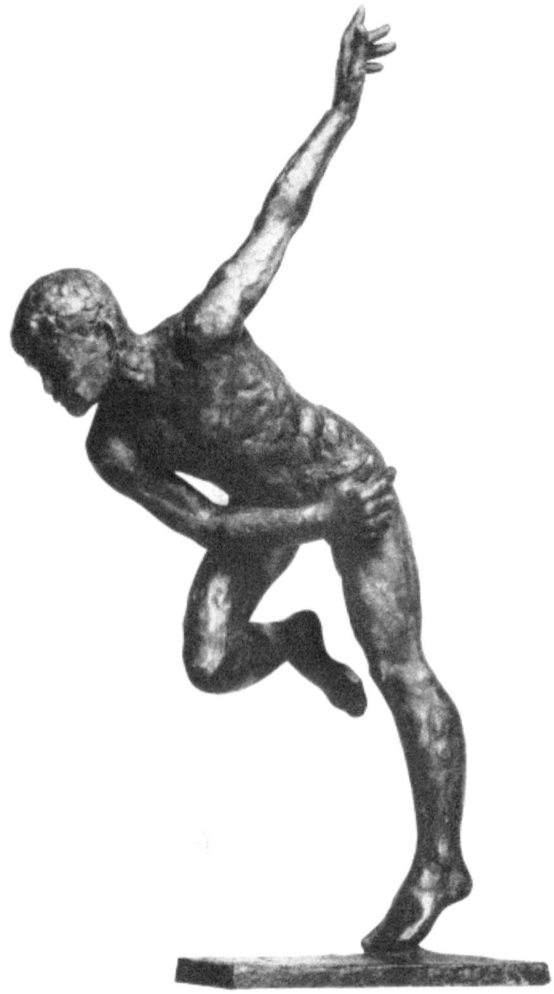

Alec Bedser

pression on Pugh straight away when they first met at a dinner party. Mrs Pugh had spilt coffee on her dress and David, without any hesitation, sprayed the stain with liberal amounts of soda water, using the siphon to ensure a good aim. Pugh was much impressed when he discovered that his wife's dress was merely damp and that the coffee had not left a stain, thanks to the quick-thinking young sculptor. Michael Pugh later introduced David to Frank Taylor, founder of the building firm Taylor-Woodrow, a meeting that led to the creation of *Teamwork*. Pugh was also responsible for David's first piece of sculpture to receive attention in the popular media. He commissioned David to sculpt the English cricketer, Alec Bedser.

The Bedser twins were a famous cricketing duo. Both played for England, though Alec was probably more popular as his bowling had often saved the day in test matches and county-league tournaments. Famous for his fast spin, Alec posed in action at David's studio, running and bowling as the sculptor struggled to capture the impression of strength and movement. There was some amusement in the press, for though the portrait, which now stands in the Long Room at Lords, has Bedser in best cricketing whites, another study was made of the subject nude. Nineteen inches high, it captures the bowler just as he has landed on one foot, having released the ball with his right hand, and seeks to steady his action by extending his left arm high above his head. The energy is dynamic.

There followed another commission from Pugh for a bronze of an even more famous cricketer, Denis Compton. Glamorous, and controversial for his notorious decision to become the public face of Brylcreem, a popular hair grease for men in the 1950s, Compton was seen as heroic by many, especially young schoolboys. Compton even sold himself as a comic-strip character. The cricketing establishment thought some of his antics brought the great game into murky areas of commercial sludge, but such was his fame that David's bronze figure of the cricketer was reproduced, approvingly, in most of the popular newspapers.

David, since Stowe, had always been a keen sportsman. Michael Pugh introduced him to real tennis, an ancient game played

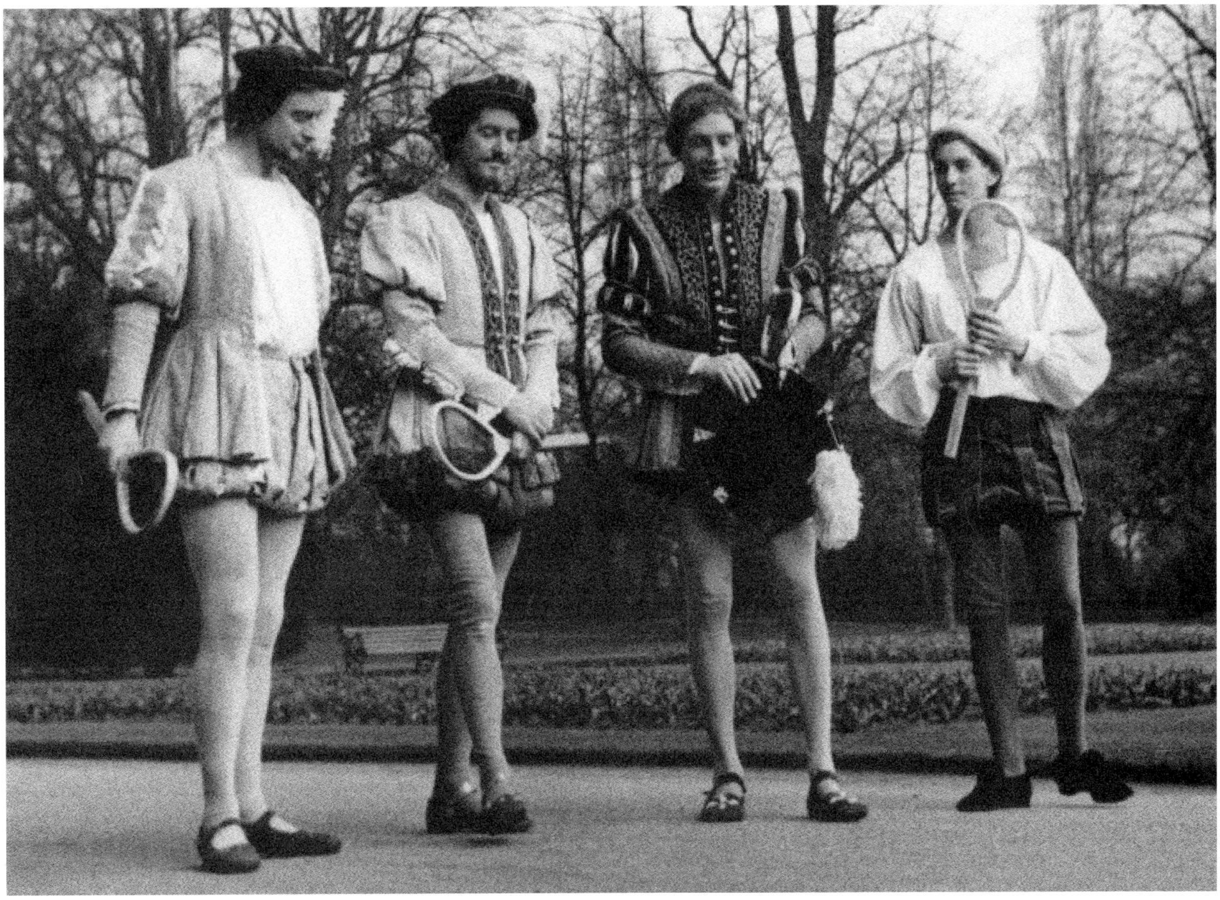

David, dressed in Elizabethan finery, playing real tennis at Hampton Court

with heavy racquets on a large covered court with thirty-foot walls. The game is capable of being played at only a few places – notably Queen's and Lords in London, and Hampton Court, which has one of the earliest courts. T. S. R. Boase observes how Wynne 'found the necessary exercise to maintain and develop that powerful physique which can today stand up to long hours with the chisel, or whatever other tool is required, and enables him, with a surprising ease, to shift the vast weights of his sculptures'. An interesting photograph appeared in the London *Evening Standard* of David, dressed in Elizabethan finery, playing real tennis at Hampton Court, alongside Lord Aberdare. Such places were ideal for a young, struggling sculptor to make valuable contacts. The Cadogan family, in particular, were to take a most important role in David's artistic and, indeed, his personal life.

Another sporting enthusiasm of David's – horseracing – found artistic expression in the eighteen-inch bronze *Jumping Horse*. It was a portrayal of the champion hurdler of 1956, Rose Park, modelled from life in a small paddock. David's abiding passion for horses, allied with his assiduous study of animal physiology, was bearing fruit. He captures the energy and rhythm of movement as the animal lands on its two front legs, head up and alert, as if it has just cleared a hurdle, with its rear legs and tail still in motion.

Because of the financial precariousness inherent in the artistic life, in 1953 David accepted an unsolicited job he was offered. Since he was recently back from Greece, one of the old girls he knew from an exclusive girls' school suggested he went to talk to the pupils about his trip. The headmistress was so pleased with their response that she offered David the chance to be the visiting art master. Langford Grove was in Sussex, set in beautiful grounds on the banks of a river. David drove down once a week to teach groups of girls aged from seven to seventeen. It was an intimate atmosphere as there were fewer than fifty pupils. He found it, and them, a total delight. Until 1957, over nearly five years, David conducted discussions, painting classes, sketching expeditions and sculpting activities for them, as well as becoming friend, mentor and, at times, confidant to many of the pupils. 'It was,' he remembers, 'working for and with the girls. Not for myself.'

He must have made a considerable impact on the girls. David is still a tall, handsome man and the girls would certainly have been impressed by this glamorous figure arriving each week in his recently acquired car. (David had just bought, very cheaply, an old, shoddy and battered Rolls-Royce.) The admiration was mutual. Now, decades later, his face lights up in sheer joy at the memory of those years. Even T. S. R. Boase would comment on David's 'appreciation of some of the talent he found there'.

Oliver Brown owned a gallery off Leicester Square. His annual midsummer exhibition, called 'Artists of Fame and Promise', had come to be regarded by many influential critics and art connoisseurs as an important event. *The Times* of 29 August 1955 observed that the 'exhibitions have grown to be, in the 23 years of their existence, an annual *salon* which is comparable, if on a much smaller scale, with the collections shown every year by the London Group or by the Royal Academy'. The format of the show was unique. Eminent artists were invited by the gallery to exhibit, as were younger artists whom the gallery wished to encourage; a third category, however, comprised painters and sculptors quite unknown to the gallery's proprietors. *The Times* reported 'as many as six or seven artists visit the gallery each day during the months of May and June, bringing pictures which they hope will be included'. The paper suggested that more than seven hundred works were rejected each year.

In the spring of 1954, David had left his recently completed bronze head, *Negro Boy*, there while the owner was out at lunch. On his return, Brown told David he would exhibit it in his up-coming exhibition. The head was admired and bought by Alistair McAlpine, a renowned art collector and philanthropist. McAlpine soon became another vital member of David's growing list of art-loving patrons.

The first one-man exhibition of David's work was held at the Leicester Galleries in February 1955. Other rooms in the gallery showed the work of two more young artists, the English painter Keith Vaughan (interestingly, also self-taught) and the Greek painter Nicolas Ghika, whose work had already been bought by the Metropolitan Museum in New York and the Musée d'Art Moderne in Paris. All three were artists whose work was growing in reputation and, more important perhaps, gaining patronage.

Some years later, in an article in the *Observer*, Alistair McAlpine was described as having 'many of the swashbuckling qualities essential to the man who backs his own fancies in the art game'. A director of the huge building firm, he was especially passionate about sculpture, owning works by, among others, Lynn Chadwick, Barbara Hepworth, Reg Butler, Elizabeth Frink and Bryan Kneale. 'When I come home,' he told the journalist, 'I don't want to read about war in the Middle East or murder in the East End. I prefer to look at the things my wife and I have collected.' In the background of the photograph which illustrates the article – a portrait of McAlpine drinking tea in the gallery specially built on to their country house near Henley-on-Thames – can be seen three works by David. The relationship between the artist and the businessman was by now close and crucial.

David's exhibition at the Leicester Galleries – he showed thirty-seven pieces – proved successful, both privately and commercially. The centrepiece was *The Entry into Jerusalem*, a distillation of all that he had seen and learnt on his European trips and his visit to Jerusalem. Inspired, in part, by Giotto's frescos in the Arena Chapel at Padua, which had overwhelmed David when he first saw them, he described the evolution of this work as an attempt to answer a question he had often asked himself as a child. 'If one had been in the crowd on that first Palm Sunday, would one have recognised that the man riding the donkey was the Son of God?'

In the previous year, 1954, David had made three maquettes of *Christ on the Ass*. The first, six inches, the second, five inches, and the third, fifteen inches high. All three were preparatory studies for the larger, thirty-six-inch, bronze, *The Entry into Jerusalem*. The animal is small, indeed Christ's bare feet seem to touch the ground. But the tiny beast seems more than capable of bearing its load, standing solidly, head pointed forward and sturdy legs still. Christ sits on the rear of the beast, hands clasped forward, eyes shut as if contemplating the epic events to come. Interestingly, the art critic of the *Spectator* thought the work had 'the considered simplicity of the South German wooden images of the same subject'. The *Daily Telegraph* discerned 'grace of form, which is the direct projection of a personal style . . . In an animated assembly of work, there is no dead weight.'

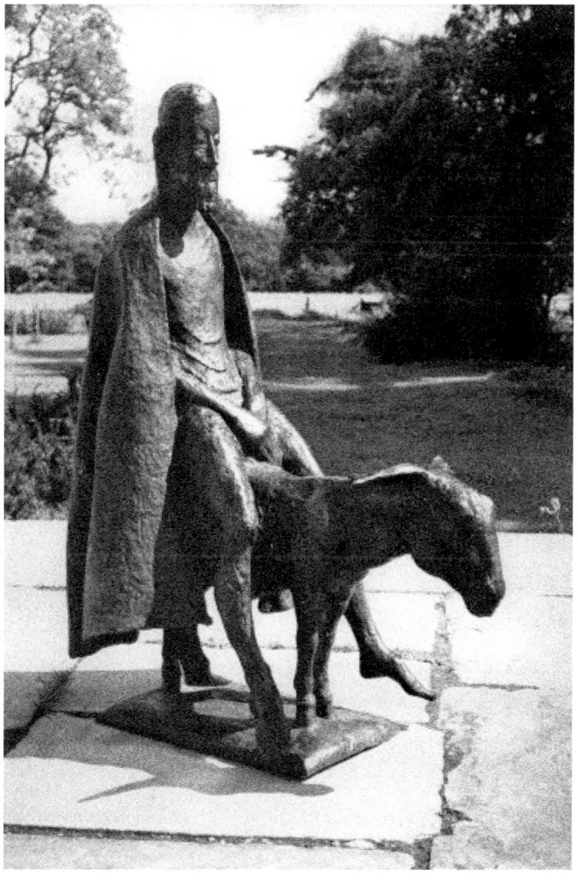

The Entry into Jerusalem

Through the exhibition David garnered another important patron, Victor Hill, an eminent collector and a solicitor. He bought the bronze of Alec Bedser and a carving David had made in Derbyshire marble of a European bison. He remained another ardent collector and supporter of David's over many years. The rapport between artist and patron was instant. When Hill invited David to meet with him, the sculptor asked, 'What time do you dine?' 'Eight o'clock,' replied Victor. 'In that case, I'll come at seven-thirty!' responded David, and their ensuing relationship never faltered.

At the Leicester Galleries, the young sculptor's parents had been able to see and share in their son's achievement. Informed by someone at the exhibition that he must be proud of his son, David's father replied with typical *élan*, 'Don't be a bloody fool. I'm proud of myself.'

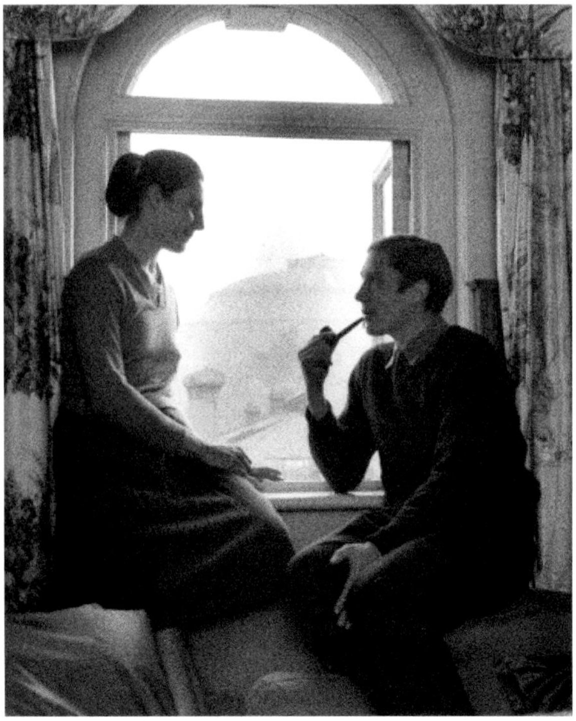

Gilli and David

From a young age, David had always embraced the world as it was and sought to experience whatever came his way. Encouraged by his parents to follow wherever his feelings and aspirations led him, supported and protected by his older brother, exposed to real life by his experiences in the Navy and embracing the flamboyant lifestyle of the young Cambridge buck, he had lived so far an exciting, even exotic, and certainly a glamorous life. Squiring attractive young women to fashionable London and Paris night spots, close friends with many among those who came to be known by an ever encroaching media as 'the fast set', he must have cut a dashing figure. Yet his disciplined approach to work maintained a balance between the easy, fun-loving bohemian lifestyle of café society, with all its temptations, and the time he needed to devote to his burgeoning talent in obeying his compulsion to create. And though he was passionate about his friends, he had yet to embark on a sexual relationship. His initiation was to coincide with his first important London exhibition.

David was twenty-eight when he discovered the electrifying wonder of physical love. The affair was with a beautiful aristocrat and its consequences were of enormous importance. Apart from the personal joy in discovering his desirability to women, allowing his self-esteem and confidence to soar, the relationship with one of the grandest – and richest – noble English families did a struggling young artist little damage; especially as the influential family encouraged him by their commissions. And other prestigious patrons followed as a consequence of the deep and enduring friendship that developed between David and his first lover. Indeed it was she who predicted that David would marry the woman he did when all three were at the party for his private view. Although Gilli and David's marriage was thus foretold at his first important London exhibition, it was not until just after his second showing at the Leicester Galleries, in 1959, that it was celebrated.

Encouraged, and in need of a bigger space in which to work, late in 1955 David converted some stables at Ebernoe in Sussex into a country studio. They stood in a forest on land near a large Queen Anne house where Gilli – Gillian Bennett, daughter of well-known novelist Joan Grant – lived with her husband, Kem. Godfather to their two children, David had been close to Gilli ever since they met in 1950 at Georg Ehrlich's studio. He had thought her the most beautiful woman he had ever seen and asked her out. It had been the start of a long and vital friendship.

As he began to earn money from his endeavours, David had moved from his small Camden Hill studio to Queen's Gate. Though there was room there for a studio, his larger works required him to spend more time in the makeshift carving studio at Ebernoe and there his feelings for Gilli, and hers for him, intensified. Gilli and her two children often spent time in Cornwall and were with David when he started work on his first huge sculpture, *Teamwork*. The three adults reached a mutual decision that a resolution to their situation was required and Kem began divorce proceedings. It was an amicable readjustment. Kem moved on and David became stepfather to Gilli's young children, Nicola and Johnny. He had found in Gilli the ultimate source of inspiration

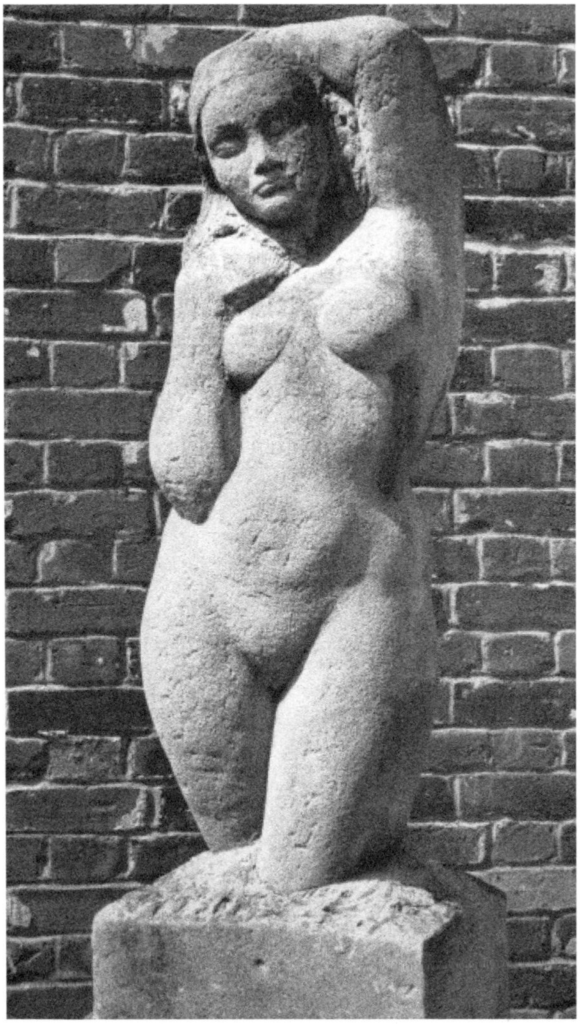

Sandstone figure

and advice: his true Muse. He himself would sum the partnership's significance up in the simple yet profound dedication of the third book which celebrated his work and was published shortly after Gilli's death in 1993: 'This book is dedicated to my beloved wife Gilli, without whose help and encouragement my sculpture would be much worse.'

The very first female figure which David sculpted in stone was carved from a sandstone door lintel which he had salvaged from a ruined building near his Campden Hill studio. Forty-eight inches high, it would be

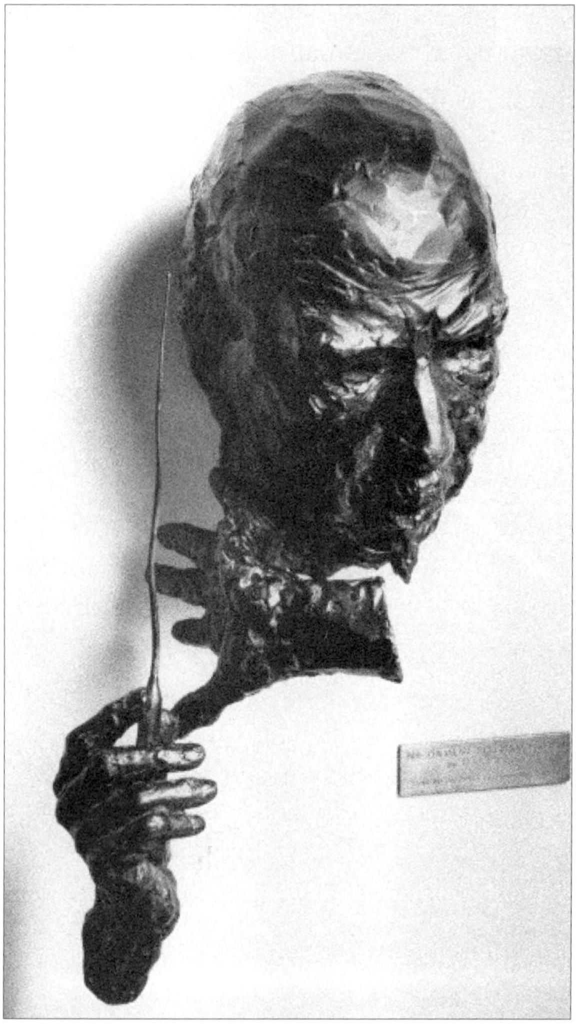

Sir Thomas Beecham

bought many years later by Graham Hill, one of David's most enthusiastic collectors, whose friendship still remains among his most cherished memories.

Carving in stone is, as David described later:

> The exact opposite approach from modelling in clay or plaster. Instead of a deft and rapid building upon a thin frame, the result destined to be cast into metal, the sculptor begins with a rough-hewn block of stone, from which about two-thirds of the mass must be removed with hammer and point. While working on this figure, I realised that carving, with its slow philosophical tempo and enormous physical demands, is the perfect counterpoint to the swift agonies and rewards of modelling.

The first of his large commissioned carvings would be the 204-inch *Archer*, for Longbow House in Chiswell Street, deep in the heart of the City of London. Rising two storeys above street level, the whole figure was carved by David *in situ*, with the help of a stonemason, from blocks of Portland stone, and completed in 1956, the same year he made his figures for the Chapel of the Annunciation at Bradford-on-Avon.

David had not forsaken the intimacy of the portrait head, however. At the suggestion of Gilbert Harding, with whom he had become friendly, the Royal Philharmonic Orchestra commissioned from him the head of Sir Thomas Beecham, as a gift for the renowned conductor to commemorate the tenth anniversary of Sir Thomas's re-formation of the orchestra. Harding was a famous radio and television personality of the day and, in the course of their friendship, David had made a number of broadcasts with him about his sculptural work. Sir Thomas would grant only one private sitting, so David had to attend all the orchestra's performances for many weeks beforehand, often sitting among the violins during rehearsals, observing while Sir Thomas conducted.

In 1958, one bronze cast would be unveiled by Sir Thomas on the main staircase at the Royal Festival Hall. According to press reports at the time – and the coverage was enormous, as we shall see – the conductor felt it reflected his 'ruminative mood, thinking of all the mistakes his orchestra had made!' A newspaper in Rhodesia, the *Bulawayo Chronicle*, went further in reporting the conductor as saying: 'I look as if I'm hearing every wrong note my orchestra has played for ten years.' When the great conductor died suddenly two years after the unveiling, the *Illustrated London News*, reproducing the head, quoted David as recalling Sir Thomas remarking, on seeing it for the first time, that he was pleased someone had put on record that he had his serious side.

The conductor's head is bent forward, his hands are in mid-air, the baton is delicately held erect. It is no surprise that the National Portrait Gallery also bought a bronze (an edition of six was made), for the piece remarkably captures the man in action. His hands are about to sweep out, almost to embrace his orchestra, and his face is in a state of exalted animation. According to David, Sir Thomas was insistent that the third finger of his left hand, which he broke playing cricket, should be made bent. David also created two small full-length figures of the great conductor in action. The figures seem to be in an almost lyrical state, as if they might, at any moment, lift off in time to the music.

For David, the making of the bust was another breakthrough. He had intended it to include the arms of the conductor, but in its execution, he realised he could, by joining only the hands and head together, strip the movement down to its very core. This realisation was of profound significance for him. The impression of movement created by joining together parts of the sculpture would become almost a leitmotif in many of his future works. Birds in flight, animals in movement, even the human figure holding the fin of a dolphin – no other sculptor had achieved such a technique. The self-taught artist had discovered an ability to convey a grace of movement which would make his work world famous.

5

ON 22 October 1958, the *Daily Telegraph* reported that 'a granite sculpture by David Wynne is due to arrive in London tomorrow after a three-hundred-mile journey from Cornwall . . . It is said to be the largest sculpture from a single piece of stone since the Pyramids were built.'

Michael Pugh had introduced David to Frank Taylor, the founder and chairman of the Taylor-Woodrow organisation. The huge building firm had recently run a competition among its employees, to see who could come up with a design for a sculpture to front the new corporate offices being built on Western Avenue, a main traffic artery running west from central London. A member of their accounts department won with the idea of a statue based on the then logo of the mighty construction company – 'Teamwork', four men straining on a rope in unison. Commissioned to execute the work, David decided the statue must be carved in granite. It was also decided, evidence perhaps of David's growing confidence, that the fee would be calculated after the massive work was completed. It was Frank Taylor who made the suggestion: 'You don't know, I don't know, what it's going to cost. Let's leave it to the end.'

A commission so huge brought great media attention, including a film crew to follow the nine-month gestation of the sculpture (and record its journey to London) for a television programme, premièred at the Royal Society of Arts, where David had recently been elected a member. David's talk to the RSA that evening gives some indication of the intense problems he and his comrades in the Cornish quarry had had to overcome.

Travelling to Penryn, where he had been told he might find granite of the size and colour required, David met a 'dour Scotsman who tried to persuade me on the railway station that not only was such a piece of granite impossible to quarry unbroken, but it would be more than the resources of his firm could withstand to allow it to be worked where it lay!'

With typical sangfroid, David –

> *assumed an air of complete innocence and rather ruefully told him that I must have been misinformed in London, where he had been spoken of as the greatest authority on the subject in the country. I followed this up with a humble plea to be shown the quarry . . . During the drive . . . he began to tell me the*

possibilities and beauties of the stone that constituted his life. I in return described my conception of the sculpture, and how possibly after all it would look finer in bronze. At this he stopped the car, flew into a passion, and asked me to wait until I had seen the quarry before deciding on matters of which I knew nothing at all. My fish was caught!

The quarry was very beautiful. The working face high above our heads was a startling sight, for there, jutting out over the edge and looking as though a punch of the hand would send it tumbling to the bottom, was a block of stone seamless and perfect, which to my prejudiced eye looked twenty feet long, seven feet high and at least five feet thick! . . . What was finally decided was this: if the stone could be tobogganed down the cliffside into the pit without mishap, and if it proved indeed to be without flaws; if the Scotsman could persuade his partners to accept a scheme which he had already turned down as impractical, and if we could come to terms whereby he would be compensated for loss of time and space over the next year and the work of his two most skilled masons; then, unless I thought better of the whole idea, he would risk his reputation, his firm's solvency and his sanity in helping me to see it through.

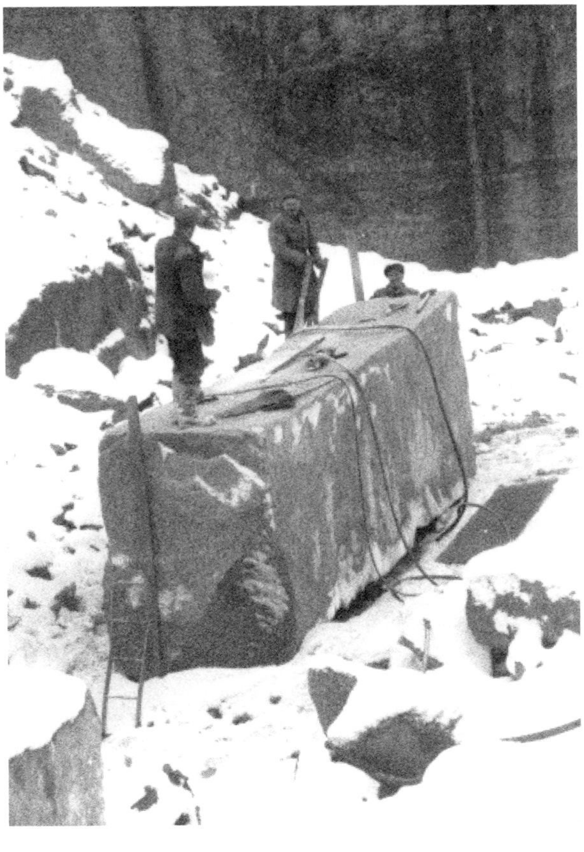
The original block of stone for *Teamwork*

And so it was. David moved into a farmhouse on the hillside below the quarry and with the help of Bert, the quarry foreman – 'a great, gentle man who was to be one of the kindest and most understanding friends I have ever had,' David told the RSA audience – work was commenced.

For many months the weight of the block would have to be slowly reduced, and each time it was turned it could be rolled by means of special tackles farther and farther from the pit, and the danger of flying fragments from blasting, till it finally came to rest under the crane, ready to be lifted on to the truck that would take it to London. In order to take accurate measurements, the base line of the sculpture had to be established before anything else. After hours of patient calculation, the flat plane was determined and worked to an extremely high degree of accuracy. This was done by Hershell, the senior mason, who worked with me throughout the entire carving, and the way he tackled this apparently impossible task of making a perfectly flat plane twenty feet by four feet across, his only tool being a three-bladed axe, made me realise how lucky I was to have acquired an ally of such skill as to amount almost to wizardry. Throughout the year we worked together I

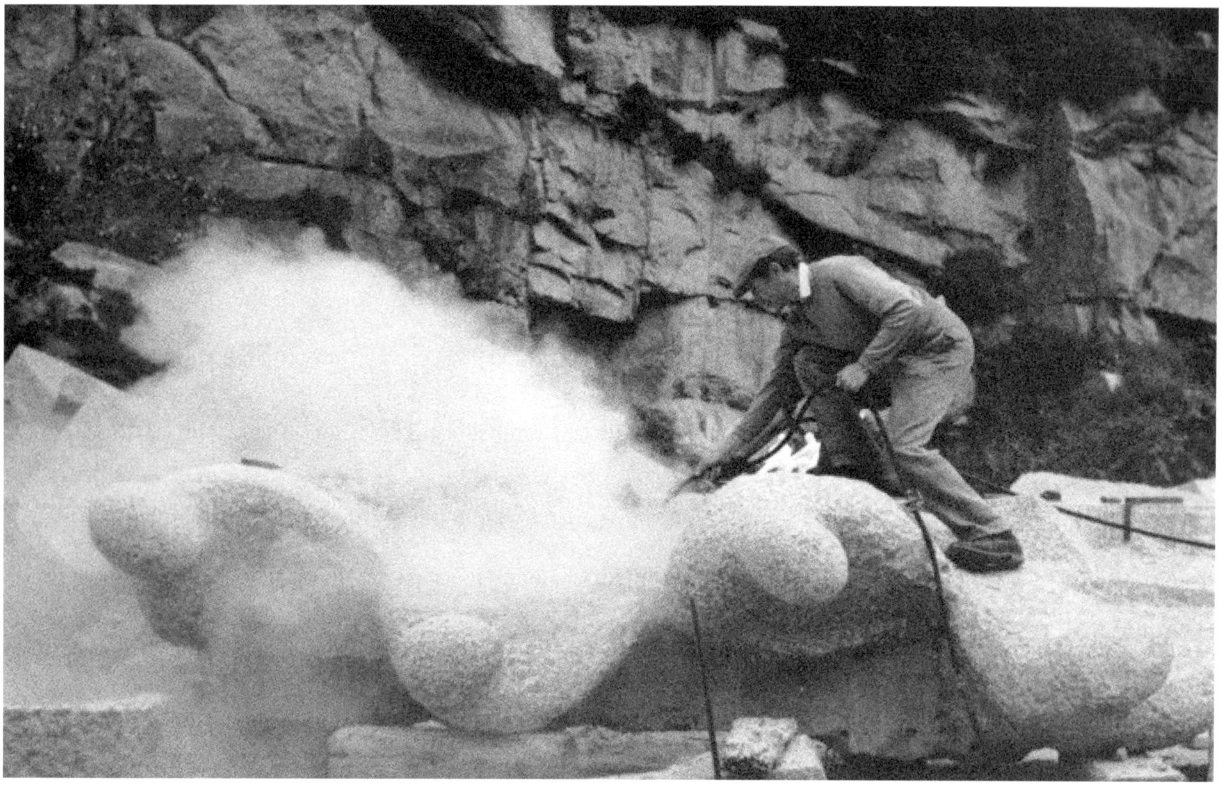

David at work on *Teamwork*

> *never tired of watching the power, deftness and beauty of Hershell's movements as he used the various tools of his craft.*

The logistical difficulties of this mammoth undertaking are still mind-boggling. Over seventy tons of granite had to be removed from the original hundred-ton block, often by hand, and the work was constantly beset by harsh weather conditions – the quarry faced the open sea. David has always completed the final carving of all his works by eye alone. The maquette would be a reference, but no method of mechanical measurement could ever convey the quality created by the artist's contact with the stone itself. So, watched by the quarrymen, David created the statue's ultimate form before it began its three-day trip to London, cheered along the way, the lorry driver reported, by crowds who had read about the hazardous journey in the newspapers.

Teamwork is a colossal achievement. Four male figures strive to move an imaginary object that strains against them in the opposite direction. Though no rope connects them, their naked bodies support each other and the harmonic pattern created from their limbs, stretched taut and strained, suggests effort of almost heroic proportions. Though they do not look at each other, they have become one. They may be Titans, but equally, they may be mere men.

David would write about *Teamwork*:

> *A large carving can occupy the full energies of the sculptor for as much as a year. The very enormity of the task seems to spur him on. As he works day after day, with little visible change to the great block, the sweat running*

down his body, he seems cleansed of all thought. He is merely the carver, the servant of that which is to be released from the stone. It is impossible, but it must be done. In time, the great mass begins to yield, and the forms now dimly visible within the block take on shape and meaning. When finally the sculpture stands revealed, the sculptor knows that he has invented nothing, he has only discovered what was there.

The publicity that surrounded *Teamwork* was immense. The popular press seized on the certainty that no other piece of granite of such epic proportions had been transported over three hundred miles away from its place of origin in modern times, and likened the whole endeavour to the achievements of the Ancient Egyptians. 'Nothing like it since the Pharoahs' was a typical headline.

As the months had gone by, David's relationship with Gilli had grown more intense. Gillian and her children had spent the summer in Cornwall while David was working in the quarry and, just after his next show at the Leicester Galleries, in September 1959, they were married. Among the fifty-two sculptures and twelve drawings in the show was an exquisite charcoal drawing simply entitled *Gillian*. They moved into a new studio. A journalist for the *Sydney Morning Herald*, found 'a light, quiet, casual 33 [-year-old] lounging in his armchair'. 'In my opinion,' David told her, 'a large piece of

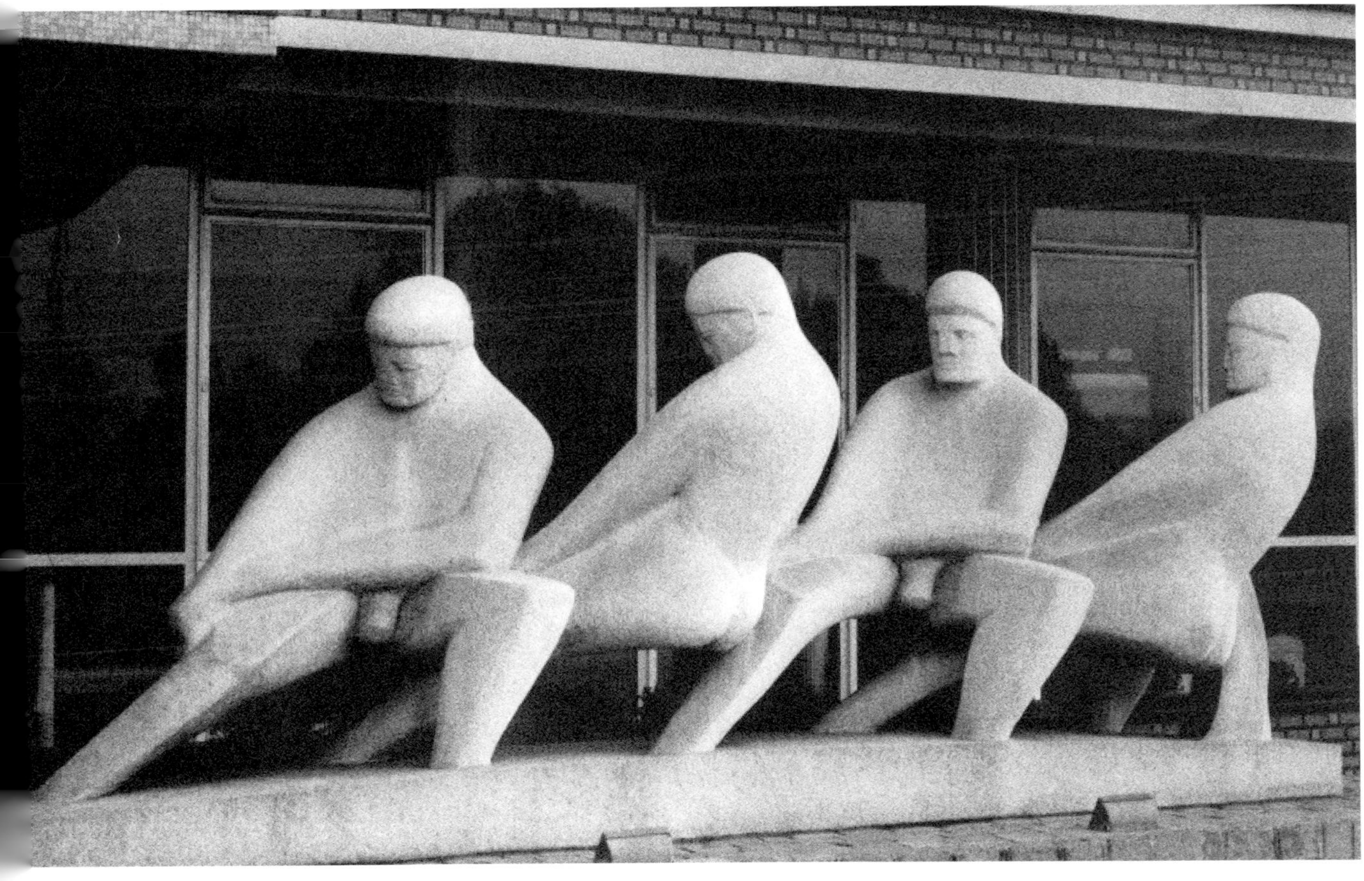

Teamwork

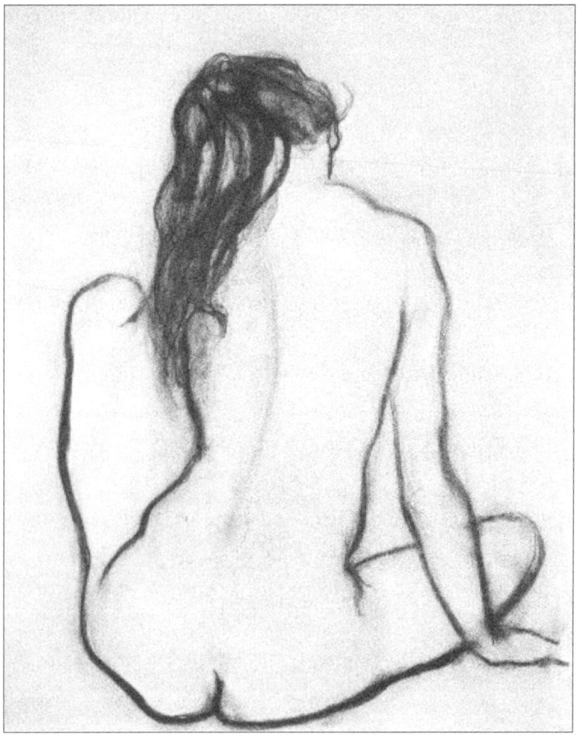

Gilli

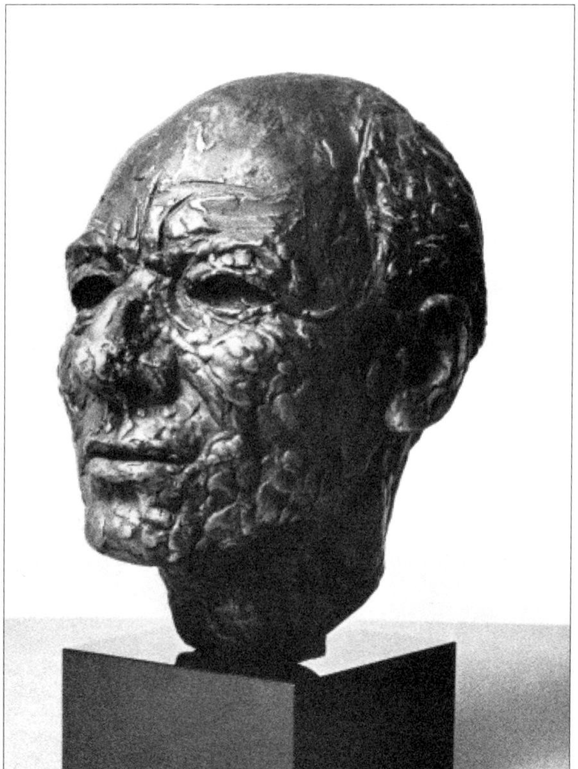

Sir John Gielgud

sculpture should never be seen in a gallery. It is like a cut flower; it may be decorative, but it never looks the same as on a plant. Like the flower of a plant, it must express the whole plant, and be only of that order of creation.' Ruefully, he added, 'Massive sculpture is a marvellous way of expressing oneself, but the difficulties are immense . . . '

David hadn't modified his intense workload. *Art News and Review*, for October 1959, commenting on the Leicester Galleries show, compliments the sculptor on his 'astonishingly catholic taste – and ability – in medium, subject, style and scale . . . Wynne is not only ready for anything, but successfully at ease in all this.' The critic applauds David's increasingly wide range: 'The reason for this range is an impartial intelligence treating each subject and medium as an individual problem of representation, expression and line, to be argued and solved from inside the idea of the completed work.'

One evening at the theatre, David and Gilli noticed Sir John Gielgud sitting near to them in the stalls. David introduced himself to the great actor and asked if he might sculpt his head. Gielgud agreed. As the sculpture was progressing and artist and actor were talking, Sir John complimented David on his knowledge of Shakespeare's sonnets – 'You know them by heart as I do!' The finished product pleased Gielgud hugely, and at the suggestion of Tom Boase, persuaded the governors of the Royal Shakespeare Theatre at Stratford-upon-Avon, anxious to commission a painting of Gielgud for their Memorial Gallery, to buy it. David conceived the portrait 'as a mask whereon moods and passions follow one another at will'. Sir John's delight at David's achievement caused the actor to suggest a meeting

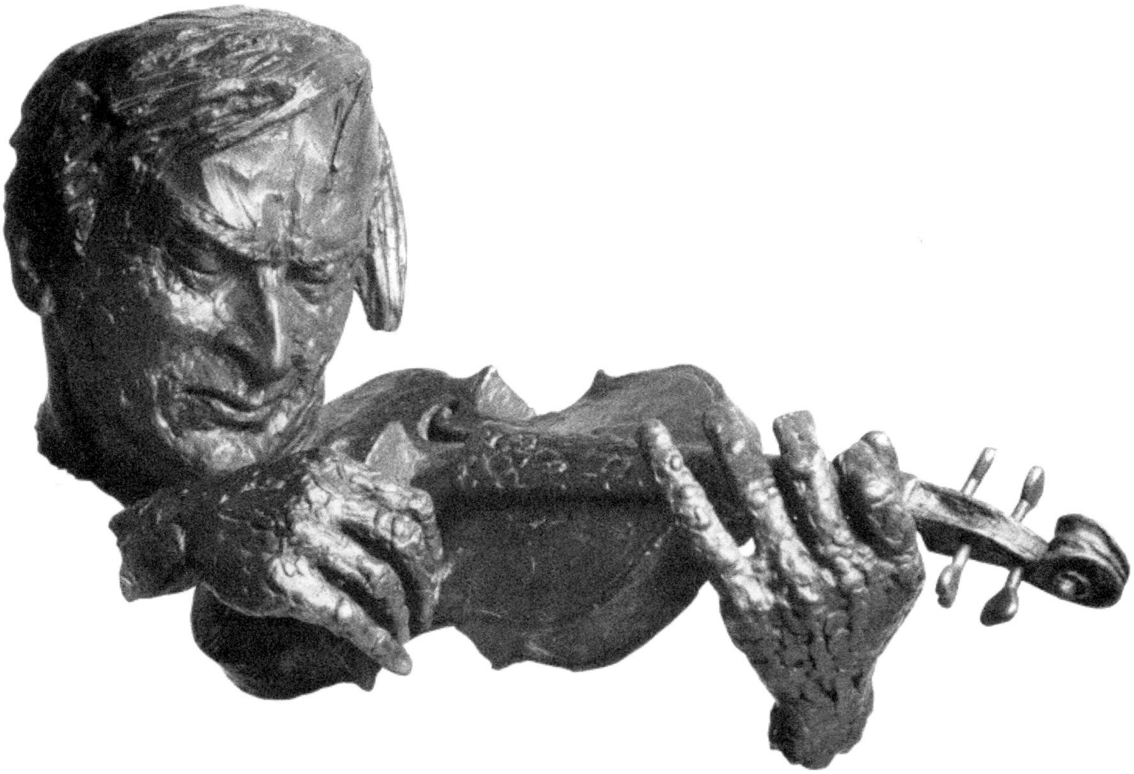

Yehudi Menuhin

with his friend, Yehudi Menuhin, to see if a portrait bust of the violinist could be made. The result is one of David's favourite works.

David began it in Menuhin's music room and brought a tiny wax maquette to the Albert Hall. When Menuhin saw that his violin was included, he agreed to pose. The violinist was learning two Vivaldi concertii, in preparation for a concert, and David worked as Menuhin played. The first attempt was to neither man's satisfaction. The sculptor and the violinist became close friends. David still remembers walking across Hampstead Heath, early in the morning, and hearing Menuhin practising scales and arpeggios endlessly. He started at five-thirty every morning, he told David, and asked the sculptor how long he worked each day. David told him seven hours. 'For a man of your promise,' replied the maestro, 'that's not enough!'

Their friendship led to Lady Menuhin's being the model for another portrait head and to David's being asked to teach at the school Menuhin had founded for talented young musicians. Menuhin went on to write the Foreword to David's first book, to complement the Introduction by T. S. R. Boase, the eminent art historian and another friend of Sir John Geilgud's.

The two men would often discuss art. One conversation left a deep impression on the sculptor. They were discussing comparisons between music and sculpture and found themselves united in the view that they were connected: sculpture was about mass and void, and music, sound and silence.

6

ONE OF DAVID'S most popular works was commissioned in 1960. Gabriel White, head of the Arts Council, suggested to the London County Council that David be included among those chosen for their £30,000 'patronage of the arts' scheme. As a result, he was asked to create a large 'animal work' for a park. David had regularly visited the London Zoo ever since the days of his zoological studies at Cambridge. Of inestimable value in all his work, this accumulated knowledge was especially useful when sculpting animals and birds.

David chose as his subject Guy the gorilla, star of the London Zoo. He told the *Daily Express* in September 1961 that he had already been working for nine months, shifting two and a half tons from the original four-ton block of black Belgian fossil marble he had chosen for the piece. He told the newspaper: 'I paid about thirty visits to Guy at the Zoo and we got to know each other well. I used to feed him liqueur chocolates and he would recognise me immediately.' The sculpture was too large for its original site and in 1963 it was finally placed in the Crystal Palace Park, high above the lake, where the prehistoric animals created by the Victorians for the first Great Exhibition in 1851 were still to be found. The work caught the popular imagination and photographs of David watching his stepson John and two-year-old Edward – his and Gillian's first son – clambering over the huge sculpture appeared in newspapers all over the world. Today, children can still be seen playing in and around Guy's massive limbs.

Another major work, *The Breath of Life*, commissioned by the British Oxygen Company to stand outside their head office in Hammersmith, was unveiled by Sir Alan (A. P.) Herbert, a famous English literary figure of the time, in 1962. The work illustrated verse 7 of the second chapter of Genesis: 'And the Lord formed man of the dust of the ground, and breathed into his nostrils the breath of life; and man became a living soul.' It was sixteen feet high, and carved from three blocks of specially cut Italian marble, and the flagship BBC arts programme, *Monitor*, made a twenty-minute film of the whole creative process, screened in December 1962. The television critic for *Punch* considered David 'splendid TV material. He spoke fluently, eloquently, of his ideas, of the sculptor's role in society,

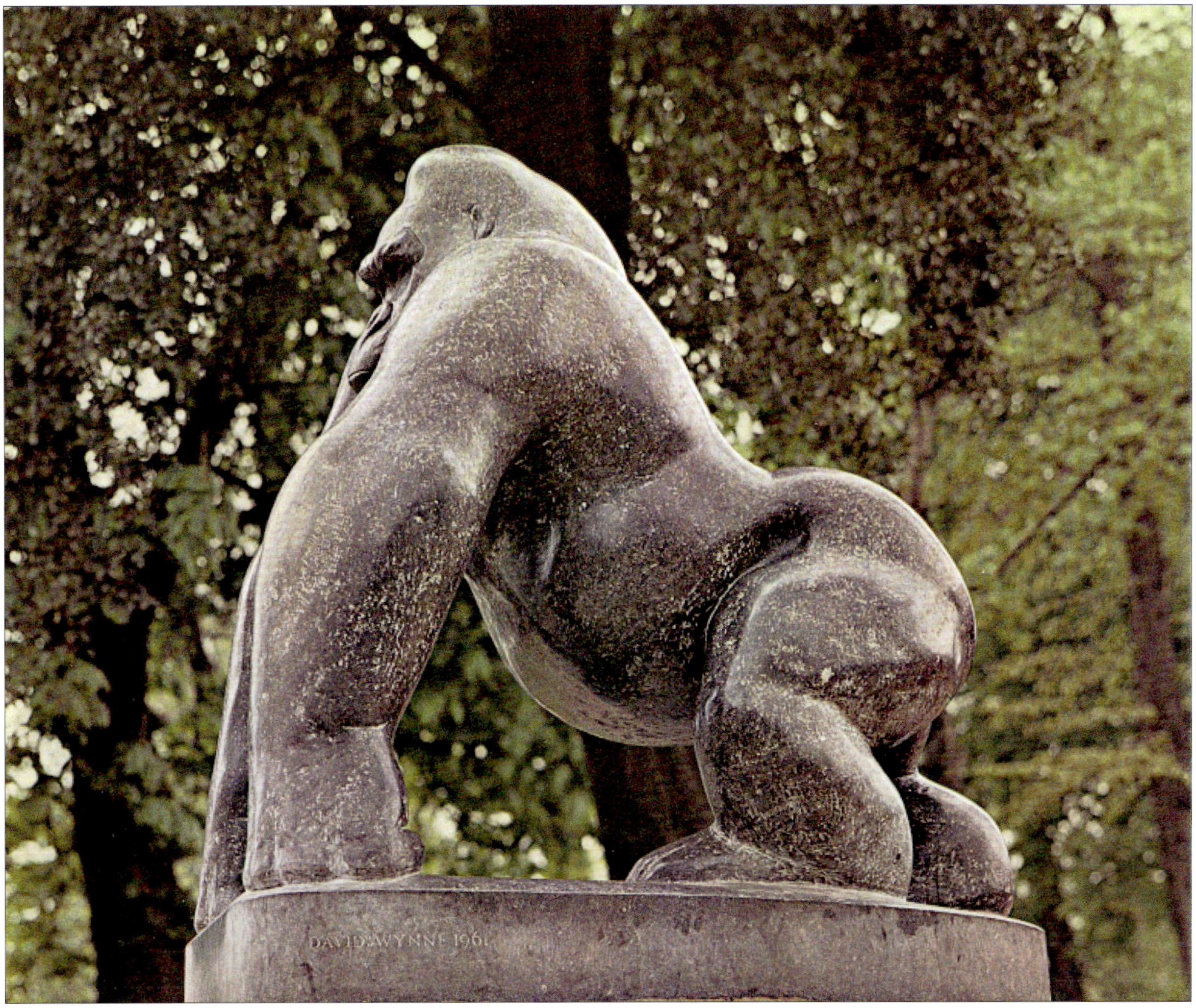

Marble *Gorilla*

of the nature of stone . . . This was an outstandingly good item.'

David's next work was to prove not so popular. Commissioned by the department-store group Lewis's to adorn their new branch in Hanley, *Fire Figure* was a nightmare to install. More than a dozen policemen had to be engaged for two days to control a quarter-mile-long traffic jam as the thirty-five-foot sculpture, fashioned from welded plates of aluminium, was erected over the shop's main entrance, with David, fifty feet from the ground, supervising the final positioning of his one-and-a-quarter-ton work. 'It looks like the devil,' said a passer-by to the local TV reporter; a Mr John Parker told the local *Evening Sentinel* it was 'far too advanced for the Potteries'. Worse was said, early one morning, by one of a group of miners passing underneath as David and Charlie Edwards were at work above:

'I think it's a fucking abortion!'

'I think you people up here know more about abortions than you do about sculpture,' retorted Charlie.

The *Evening Sentinel*'s editorial was more

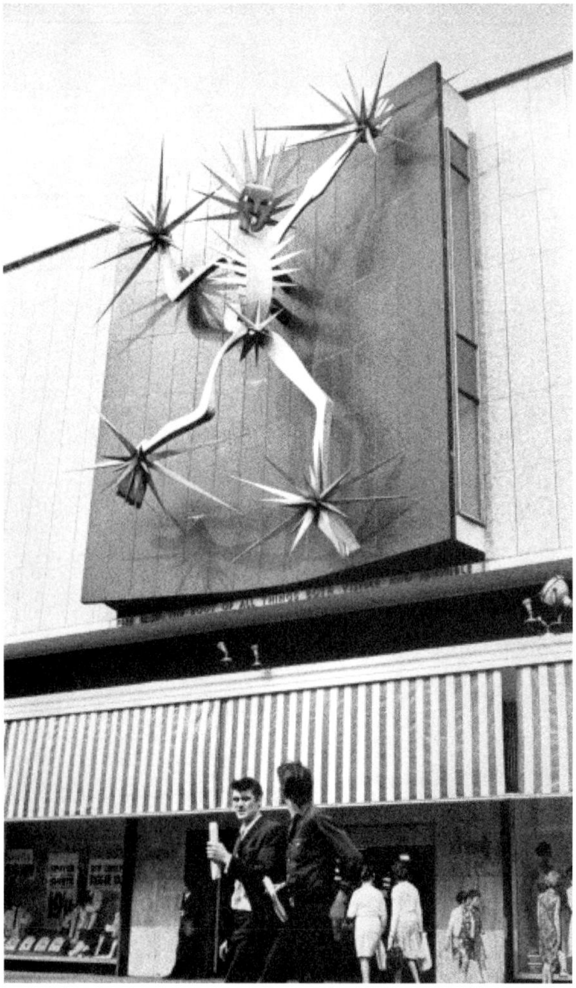

Fire Figure

encouraging: 'The striking piece of modernistic sculpture . . . has turned Stafford Street from a humdrum thoroughfare into a place of wonder and excitement.' The BBC's popular news programme *Tonight* featured a report on the whole enterprise in which David descibed his inspiration for the work as being the flames shooting from the pot banks, furnaces and foundries as they illuminated the night sky around the town. Underneath the work was inscribed a line from Thomas Vaughan: 'Fire is at the root of all things both visible and invisible.' David had the last say, telling the annual dinner of Lewis's employees, 'I like my sculpture even if nobody else does.'

1961 was an eventful bitter-sweet year. The commissions for *Gorilla*, *The Breath of Life*, *Fire Figure* and *Christ and Mary Magdalene* exposed the limitations of his studio. Gilli was pregnant. A larger home was required and now, thanks to this plethora of work, affordable. The young family moved into a modern flat-roofed house near Wimbledon Common and there, in the garden, David built yet another studio. Their first son, Edward, was born and David met the Maharishi, both landmark events. Then, in December, David's mother died.

There had been a fire at his brother's house and their mother had been terribly burned. Knowing she was dying, David spent a week with her at the Special Burns Unit at Stoke Mandeville Hospital. Her injuries were appalling. She was terribly disfigured and reluctant for anyone other than David to be with her. He drove down to the hospital on Christmas Eve, convinced the end was near, but returned home for Christmas with the family. When he arrived, Gilli was waiting to tell him that the hospital had rung to say his mother had died.

He travelled back through the snow-laden countryside, stopping around two on Christmas Day morning to walk into a field where he had noticed a large oak tree. There was no wind, yet as often happens in very cold weather, what few leaves were left on the branches were falling gently on to the snow-covered ground. The quiet, stark beauty of that moment gave him some consolation. Everything dies. Everything passes. Comforted, he went back to the car and, moving off, noticed a figure walking along the road in front of him, a stranger to

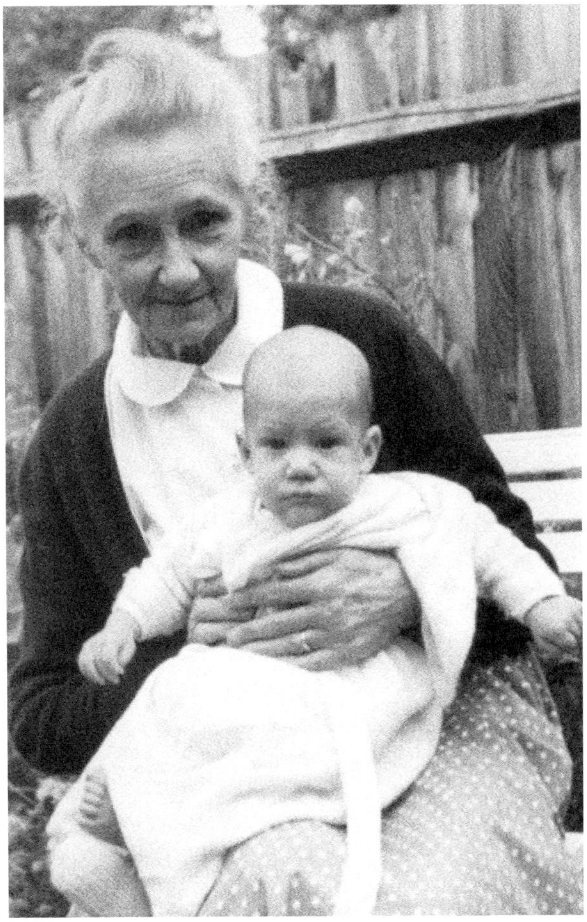

David's mother with Edward

whom he offered a lift. David realised, as soon as they fell into conversation, that he had picked up a man just released from prison, where he had worked sewing mailbags. On questioning his passenger further, David discovered it wasn't possible for him to get a room for the night without proof of work or money. The ex-prisoner had neither. Giving him what was to David at the time quite a sum of money, David dropped the man in the town and drove on to the hospital. Both incidents had given the sculptor comfort, as if both were symbols of the never-changing pattern of earthly existence.

A year after the success of his Leicester Galleries exhibition, a further show was planned for Tooth's. One of the gallery's directors, Martin Summers, asked David if there was any subject he'd like to model in time for the event. David suggested the Beatles, then just beginning to achieve adulation verging on the maniacal. Tooth's talked to Brian Epstein who felt it would do his clients' image good and said he would put it to the Beatles – but the work could only be done in Paris. The group were performing at the Olympia and also recording part of a new album there.

A ten-day period was found when David could work with them and it was decided that the sittings would take place in their suite at the George V Hotel. Police had to help David get through the hysterical fans surrounding the hotel and when he finally met the group, according to the account written for *Queen* magazine of the project, Epstein had forgotten to tell the four musicians that he was coming. David told the journalist from the magazine how he:

> flew to Paris . . . and got to their hotel around teatime. They were still in bed and they simply ignored me. Ringo seemed the most sympathetic, so I worked on him and he finally agreed to pose. He was very sweet. All he said was, 'Can I have my breakfast first?'

Paul agreed to pose next, then John, then George. David told *Queen* that modelling George Harrison reminded him of the time he attempted to persuade a family of kangaroos that he meant them no harm. 'They finally understood that I wasn't going to tread on their tails; and George has exactly the same kind of animal caution that has to be overcome.' George subsequently became a life-long friend of the sculptor and it was David who introduced George, and then the others, to the teachings of the Maharishi Mahesh Yogi, whose head David had modelled in 1962.

Once again, the press coverage for the enterprise was enormous. David told the *Daily Express* how he had had to find the clay himself, outside Paris, and dump two hundredweight of the stuff ('it smelled horrible') in the bath tub in the Beatles' hotel suite. 'They had,' David told the reporter, 'quite a lot to say about it.' A warm bond developed over the next few days. David took the boys to dinner at a fine restaurant in the Rue Jacob, where they upset the management by demanding Coca-Cola, roast quails and boiled potatoes. In return, the group took David to the recording studios where, over seven hours, they composed and recorded 'Can't Buy Me Love', while David modelled individual figures of them playing.

One night, at another restaurant, a cabaret act dressed as troubadours approached them. David asked John to say something complimentary which David would translate to the lead singer into French. 'Tell Danny Kaye,' said John, 'he's got the makings of a great deaf-mute act.' He was, David felt, the brightest of the four, while Ringo had disarming appeal. Back in London and now on friendly terms with them all, David visited their apartment in Park Street. The building was besieged by screaming fans and once again police had to help him gain admission. When he finally

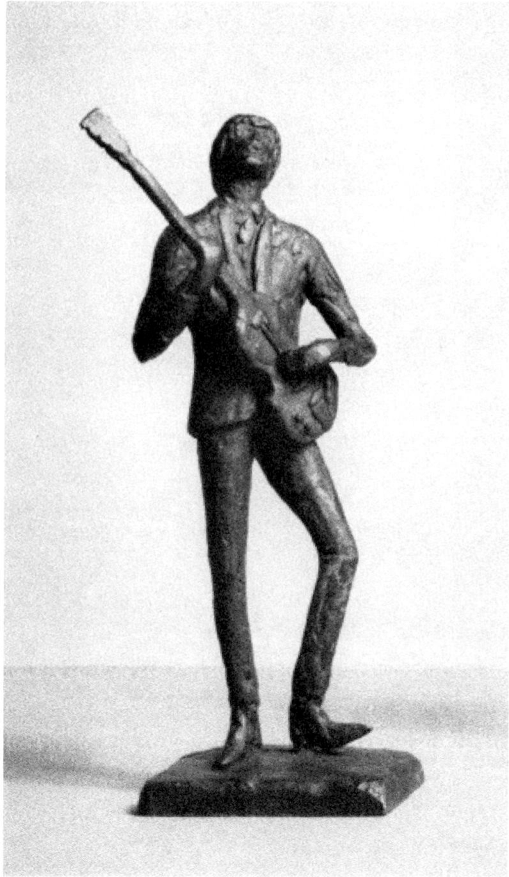

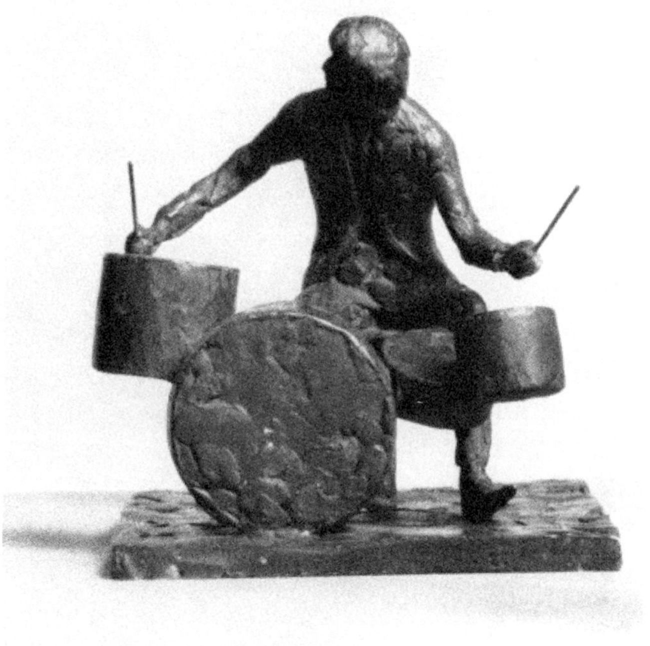

got in, Ringo was the only Beatle at home. 'Here, Dave, have a beer,' said the drummer. 'Drink my health!' 'Right ho, Ringo,' said David. 'What else should I drink to?' 'Well,' said Ringo, 'we've just heard we're millionaires.'

The final bronze was a composite portrait: Ringo at the bottom, Paul and John next, George at the top. Done while there was still, as David would later write, 'comparative shelter from the mounting wave of popularity which for a time engulfed [them], the heads portray four young artists, in accord with one another and intensely aware of the strange world that they are entering . . . '

As well as introducing the Beatles to the Maharishi, it was through him that David met a man who was to become one of his greatest friends, the painter Peter Rogers. At the suggestion of someone who was at a gathering with the Maharishi, David went to an exhibition of Peter's paintings in the crypt of St Martin-in-the-Fields in Trafalgar Square. The Maharishi was to visit the show at the same time. David and Peter would become inseparable friends. Not only did David consider the painter's work extraordinary but they discovered that they agreed almost totally on what their artistic aims were and what their work was to be about – the sense of the spiritual in the world. It was significant that David's first impression of Peter, with his flowing beard and white robe, was that he looked just like Jesus might have done. During the 1960s and 1970s, Peter lived in New Mexico and David visited him

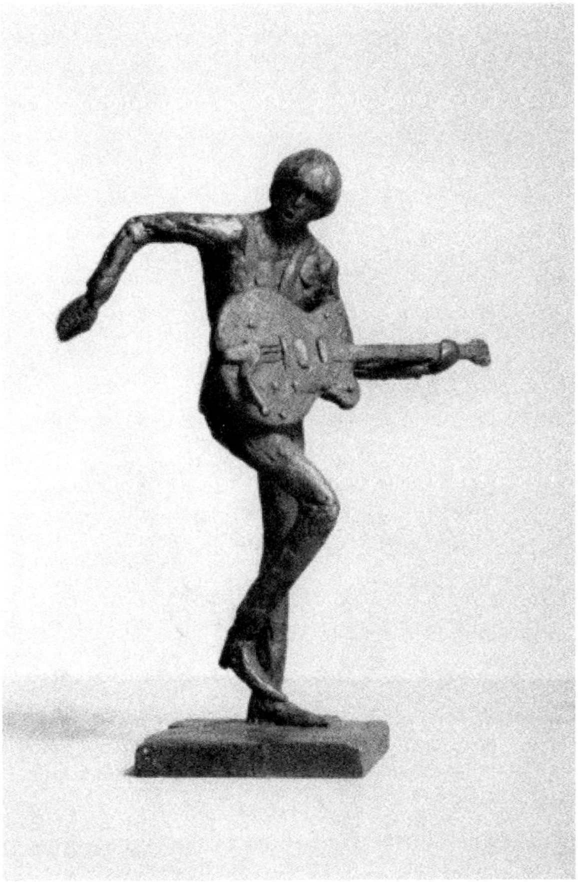

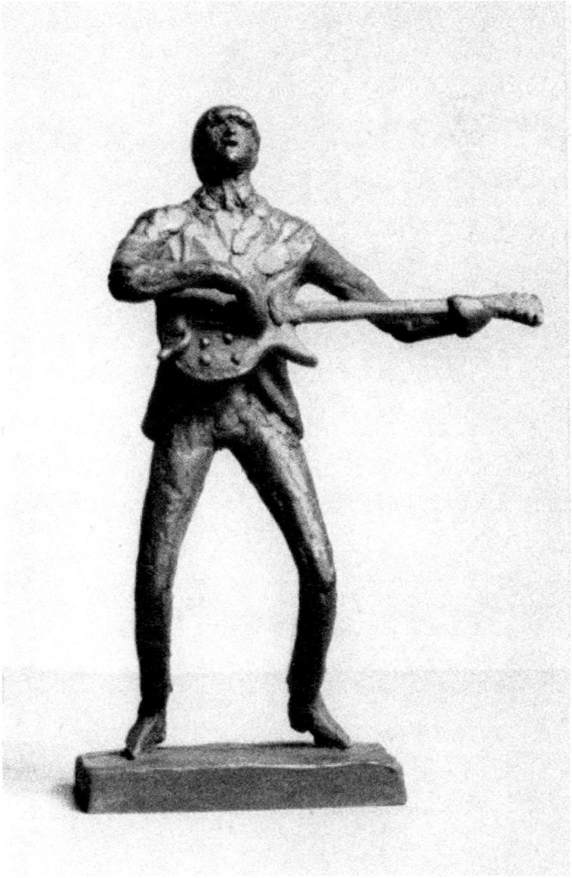

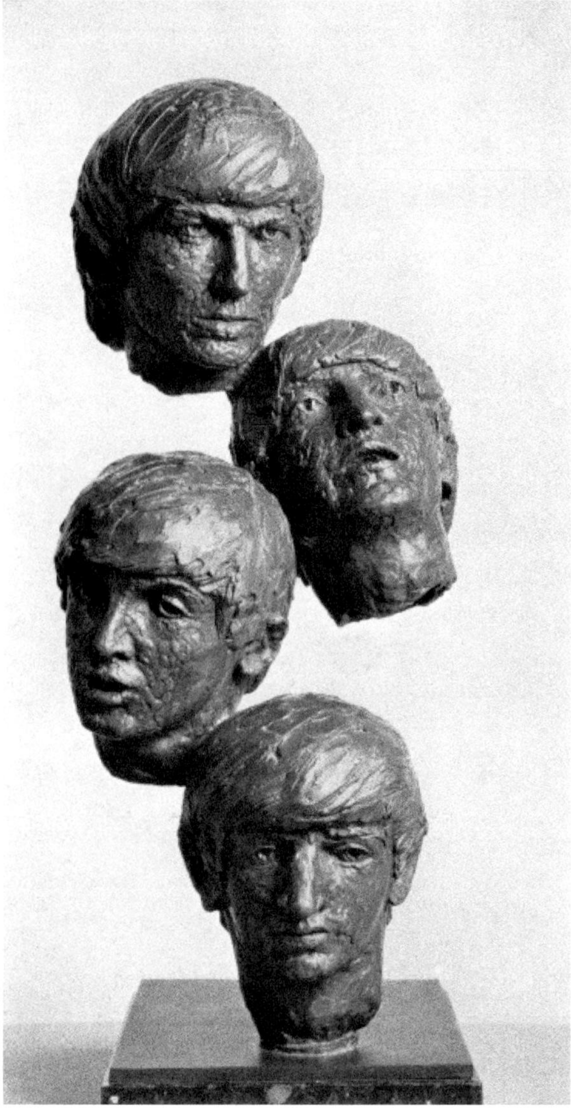

The Beatles

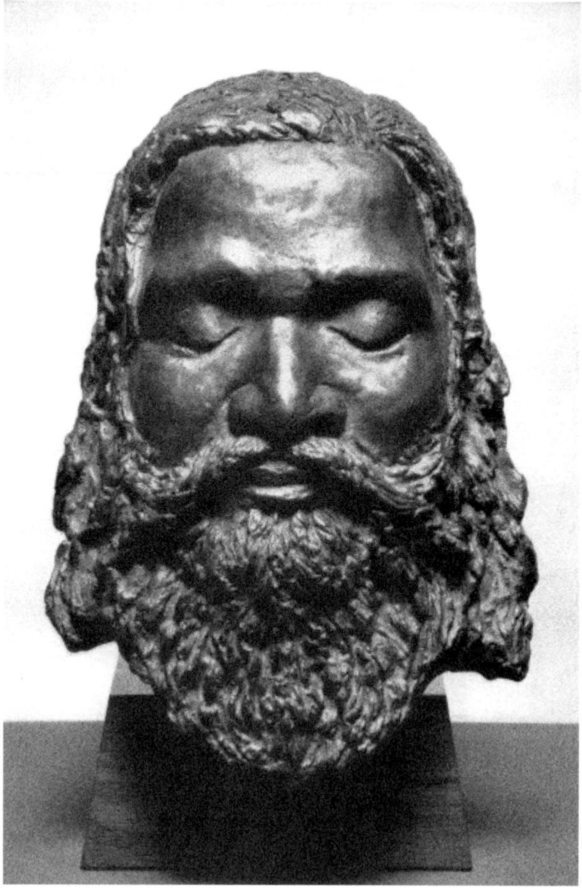

H. H. Maharishi Mahesh Yogi

whenever he could. Peter's canvases adorn David's Fulham studio, among them David's favourite portrait of Gilli.

The exhibition at Arthur Tooth's opened in May 1964 and attracted considerable coverage. The Beatles saw to that. Twenty-eight pieces were on show, including one of David's most important religious works, *Christ and Mary Magdalene*. Completed in 1963, the bronze stands seventy-two inches high and represents the moment when Mary Magdalene found the stone rolled away and the sepulchre bare. Not recognising Jesus and thinking him a gardener, she asks if he knows where the body has been taken. David chose the text from St John's Gospel 20:16–17:

> Jesus saith unto her, Mary. She turned herself, and saith unto him, Rabboni; which is to say Master. Jesus saith unto her, Touch me not; for I am not yet ascended to my Father: but go to my brethren, and say unto them, I ascend

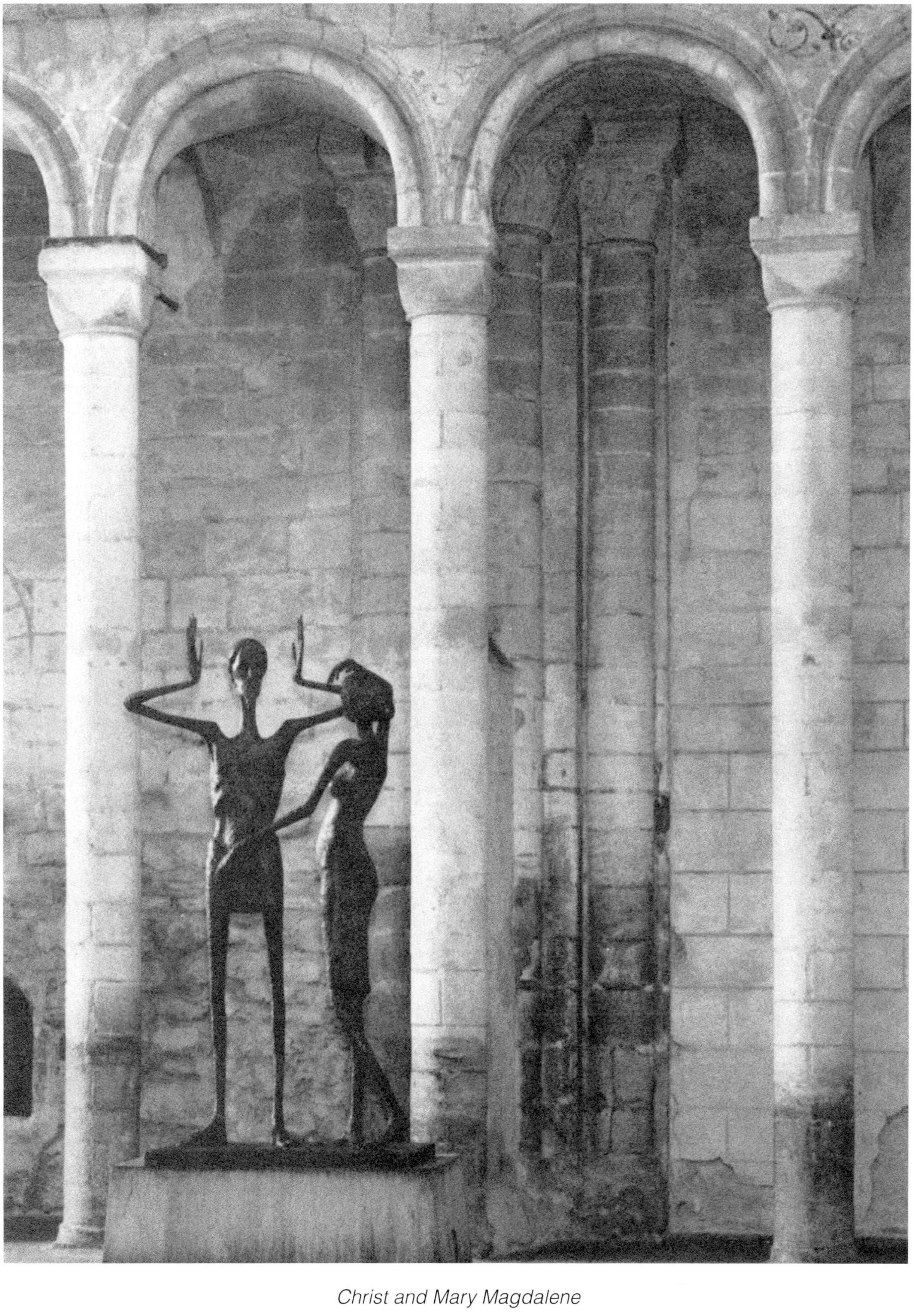

Christ and Mary Magdalene

> unto my Father, and your Father; and to my God, and your God.

The work was destined for Ely Cathdral where it stands in the south transept. Two more casts were made: one for Magdalen College, Oxford, and the other for a site in Venice. *Art News and Review* recorded:

> The emaciated rigid, wounded body of Christ, the graceful femininity of the Magdalene and the thin upraised arms, offered and rejecting, contain all the drama of the moment and the poignant relationship between spiritual and profane love. Aesthetically, in the age of abstraction, it is disturbing: we cannot bear very much reality. Perhaps that in itself is its triumph.

Tooth's also exhibited bronze heads of David's sons: *Edward Sleeping* and the baby head of Roland, just born in 1964. The press, however, focused on the sculpture of the Beatles and newspapers around the world reproduced photographs of the group's portrait heads with David smiling up at them. The portrait head of Yehudi Menuhin was also on show. His set of six sold out faster than the Beatles, a feat the great maestro was very proud of and amused by.

Concurrently with the Tooth's show, at the Temple Gallery, an exhibition of David's drawings and watercolours was arranged.

> The whole collection [reported *Art News and Review*] gives one that rare pleasure that comes from a painter who appears to be looking and delighting in nature for the first time . . . a hand of exceptional skill has translated the impressions of an eye that has cherished the single object and the shifting patterns of light and colour.

In July 1964, David received a gratifying invitation due, no doubt, to the success of the Tooth's show and the attention it received. He was asked by Roy Plomley to be his guest on the enduringly popular BBC radio programme *Desert Island Discs*, a rare accolade (repeated many years later when David was asked to appear on the show again, this time with Sue Lawley).

The years were bringing David increasing success and security – and it seemed his fame was spreading.

7

THE NEED for David to acquire a larger studio to provide a better space to work within was becoming imperative as his sculpture became more and more sought after. The requirements of his growing family only added to the urgency to find a suitable home. A very large, twenty-seven room, eighteenth-century converted farmhouse on Wimbledon Common seemed to him ideal. Besides the sheer size of the house and the possibility of converting the various outbuildings into studio space, it was also set in gardens of great beauty. There was even enough room, under the ancient trees, for a croquet lawn. But Gilli had her doubts.

In 1965, the day the Labour Party was returned to power, a run on the pound, coupled with an uncertain economic future meant that nobody else was bidding for the empty property. Once again, two of David's patrons stepped in to help. Victor Hill arranged a private mortgage and Alistair MacAlpine offered to convert the house and outbuildings into a custom-made dwelling, suitable for family life but also providing three studios of varying sizes. After six months' building work, David would have a large studio space for modelling portrait heads, etc., a second plaster studio and a brick-built garage transformed into a studio where his carvings could be made. The cost of the conversion was covered by the ever generous Alistair MacAlpine, in return for more of David's sculpture in eventual repayment.

The choice of Rushmere would prove to have been inspired. It was the place from where David would finally achieve international recognition. Two years after Rushmere's conversion, David held his first exhibition in New York. It was a sell-out. His work was bought by multi-millionaire collectors for their private estates and huge international corporations for the forecourts of their flagship offices. David's success would vindicate his belief that Rushmere was the right thing to do and Gilli's initial reservations would be dispelled. Indeed she would become a vital partner in what became known by David, his family and their friends as the 'Rushmere Foundation'.

Over the next decade, as their children grew up, Rushmere provided an environment which is still recalled by those who experienced it as verging on the magical. Gilli provided the loving, warm, maternal centre and no one was turned away; most

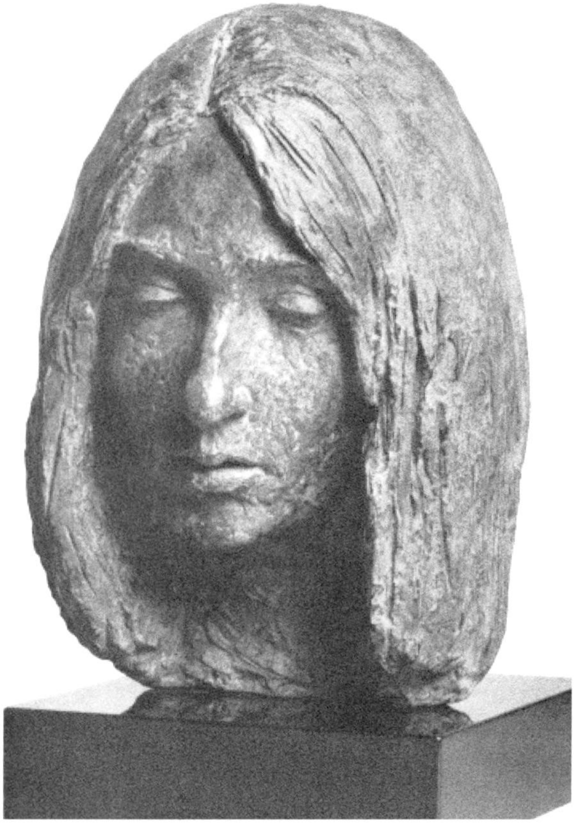

Joan Baez

things seemed possible, and so long as the noise level did not interfere with David's work, anything went. Local children from the nearby school were as welcome as the Beatles.

It was at Rushmere that David modelled his portrait of Joan Baez. The singer Chris de Burgh, through David's friendship with his parents, came to stay, often for months on end, to write many of his songs there (he would eventually become one of the biggest collectors of David's work), and the folk singer Donovan, then a young, aspiring newcomer, moved into a small flat within the complex and was welcomed as warmly as if he were a member of David's own family. The *Evening Standard* reported some time later, on 8 December 1969: ' "Come home and sing with Donovan," Edward and Roland Wynne urged their friends at Bishop Gilpin School, Wimbledon. So thirty of them came and helped Donovan record his new song "The Lord of the Dance".' The double-page article goes on to describe how they all sat in Rushmere's living-room and learned the words from posters stuck up on the window, as Donovan's father pointed them out. The newspaper concludes by informing its readers: 'Donovan once had a flat in David Wynne's house overlooking Wimbledon Common. The sculptor, who has already made a famous portrait of the Beatles, will show his head of Donovan in his March exhibition. Donovan has promised to play at the opening.'

Jimi Hendrix was another guest, whom David remembers fondly as a quiet, polite and thoughtful young man. But it would seem that all this high-profile activity in no way diminished David's creative energy. An impressive portrait head which David made of Sir Edward Beddington-Behrens, a well-known financier and art connoisseur, resulted in Sir Edward suggesting David model the head of Oskar Kokoschka. As he revealed in the *Tate Gallery Report* (a cast of *Kokoschka* was presented to the gallery by David), Kokoschka 'showed an intense interest in the progress of the work, giving frequent advice interspersed with entreaties not to take any notice of what he said!' David worked on the portrait in the artist's house at Villeneuve. It was completely modelled in two sittings of four hours on consecutive days.

> It is [David wrote] nearly impossible to describe in words what one aims at in a work of this kind, but would it help to say that I approached it from the point of view

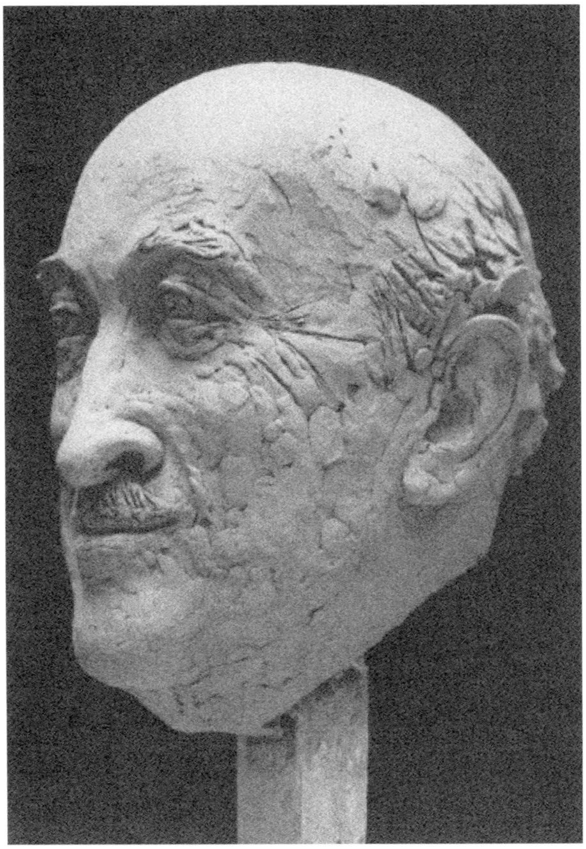

Sir Edward Beddington-Behrens

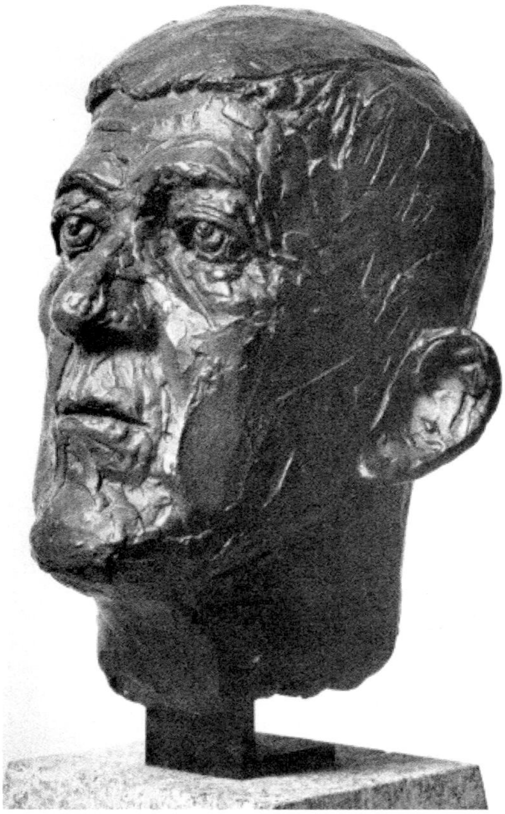

Oskar Kokoschka

that he was a solitary genius, who had gained rather than lost from reverses of fortune which would have broken a lesser spirit? I attempted to show a visionary painter who, in age, had lost none of his sense of wonder, but had gained a vast compassion for other people, which he was able to communicate through his work.

Kokoschka later told David it was the best likeness of him that had ever been made.

It is worth recording that initially the curators at the Tate were not enthusiastic about receiving the bust of the great painter. Sir Edward reported this to Kokoschka, who viewed the matter most seriously and informed the gallery that he might reconsider the gift of his works in his will. Many other galleries would undoubtedly welcome the gift. The Tate capitulated, accepted the bust and, as far as can be determined, the magnificent portrait still loiters darkly in the storage cellars. It has never been put on permanent display and can only be viewed by appointment.

Spring 1966 saw the second exhibition of David's work at Tooth's in Bruton Street. It was called An Exhibition of Bird Sculpture and Recent Portrait Heads. Just one year before, David had received his first commission from the United States. Many of the sculptures in the Tooth's exhibition derived from David's protracted study for this massive work. Eighteen of the twenty-six bronzes (all in editions of six) were birds.

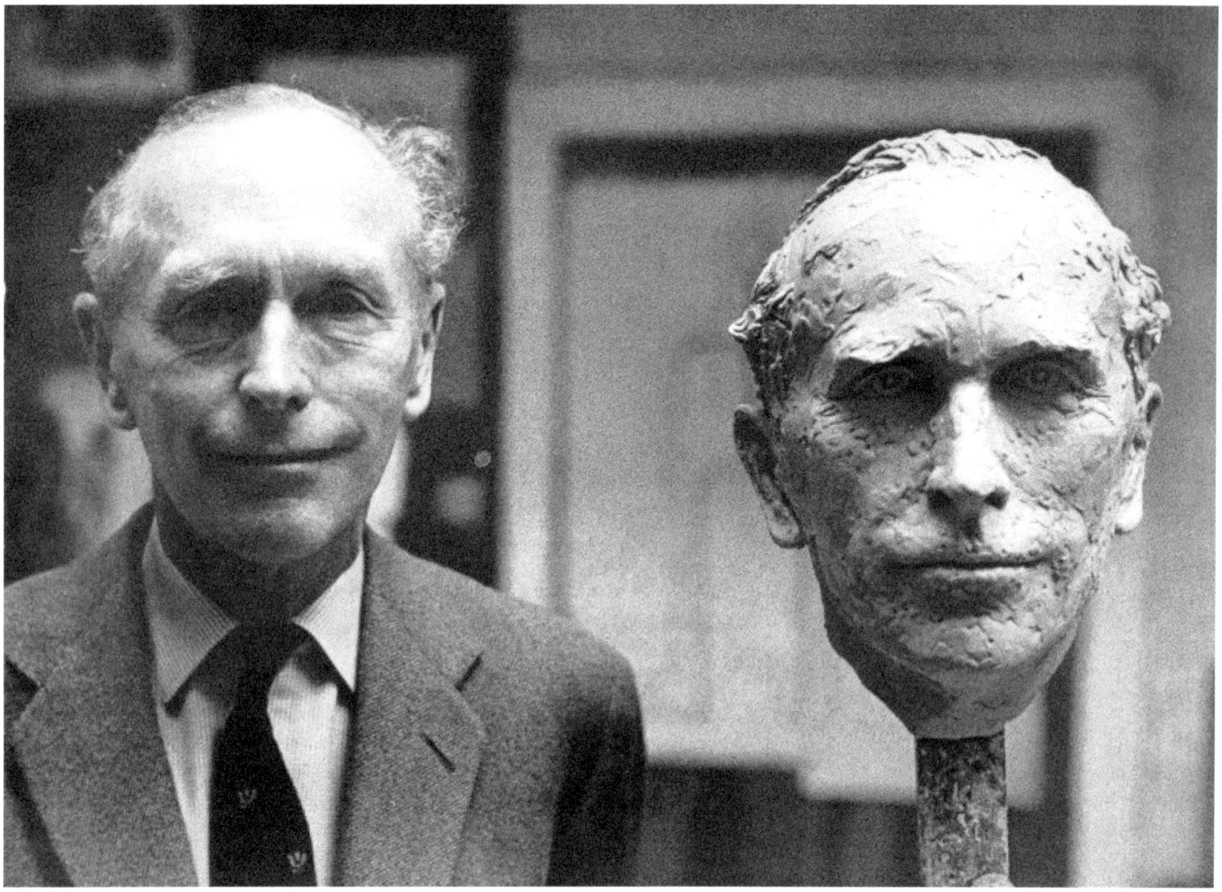

Sir Alec Douglas-Home, commissioned by Christ Church, Oxford

All were dated 1965 and 1966, a phenomenal amount of work in such a short period, and at Tooth's they joined the heads of Kokoschka, Lord and Lady Brabourne, Joan Baez, Sir Edward Beddington-Behrens and Evelyn de Rothschild. A portrait of Sir Alec Douglas-Home, commissioned by Christ Church, Oxford, completed the exhibition.

Sir Alec came to Rushmere for the sittings. Two memories remain with David which may indicate how intimate the relationship between sculptor and subject can become. During the second sitting it was decided that the afternoon should end with a game of croquet. As it had begun to rain, Lady Hume and Gilli supposed playing a game was not possible, but Sir Alec insisted, holding tight to an umbrella, that it went ahead. At another sitting, the ex-prime minister asked David if he had ever voted, and on being told by the sculptor that he never had, Sir Alec replied, 'If I was in your position, I wouldn't either.'

8

DAVID'S FIRST American show was held in New York, at the Findlay Galleries, on East 57th St, during May and June 1967, a year after the successful exhibition at Tooth's. The show had been organised through Tooth's, whose close relationship with the mid-town Manhattan gallery had facilitated the event. David had forty pieces on show. Maquettes were again on display of the work for which he had already been commissioned by his first important American patron, Herbert W. Armstrong, the president of Ambassador College. A private, evangelical Christian higher-education institution, the college had campuses in Pasadena, California and St Albans in Hertfordshire, and a new college was being built in Texas. In time, David's work would reside at all three. Armstrong had been in England to select a piece of sculpture for the Pasadena campus. Not liking any that he had seen, including even those of Henry Moore, he was visiting MacAlpine's to discuss an unrelated building scheme. There, in the chairman's office, he saw, and liked, one of the edition of David's Menuhin sculpture. Alistair MacAlpine, the chairman's son, arranged a meeting in David's studio.

'They said they wanted something along religious lines,' David told the *Newark Evening News*. 'I said I wouldn't do that but if they were interested in a work of aspiration and hope I would be glad to oblige.' He told the college delegates he had in mind a flight of birds, egrets possibly, circling upwards around a column of stainless steel. The piece would be set in a fountain and a column of water, reflecting lights in the bottom of the pool, would give the birds an appearance of flight. 'They said it would be fine. Then I said it would cost $100,000. But they liked the idea more and more. And they commissioned it.'

The Findlay show catalogue describes the fountain's maquette as 'the culmination of a protracted period of studying birds in flight, particularly egrets and swans. The bronze group when cast will weigh about five tons and be thirty-six feet high. It is to be erected in the summer of 1967.' Two days after the New York gallery opening, the US press were reporting that eleven huge crates were now on their way to California by ship. Two blacksmiths would fly to Pasadena from London when David gave the word. It would take, he estimated, a month to erect. An interviewer challenged,

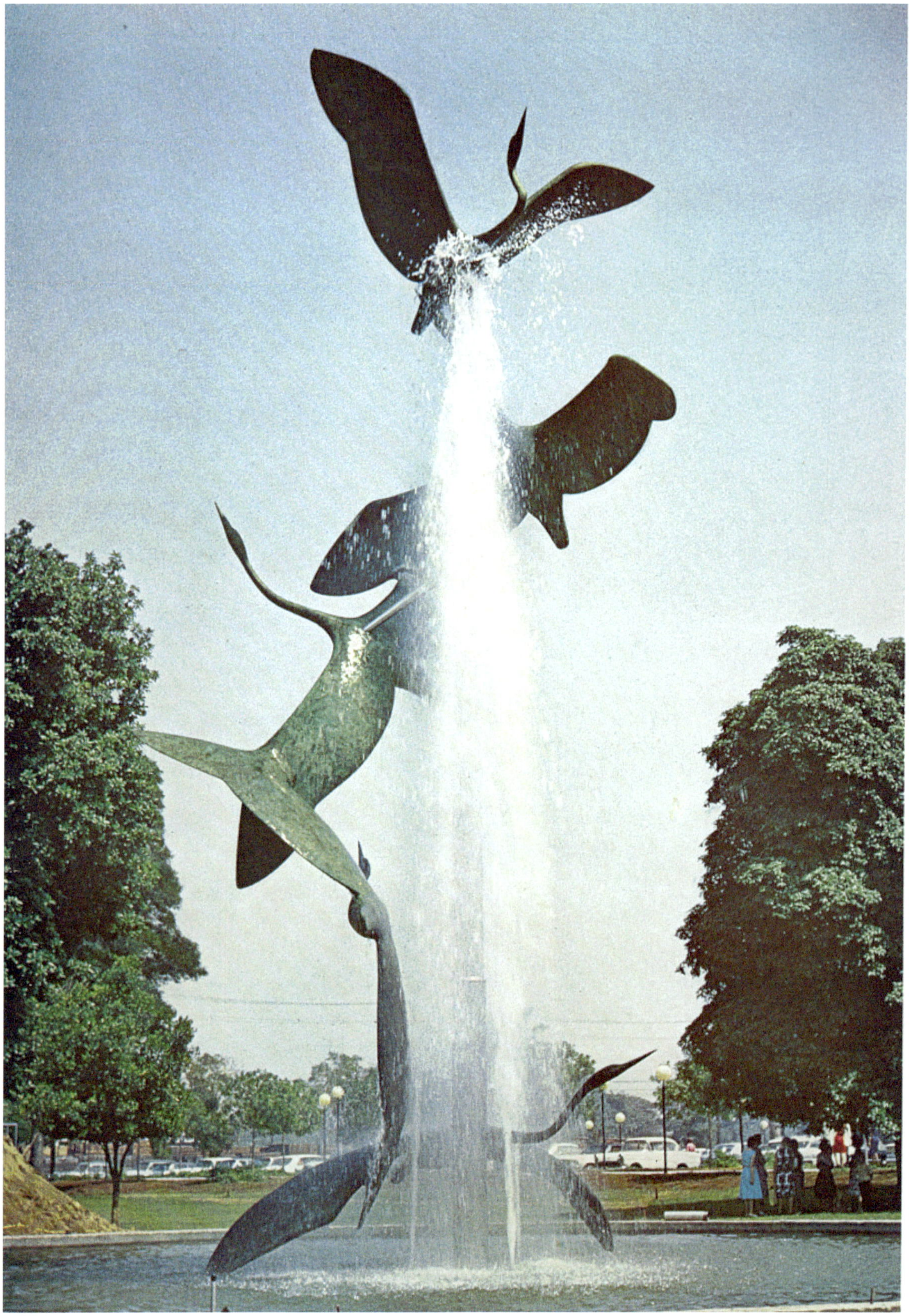

Pasadena bird fountain

'I hear that you claim this is to be the tallest sculpture on the West Coast of the USA.' David replied: 'I now believe it to be the only piece on the West Coast!'

Later, in a celebratory monograph of his public commissions, published by Phaidon in 1974, David described the Pasadena Bird Fountain:

> Five enormous birds wheel into the sky from the surface of the lake. Behind them the moon rises over the Pacific. They express aspiration. Up and up like the thoughts of man, water falling back into the lake. Light touches the palm trees and the topmost bird.

There is a moment of stillness in any action which explains it. First the sculptor drew the birds in flight for many weeks: egrets passing and re-passing overhead to their nesting site. Then he made studies of flying birds in wax, clay and plaster, next the maquettes for the group itself; the engineering problems had to be overcome at this stage. Each bird was to have a wingspan of seventeen feet and would weigh a ton. Finally, the five birds were modelled, united under cranes and the unions formed between them, and cast into bronze. They were erected on site and welded into one by the sculptor with two assistants in four weeks. During an earthquake, three years later, the steel pole whipped like a tree in a gale, but the sculpture was quite unharmed.

David's New York show was slow to take off. After a few days there, he decided to go sailing with an old friend, Steve Colhoun, along New York Sound to Martha's Vineyard. He arrived at the resort to find the gallery demanding to know where he had gone. They wanted him back fast. The entire show had been a sell-out and some important clients were interested in discussing individual commissions. He flew back, by private plane, to discover he really had made it there. He had achieved such recognition that, from then on, his sculpture would be as eagerly sought after in America as it was in his own country.

Yet he managed to retain his ironic disregard for convention. He recalls one day in the gallery a very grand-looking man bowing to him, introducing himself as Grant Simmons and telling David he'd just bought 'two of your big pieces'. Inviting David to his home in South Carolina, he threw a party for the sculptor by the huge octagonal swimming pool. A US senator approached David, saying: 'You know, Mr Wynne, if you weren't here we'd be skinny-dipping now.' David asked the senator if the lady next to him was his wife. On being told she was, David zippered down her dress, shook her out of it and chucked her in the pool. 'Mr Wynne, you shouldn't have done that,' said the startled politician. 'I'm so sorry,' said David, 'I must be the biggest fool in North Carolina.' 'Mr Wynne, you're in South Carolina.' 'Yes,' said David, 'but you've got to be the biggest fool in South Carolina.'

David played real tennis at the New York Racquet Club with another patron, the architect Sammy Van Allen. David knew the club's pro, Jim Deare, from the Queen's Club in London. Asked if he had improved, David said he hadn't really, so the pro suggested they practise a few baskets before the game as they were up against the hardest hitter of them all, Alistair Martin, the best player of the game in America. Though David acquitted himself well, they lost. Later that night at a grand New York restaurant, the Côte Basque, David dined with Van Allen, met Nelson Rockefeller and John Lindsey, then the Mayor of New York, and was sat next to four young men. David reckoned they were professional football players with their clean-cut looks and quiet good manners. Telling one of them about his exploits on the court that afternoon, David suggested he was the bravest man in America, 'trying to defend the dedans' against the hardest hitter in the game. The young man listened politely to the joke, then answered David's next question as to what the four young men did. 'Don't you know?' he replied. 'We're just back from the moon.'

Another evening, at dinner with Grant Simmons at Orsini's, David confided that he had a problem and asked what he could do. He had realised, suddenly, that he had just made a great deal of money and it scared him. David has never forgotten the reply he was given that evening. 'Don't forget, David. You can always give it away.' Those words have stayed with him ever since. A few days later, jogging through Central Park (then a regular activity for him) and stopping to rest on a bench, David was approached by a beggar wanting the price of a cup of coffee. The man must have thought he'd won the lottery when David handed him a fifty-dollar note.

David's explanation of his New York success is a simple one. Just before the exhibition opened, Kenneth Clark's television history of art, *Civilization*, aired on American public broadcasting networks. As in England, the series had been a huge media event. Ratings for a cultural television show had never been so high. Clark's defence and explanation of traditional art, the figurative in painting and sculpture, allowed many collectors, bombarded by the more aggressive forms of abstract art, to embrace a gentler aesthetic, one based on a more accessible provenance. Quite certainly, the gallery anticipated what was happening. They quoted from Vasari in David's catalogue: 'Sculpture is an art which, by removing all that is superfluous from the material used, reduces it to that bodily form which is designed in the artist's mind.'

The industrialist Grant Simmons, unfazed by his guest's pool-side exuberance, went on to collect many of David's sculptures. He became a close friend and recorded, in 1993, his view of what made the work so special for him:

> Only by living with a sculpture can one fully extend one's understanding beyond the reach of photographs or words . . . I have enjoyed [the privilege] for some two decades of having in our home a number of David Wynne sculptures, now totalling twenty-one . . . David Wynne would have been far more celebrated in any century but this. At about the time of his birth the high priests of chill 'abstracts' seized the citadels of the art world, the schools of art, the art media, and a big part of the art market. This priesthood sneers at 'mere' representation, idolising only the abstract. David's work celebrates life. Hence it will be more and more treasured in years ahead, long after the vogue of the twentieth century has passed. To enjoy fully a piece of David's sculpture requires an appreciation of its *balance*; its *honesty*; its *life energy*; and its *love* . . .

And yet another of David's US patrons, Donald M. Kendall, the chairman of PepsiCo Inc, who commissioned one of David's most

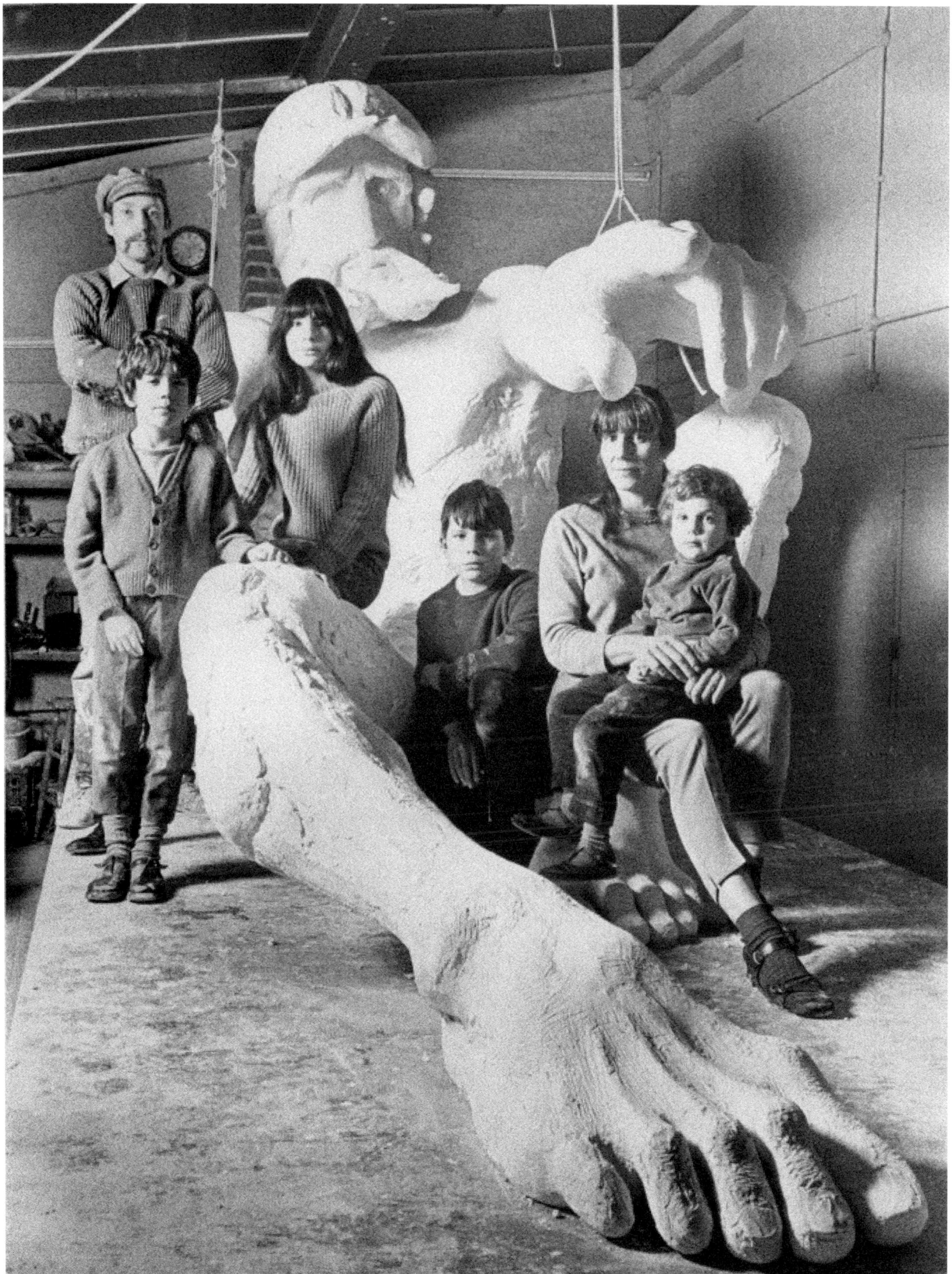

Tyne God Fountain with David, Edward, Nicki, Johnny, Gilli and Roly

famous sculptures, *Grizzly Bear*, wrote in the same Festschrift (*The Sculpture of David Wynne 1974–1992*, Lund Humphries 1993):

> . . . you wonder how David could find the time and energy to create the wonderful things he does. Maybe somewhere in his eternal search for the good in life lies an important secret of creativity.
>
> Whenever I think of David Wynne, I think of two things. First is the extraordinary *Grizzly Bear* sculpture on the back lawn of PepsiCo. Each day in the springtime when classes of students visit our grounds, you invariably see them running across the lawn toward the huge piece. What makes that old bear so magnetic? Our place is filled with the greatest sculpture of the twentieth century, from Moore and Calder to Rodin. Yet I bet more visitors remember *Grizzly Bear* best and love it most.
>
> The other thing I think about is the dinner party we held celebrating the arrival of the sculpture. My clearest memory is of David dancing on a table drinking champagne out of my wife's shoe. I didn't think people actually did that sort of thing . . . until I met David!'

No sooner was he back from his New York triumph, than another massive piece of public sculpture awaited David's attention. Commissioned by the local council to adorn the new Civic Centre in Newcastle upon Tyne, *Tyne God Fountain* would cause some controversy in the first few months after its unveiling by King Olav V of Norway in November 1968. David described the work as:

> a great figure conceived as a river. He is old and strong, and as direction gives shape to a river, so he is pointing. A river grows from a tiny source, gains strength and then is lost in the sea. So the water, spurting from the raised right hand of the figure, flows out over the body and is lost in waterfalls from his pointing finger, his toes and his long forked beard.

Mounted on a huge Otta slate wall, which formed a link to the new council chamber at the end of a ceremonial walkway lined with a long row of nine flambeaux which when ignited threw up five-foot gas flames, the majestic bronze sculpture of the river-god Tyne weighed two and a quarter tons and stood some sixteen feet high. It was one of the biggest free-hand sculptures made in Europe since the work of Rodin, nearly ninety years before. There was some annoyance in the media from local arts associations complaining that an artist from the North-East had not been commissioned, and twenty-two local artists signed a letter of protest saying any one of them could have done a better job. This criticism did not deter the council from commissioning another huge piece from David, a fountain with five swans in flight, taking off into the stream of water rising out from the eighty-foot pool which provides the statue's base. The swans were to symbolise the city's links with the five Scandinavian countries.

The fountain was based on a design originated for London Airport, but the management team decided it was too expensive a project. David sold a cast of the work, with a one-hundred-and-twenty-foot pool, to the new Ambassador College complex in Big Sandy, Texas. The group of the

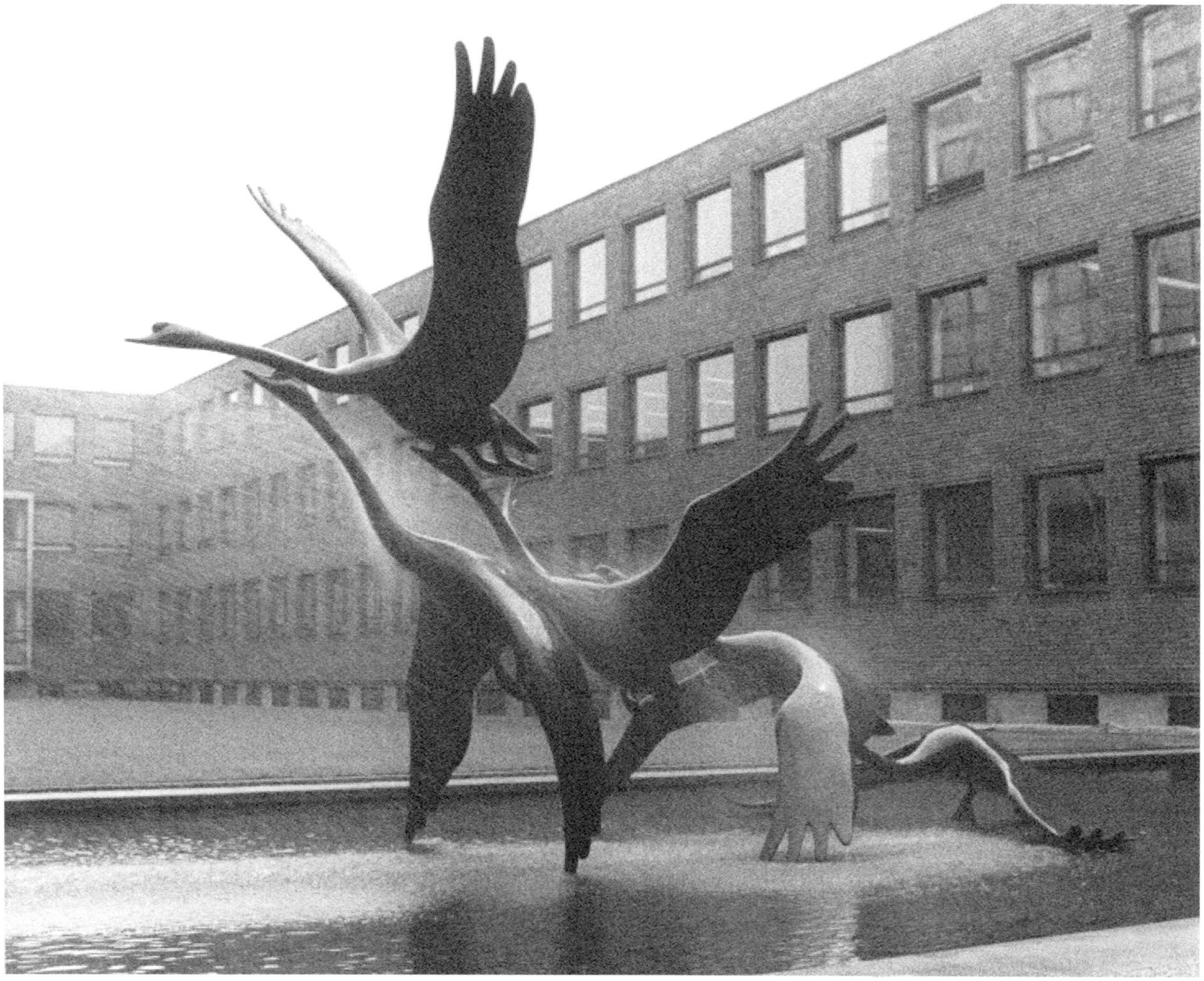

Swans, Newcastle

five birds was thirty-eight feet in length and fifteen feet at its highest. When it was unveiled in May 1969, the *Dallas Morning News* reported the ceremony:

> Wynne is a tall, shaggy-haired and personable fellow, dressed in a mid-Victorian-style mod suit, and he speaks in careful, resonant tones . . . In response to Chancellor Armstrong's calling him the No. 1 sculptor, Wynne said: 'By Jove, I don't know about that. Yet Mr Armstrong is certainly the No.1 art patron.'

Having been a momentous year, 1967 culminated in a modest but prestigious show at the Mercury Gallery, in London's Cork Street, of small animal sculptures. Seven bronzes of studies he had made at the London Zoo were on show, along with a bear and a seal created in glazed terracotta.

By 1968, David's career was secure. The New York gallery arranged for another show, to be held in 1969, and plans were started for a large one-man show in London during 1970. His first monograph was published by Michael Joseph in 1968. With a Foreword by Yehudi Menuhin and a critical introductory essay by T. S. R. Boase, the book was extensively illustrated with 134 large plates and listed more than 200

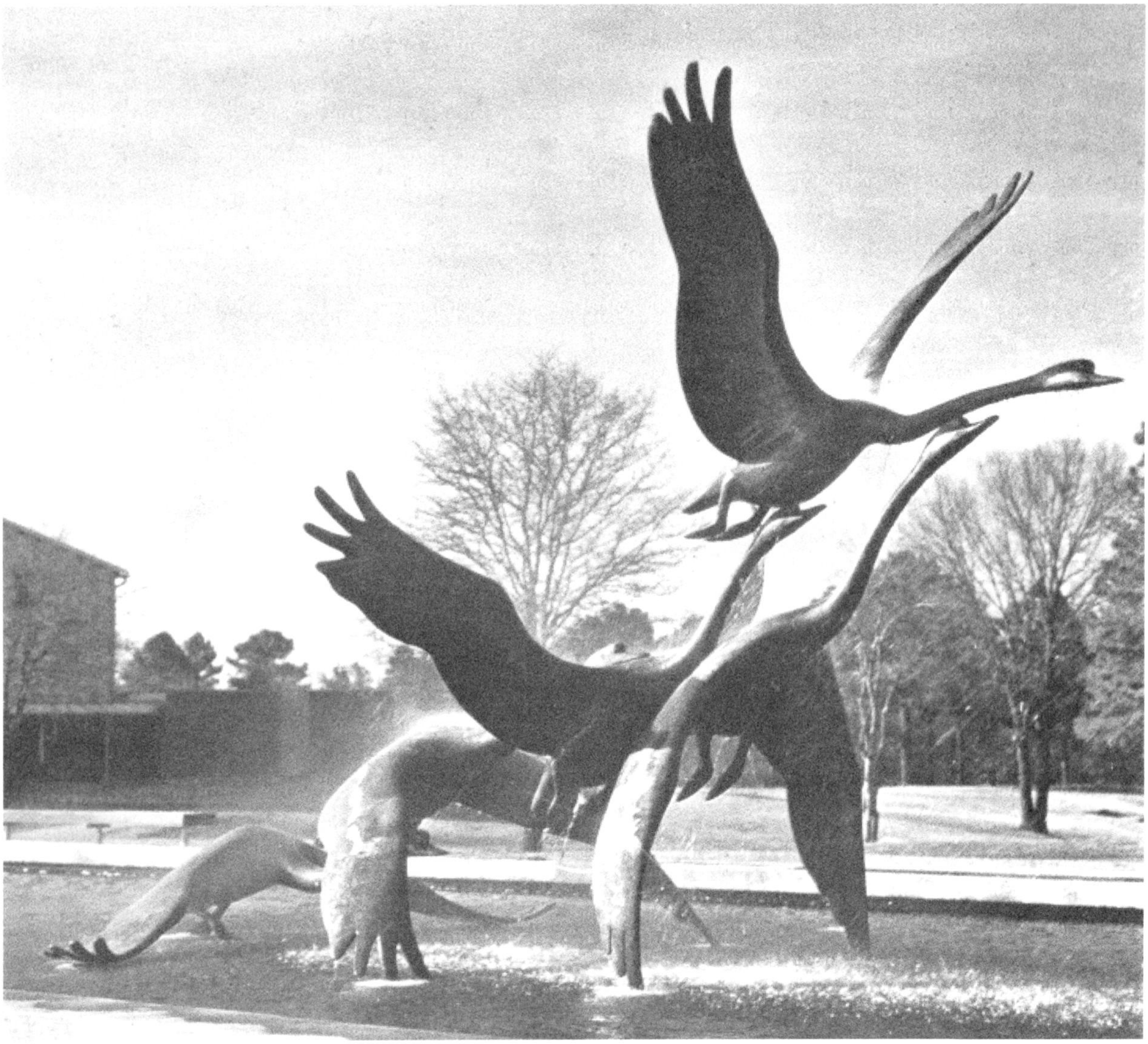

Swans, Texas

finished sculptures of all sizes, dimensions and materials. Alistair McAlpine provided the funding for what was to be a lavish celebration of all David's work to date. A rather superior review, written anonymously, in the *Times Literary Supplement* complained that David had a 'limited knowledge of art history, while instinctively refusing to become acquainted with modernism'. The reviewer did concede, however, despite this attitude, that David 'has made for himself a commercial success'. Snobbish asides apart, the review did point to an explanation for David's popularity, though its mandarin tone and elitist assumption did somewhat diminish its point. 'Those who are frightened by change, inspiration and daring find consolation in Mr Wynne's cool traditionalism, because they see proof there that a living art exists which is not challenging and modern.' There were few other dissenting comments and the book sold out.

Early the next year, David was asked to

create a life-sized head of the Prince of Wales. In July 1969, at a great pageant to be held at Caernarfon Castle, Prince Charles was to be invested by his mother in front of the Welsh nation, in an ancient ceremony of great historic provenance. Louis Osman had been commissioned by the Goldsmiths' Company to design and create a special coronet for the grand occasion. In order to ensure the coronet fitted correctly, a life-sized head of the prince was necessary. David was granted a number of short sittings at Buckingham Palace. It was reassuring at their first encounter for David to be told by the twenty-year-old heir to the throne that having seen *Guy* at Crystal Palace Park, Prince Charles hoped he would prove a sitter of equal merit. The sittings were informal – the prince's younger brothers played with the clay on the carpet as David and the prince worked.

As the bust was completed and made into solid plaster of Paris, David felt a growing sense of unfinished business. Though Osman was pleased with the end result, David had misgivings and mentioned these to the prince. He would relish the chance to make an over-life-sized version of the head, adding a gravitas and dimension which both felt was absent from the plaster cast. A few weeks later, David was telephoned by a City of London alderman who had once been coach to the Trinity boat at Cambridge. The Guildhall, as the premier guildhall in the land, had been granted permission to commission a proper portrait head of Prince Charles and, much as before, a schedule of sittings was arranged.

David needed to go not only to the Palace but also to his old college, Trinity, where the prince was now a student. Made very welcome by the Master, R. A. Butler, David felt a rare sense of achievement at being invited to stay as his guest. During a sitting at the college, Prince Charles raised a problem. The investiture at Caernarfon was only ten days away and no one organising the great event could tell from what Louis Osman was saying whether the coronet would be ready in time. Asking if he knew Louis well, the prince wondered if David might make some enquiries. David did indeed know Louis well and told the prince, accordingly, that he would do his best to find out.

Next morning, David drove to Osman's Elizabethan manor house in Northamptonshire where he found the architect hurling a

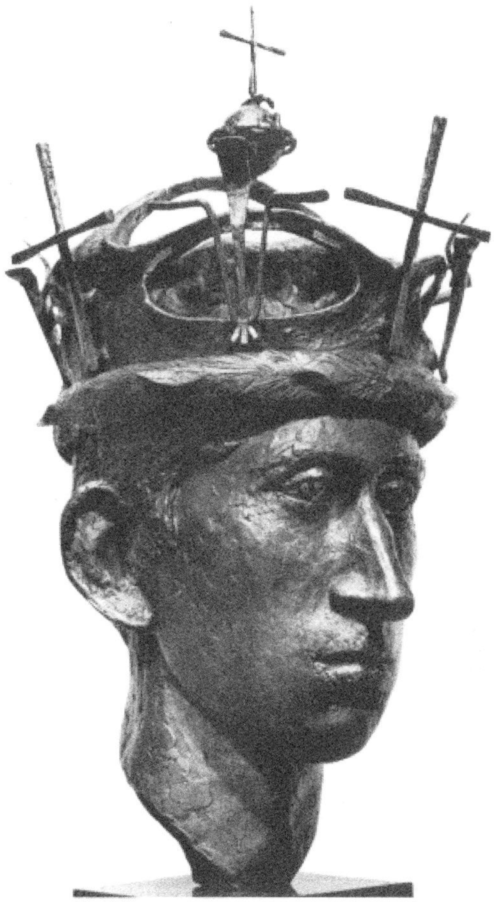

Prince Charles

two-inch golden ball against a brick cellar wall. It was the orb which, once incorporated into the coronet, was intended to represent the moon, and Louis was creating the tiny craters on the moon's surface. After showing him the intricate coronet, composed of hoops and arches and cast by electrolysis, using rare gold from a Welsh mine, Louis decided they both needed a ploughman's lunch from the nearby village pub. As they walked out into the courtyard, Louis nonchalantly hung the coronet on a coat hook beside the front door, in full view of the road to the village pub. An appalled David was reassured no Welsh anarchist would run off with it, and over lunch, Louis promised to deliver the completed coronet, ready for its fitting around the cap of maintenance, in one day's time, at eleven o'clock sharp. And though Louis arrived one hour late, covered in straw, having had to feed his cows before he left, all was ready for the great event. David completed the second portrait, which was cast in plaster. He added the coronet in plasticine, working from photographs and drawings he had borrowed from Louis, and the final bronze was unveiled at the Guildhall later in the year. A second cast went to Rothesay Castle, on the Isle of Bute. Chosen as the centrepiece for the re-constructed Great Hall, the bronze bust was unveiled by the Secretary of State for Scotland in July 1970. David also made a miniature gold bust of the prince for the Worshipful Company of Goldsmiths' world-renowned collection of antique and modern pieces in gold and silver. The 18-carat, eight-inch-high bust was set on a block of beryl, with five rubies, four emeralds, a large pearl, sapphires and a piece of lapis lazuli. It was stolen later that year from David's London exhibition, an event reported in newspapers around the world.

Though no doubt interested due to its royal connection, the Australian media's reporting of the theft coincided with David's first antipodean commission. *Circling Birds*, a five-foot bronze, was made for a site in Perth, Western Australia. It was one of the sculptures chosen by the BBC in the autumn of 1970, when David and his work were the subject of a series of broadcasts for schools. The visual material produced for the teachers to use, in conjuction with the broadcasts, comprised reproductions of ten of David's works, as well as his comments on them. *Circling Birds* was designed for a city:

> which is an oasis in an enormous desert . . . I felt people . . . would like to see something which was not at all like a hot desert thing . . . that they could apprehend from where they were, relaxed with probably a drink in their hand. The shapes are smooth and simple because the light is very hard.

Writing about his *Alec Bedser* bronze, David gave his schools' audience a fine description of his approach to his work:

> He and his brother used to come to the studio and he would thunder up and down and the whole house used to shake . . . In every beautiful movement there is one moment of stillness. You can say it's a moment of stillness within an action – find the moment when a flying bird is for one second still, and this split second achieves a most extraordinary symbolism about the whole art of whatever movement it is.

The *Swans* at Newcastle was his attempt:

> to lighten the square and complement the necessary dullness of an enormous complex of office blocks. I don't think that any of us can afford to be without a hint of the natural world when we live in an urban environment, and this is just in order to help people to enjoy their day.

On his *Gazelle* (1955):

> . . . I drew it and drew it and drew it, and I had to really look at it because I had . . . a long journey [home], and then make it and . . . because all the superficial things dropped away . . . and you could only put in what you understood, . . . because you can't make a model of a gazelle as beautiful as a gazelle is. You're not trying to do that, you're trying to make something.

And the need always to be making something continued to dictate David's rigorous and intensive work regime. However, an amusing anecdote, reported in the *San Francisco Chronicle* in Herb Caen's column, revealed David's time was not always concentrated on his art. When he was in Pasadena to complete the fountain, David's daughter wrote from London requesting a typical American mini-skirt. He sent her the miniest one he could find –

> and a short time later, back came a package from her with a note reading: 'Dear David: Here's a tie I made for you from the bottom five inches of that so-called miniskirt!' . . . She also wanted some Haight-Ashbury beads and bells, so poor Mr Wynne (Father of the Year?) walked the streets till he found a hippie wearing some. 'Where can I buy these?' he asked. 'You can't,' replied the hippie, 'I made these myself.' (Pause). 'Come to think of it, I guess I can make some more,' with which he draped the beads and bells around Wynne's neck.

9

DAVID'S NEXT LONDON show was held at the Covent Garden Gallery during most of March 1970. Chosen by the Crafts Centre of Great Britain to launch their brand new gallery in Earlham Street, the exhibition opened on 4 March with Donovan playing and singing among David's sculptures. The new gallery had been created from a converted brewer's warehouse. Covent Garden was already beginning its transformation from London's fruit and vegetable market into one of the city's more fashionable areas, emulating what had already happened to Les Halles in Paris. Boutique shops, galleries and elegant restaurants began to appear and the new gallery and its first exhibition generated considerable interest in the media.

The *Evening Standard* devoted a whole page to the subject, complete with a large photograph of David guiding *The Lovers* – the work, the newspaper informed its readers, took five years to carve from a four-ton block of Norwegian rose marble – into the gallery, using heavy lifting gear and scaffolding. It was, said the article, 'an epic one-man show, one of the largest ever presented in a private London gallery'. Fifty new sculptures were on display and there were screenings in the lower gallery 'of the new film, *Heads and Hands: A Portrait*'. The ten-minute colour film, made by Steve Colhoun as David modelled Donovan's portrait head, had George Harrison providing the soundtrack music. Donovan's performance in the gallery, meanwhile, was not without drama. According to *Petticoat* magazine: 'Don made a warm, intimate occasion of his set and was only thrown once when a huge bronze bust of himself tottered from its pedestal and crashed to the floor. Happily neither the head nor anyone in the audience was injured.'

Ten days later, Yehudi Menuhin gave a recital by candlelight, among the marble carvings and bronze sculptures, playing Bartok's *Sonata for Solo Violin* and a Bach *Partita*, unaccompanied. When the doors closed on 26 March, most of the exhibits were shipped over for an equally successful repeat show at the Findlay Gallery in New York. Yehudi Menuhin wrote the Introduction to the catalogue for the New York exhibition, and it's worth quoting in its entirety as one artist's tribute to another:

> David Wynne is a born sculptor. His work seems to spring from some arch

mould of which he himself is a true prototype, having that quality the Germans call an *Urnatur*. His hands are made for the task – whether he handles clay or a bird itself, they are as strong and compelling as they are sensitive and tender. And as his hands, so his heart and mind, for mind and heart and matter are extricably entwined.

He has the simple conviction of one who knows and trusts his own nature, because it is a good nature. He does not live, therefore, by law or by any abstract, preconceived, deliberate compulsion by principles, and as he is 'all of a piece' he can afford to trust his impulses, and his fancy.

Because his emotion is as a constant refreshing spring, he also prefers to work from the motion of life itself. He will watch his subject, in flight, playing the violin, in song, or in thought, and tracing quickly and accurately, will catch an endless number of moods on the wing revealing the urge behind the movement. When he came to my music room I remember how he listened and the way he watched, for he is guided by what the eye cannot see, and only the heart can perceive. In general he likes to work to music. It is also so reassuring to any sense of 'wholeness' to see an artist (of which there are still quite a few) who is in the very centre of life, not divorced as it were through his art, but rather united with the unbroken flow of all living creatures – in his case as much 'at home' in his studio as with his lovely wife and sweet children.

Commissions continued to come along. A portrait head of Olave, Lady Baden-Powell was made for the Girl Guide Movement, a commission which would later result in one of David's very few posthumous portrait heads, that of her husband, the founder of the Boy Scouts, Lord Baden-Powell of Gilwell. Both portrait heads were unveiled at a ceremony attended by more than two thousand scouts representing thirty countries, the culmination of the forty-fifth Annual Reunion Camp for world scout leaders at Gilwell Park. It also turned out to be one of David's most financially successful commissions as most Boy Scout and Girl Guide Associations around the world bought editions of each head for their various head-quarters.

The Friends of Covent Garden and the Royal Ballet School commissioned a portrait head of Sir Frederick Ashton, which was unveiled in the crush bar at the Royal Opera House. The *Daily Telegraph* reported the event: ' . . . it portrays him with hair less immaculate than it was yesterday, so when

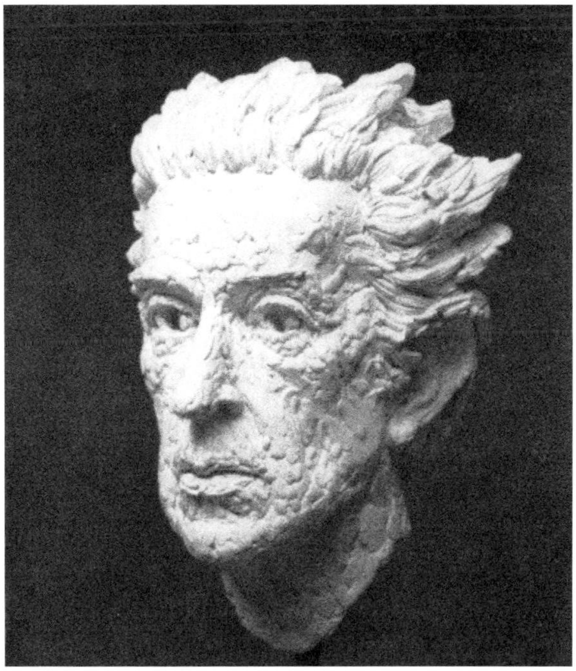

Sir Frederick Ashton

he posed beside it Sir Frederick ruffled his hair to improve the resemblance.'

David received another commission in 1971 which led to the creation of three of his best known works, the bronzes in the gardens at Cadogan Place and in Cadogan Square, the most visible of which is *The Dancers*, outside the then Carlton Tower Hotel. Viscount Chelsea would later recall: 'Our family relationships with David Wynne go back to the early 1950s and to his days as a young artist in a small studio room in Notting Hill Gate.' David had known Primrose Cadogan for many years and through her became a family friend. His portrait of Viscount Chelsea, made in 1953, was created from sittings completed at Snaigow, the Cadogan family home in Scotland, during the young man's school holidays. Viscount Chelsea records that the work 'now acts as my hat-stand in the office', and remembered:

> It was during this time that David in his eloquent and enthusiastic manner persuaded my father to lend him sufficient money to buy the materials required for a full-sized model of his *Christ on a Donkey*, which I subsequently bought . . . and also to give the party after his first major exhibition at the Leicester Galleries in 1955.

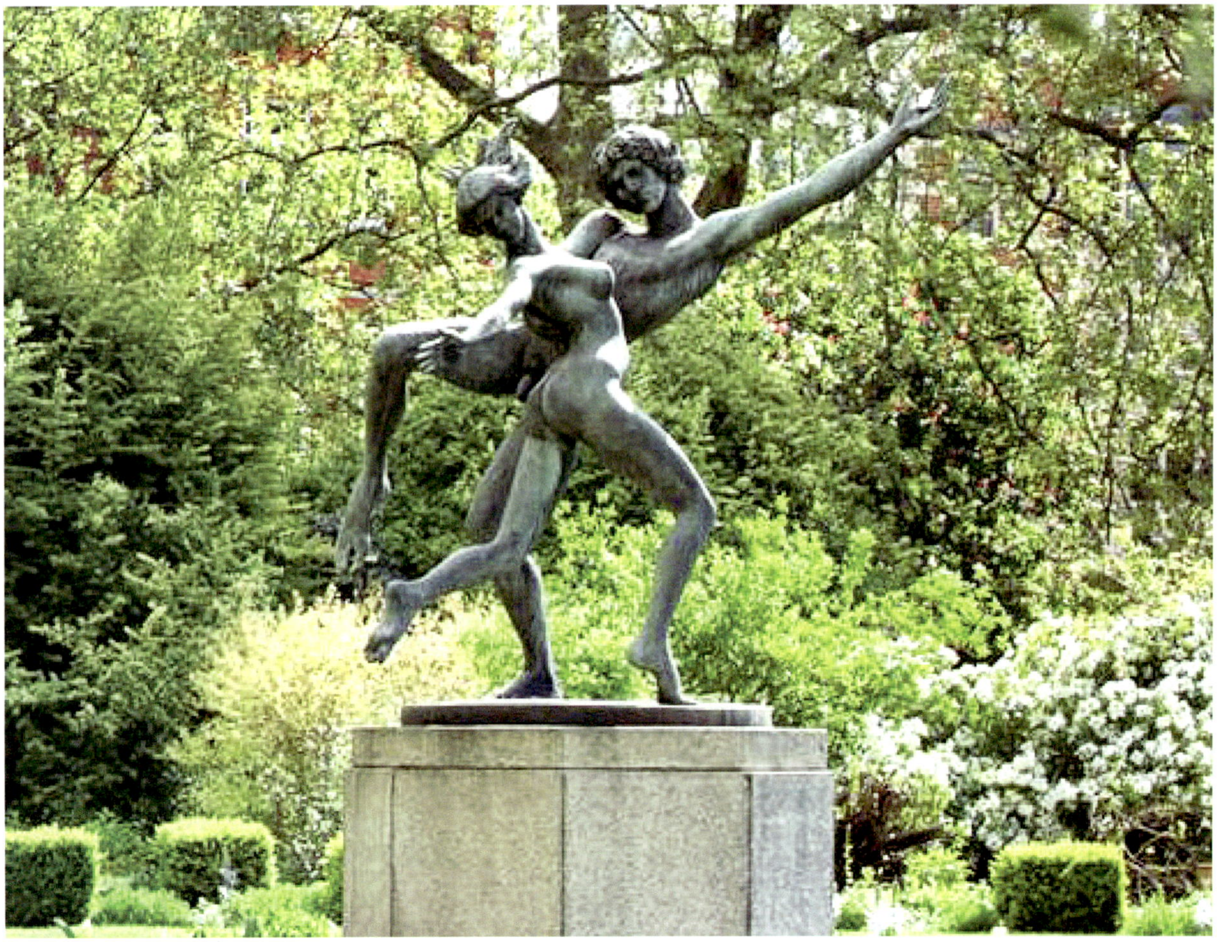

The Dancers

David's inspiration for *The Dancers* came from watching a couple, clearly very much in love, dancing with each other on a beach in Corfu. It made him think of Bob Dylan's 'Mr Tambourine Man'. He asked them if they would mind posing for him when they returned to London and it was seeing his maquette of the work in David's studio that led Lord Cadogan to commission the three Cadogan Bronzes. It is probably the most familiar, especially since the Carlton Tower for many years used a drawing of it to embellish its stationery and marketing materials. The statue's siting, directly opposite the hotel's main entrance, made it an ideal logo. *Girl with Doves* is hidden somewhat from view by the bushes and trees which cover the perimeter of the gardens along Cadogan Place and Sloane Street. Life-size, a girl with arms outstretched releases seven doves up into the air. David's realisation, when working on his portrait head of Sir Thomas Beecham, that sculptural movement can be made to look as light as air is brilliantly demonstrated.

David had first seen the model he used for *Girl with Doves* in a flower shop in the Fulham Road when he was with his father, who noticed her and encouraged David to ask her to pose for him. ('What a beautiful girl,' his father had commented.) *Rosie on a Stool* was the first of a number of sculptures of one of David's favourite models. She became part of David's extended family, even spending her honeymoon at Rushmere, David's Wimbledon home, and Gilli assisted in the birth of Rosie's baby. She returned to Boston with her family where, sadly, she later died of cancer.

The Findlay Gallery catalogue for the 1970 show ended the biography of David with the sentence: 'Today, with patrons watching over his career, many offers of commissions and a long waiting-list of potential sitters, David Wynne is a man who has brilliantly fulfilled his early promise and has established himself as one of England's foremost figurative sculptors.'

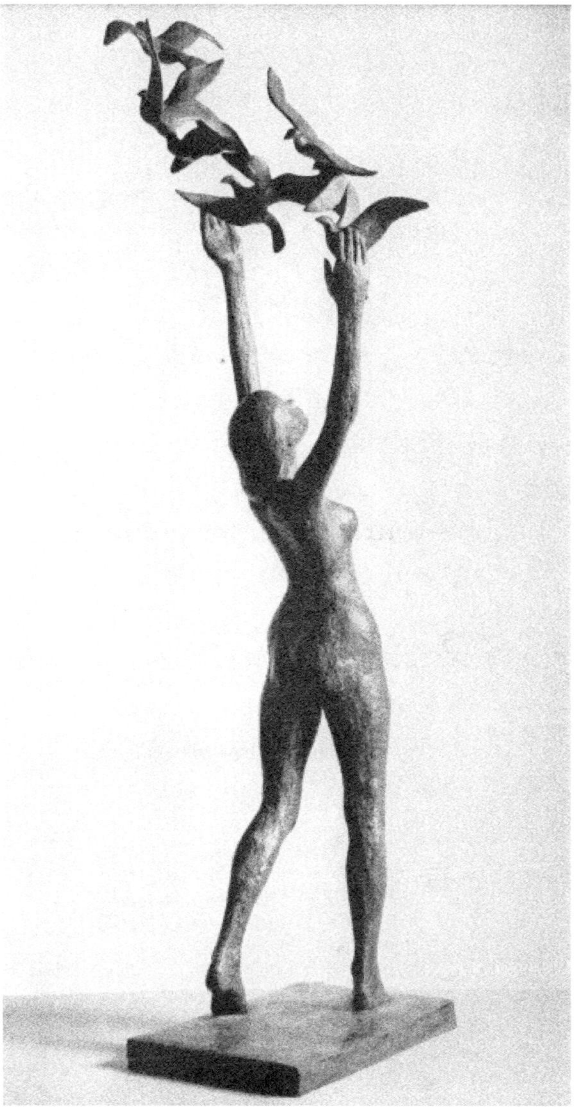

Girl with Doves

Gallery sales pitch aside, there was undoubted truth in the hype. *The Times* reproduced a large portrait of David sitting by *The Dancers* on 7 December 1971, and an equally large photograph of Virginia Wade, the tennis player, 'beside a statue of her which is being sculpted by David Wynne at his Wimbledon studio', was printed the very next day. Fame indeed.

Yet another one-man show, of recent bronzes and lithographs, was organised at the Covent Garden Gallery in October 1971. Twenty-seven pieces and ten lithographs, all made within the previous twelve months, were on show, and the following May, the Fitzwilliam Museum mounted an Exhibition of Portraits in Bronze by David Wynne. Once again Donovan performed at the opening evening. The local Cambridge evening newspaper proclaimed: 'The times they are a-changin' at the Fitzwilliam.' Later that year, in an article in the magazine *Vanity Fair*, David was asked to give advice to a young girl anxious to become a sculptor. His somewhat unorthodox views provide yet more evidence of David's maturing confidence and certainty:

> Don't go to art school, learn from life. Look at nature. If you want to work with steel, go to a foundry, if you want to carve, go to a stonemason. There are 100,000 art students in the country and perhaps six ever make it to the top. The benefit of art school is security. That in itself in dangerous. You don't pay for your mistakes at art school. Art is just for you and the piece of slate – your *truth* . . .

And it was not only as a sculptor/sage that David was treated by the media. *Harper's & Queen*, in August 1973, ran a whole page on how David would cope alone: 'Mrs Wynne will be in Switzerland this month looking for wild flowers, while Mr Wynne pays the milkman . . . ' Gilli was off on a painting holiday. She told the magazine:

> . . . there are lots of things which we both do which aren't nice for the other that we can do when we're apart. David likes driving very fast cars and jet-set sort of things. I like long walks. I'm a much slower person. I like eight hours doing the same thing whereas he likes the day to be chopped into short passages of different sorts of things . . .

David was uneqivocal: 'I shall go on working. Just as I work all the time . . . I shall spend a certain time with Graham Hill, playing about in motor cars . . . '

David's friendship with Graham Hill was one of the most profound relationships of his life. Through a mutual friend, Herb Jones, Hill asked if he could visit David at Rushmere. David did not even know who Graham was. The racing driver, as David still vividly remembers, 'stomped' around the studio. His knees had been hurt in an accident. He told David that he hoped the sculptor wouldn't mind if he didn't say anything as he didn't know anything about art at all. After more stomping in silence, Hill spoke. 'Right. Tell me something. Is anything for sale?' When David answered yes, Graham asked if he could return. By then it was eleven o'clock at night. Twenty minutes later, the racing driver came back, this time with a longer question. He told David that whenever he won a big race, particularly in a Latin country, people would come running out, wanting to touch his car. He had wanted to touch David's sculptures when he first saw them and he wanted to know if David thought that was anything to do with art appreciation. 'Of course,' said David. 'It's got a lot to do with it.' Hill's response was vivid: 'Why the fuck have all these people been filling me up with nonsense?' Graham told David he wanted to buy 'a lot of your sculpture. I've got three children and I want them to be brought up with lovely things.' David told him his work was expensive and Hill said, 'Yea? Well I'm pretty rich. I don't go doing this sort of lark for nothing – round and round the circuits. Which one's for sale?' David suggested they met again to decide what he should buy and invited Graham next time to sit with him and Gilli, drink some champagne and just talk. The driver told Gilli before he left that night how happy he was. 'I've just made a great breakthrough. I've got into another world.' This, for him, was art.

Next morning, David's telephone rang at nine o'clock. 'Graham Hill. Do you remember me?' David obviously did and the racing driver asked what the sculptor was doing that day. David was vague so Graham told him, 'Get yourself over to Elstree Airfield as soon as you can. Ask in the hut for Graham Hill.' When David arrived he saw Graham in a plane with the engine ticking over. 'Come on, Ace,' said the racing driver, 'hop in. You did me a great favour yesterday. You showed me your life and I'm going to show you a bit of mine.' In minutes, they were airborne and away to Brand's Hatch. They landed on the course and got into a souped-up Ford. 'I'll give you a normal run round.' They tore off, extremely fast. When the car stopped after the first circuit, the racing driver turned to enquire: 'You shitting your socks yet?' 'No,' said David, 'I'm having fun.' After a cup of coffee, they jumped back in the car, and to his cry of 'Hold tight!', the new friends went round again as fast as the expert racer could manage. It was the start of a deep and loving friendship that lasted till the day of Graham's death. The racing driver's fatal crash happened while he was *en route* to David's son's twenty-first-birthday party. Of all David's patrons, Graham Hill would eventually buy the largest collection of his work. David still remembers Graham's wife Bette's exasperated comment as he opened the boot of the car: 'Not another David Wynne!'

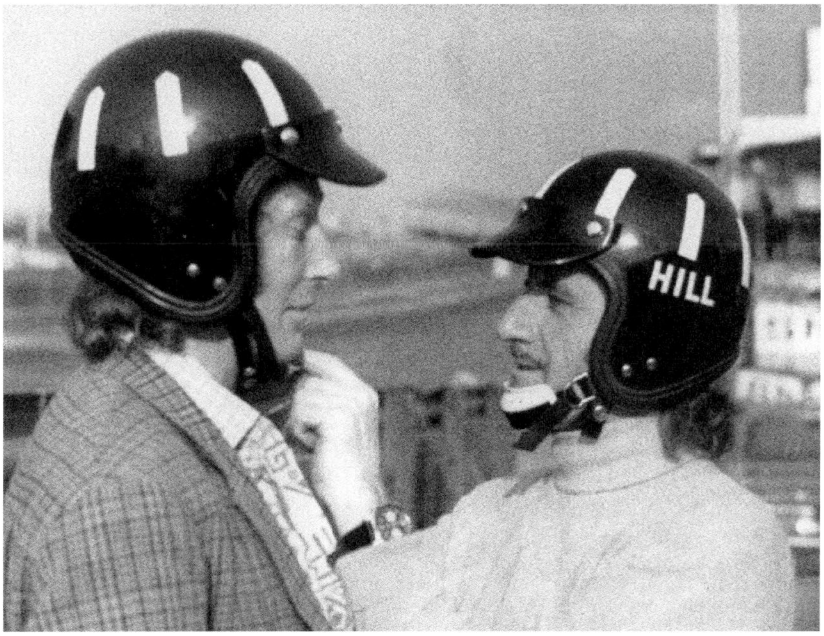

David with Graham Hill

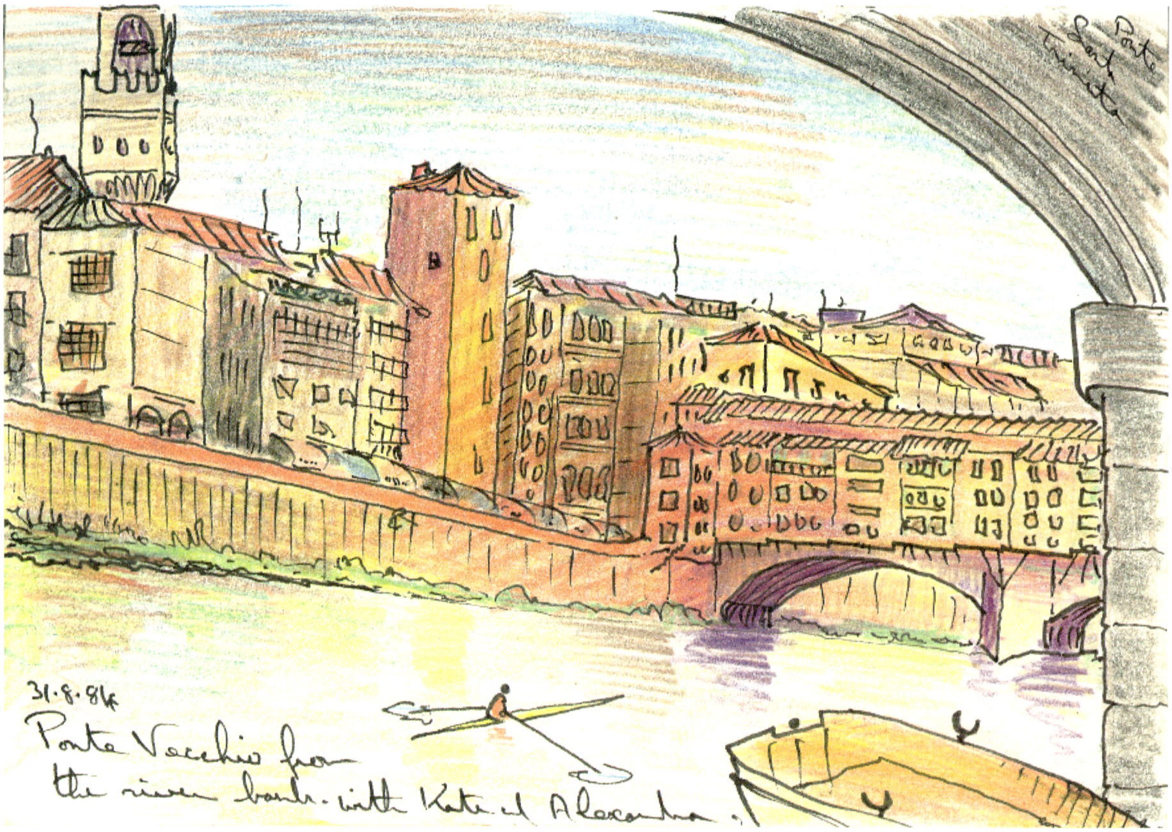

Sketches from David's Italian notebook made on his trip to Italy in 1984

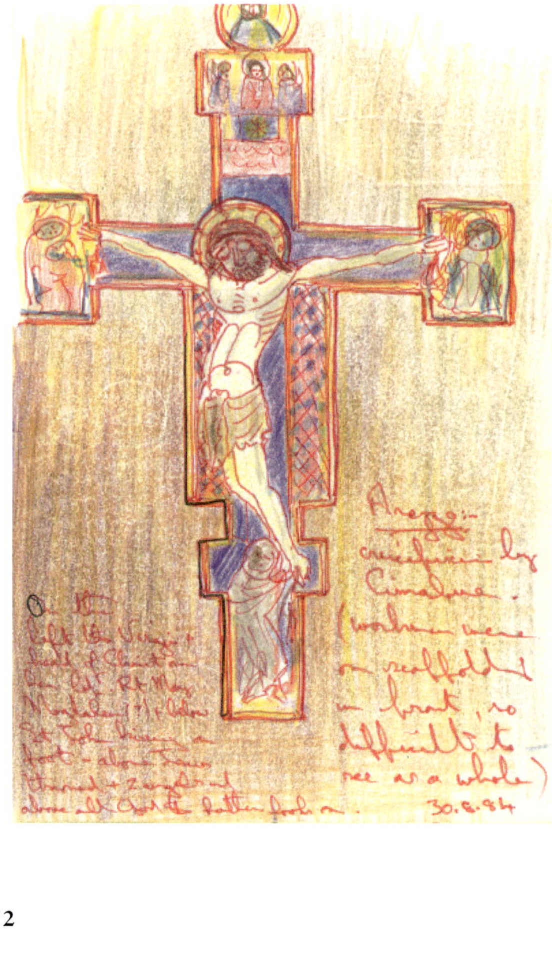

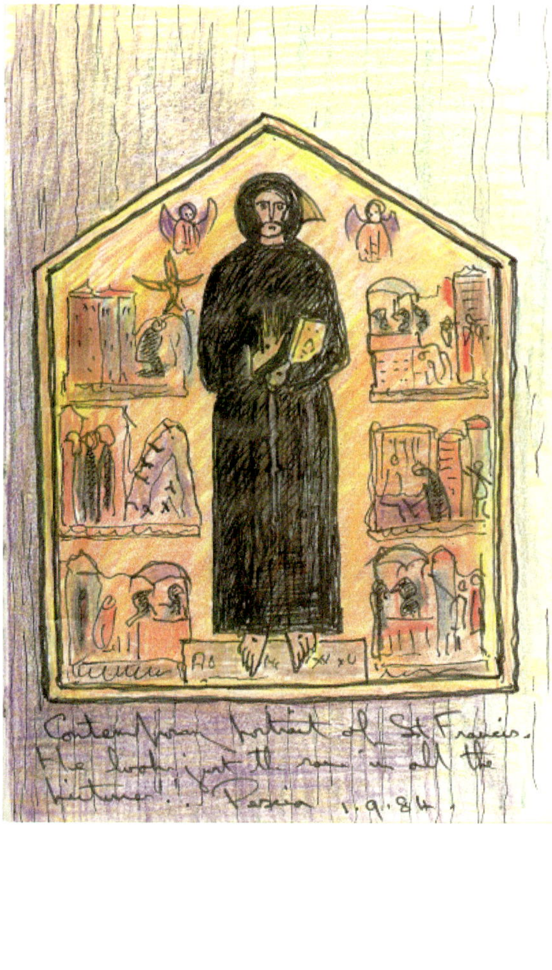

10

DAVID'S LONG LOVE AFFAIR with wild animals found an agreeable outlet when he offered to work, without recompense, with with Gerald Benney, a master goldsmith, and Bill Shand-Kydd in creating a four-ounce medal, in 22-carat gold, to be sold for the benefit of the World Wild Life Fund. The obverse bore the head of an adult male gorilla and the reverse, the image of a blue whale. It was minted by Johnson Matthey from dies cut by the Royal Mint. It was unusual for David to work in two-dimensions, but its artistic success led to a commission to design the reverse of a fifty-pence coin, to be specially minted to celebrate the United Kingdom's entry into the European Common Market in 1973. Word of the design, featuring nine interlinked hands, first leaked out in November 1972, with William Hickey, in the *Daily Express*, announcing that 'with unbecoming furtiveness, the Royal Mint has asked sculptor David Wynne to submit a design. It will then be considered by the Queen.' The newspaper went on to speculate that the Royal Mint's 'furtiveness' was due to the problems of the power cuts caused by the as yet unresolved conflict with striking miners, and 'it would be embarrassing to make an announcement and then not be able to produce the new coin'. When the *Daily Telegraph* ran with the same story the next day, 'Mr David Wynne . . . was not available for comment'!

As the requirements for striking coins were more stringent than those for medals, David had to work closely with the Mint's technical staff to achieve success. He designed the reverse of the coin, the obverse being a portrait of the Queen, created by

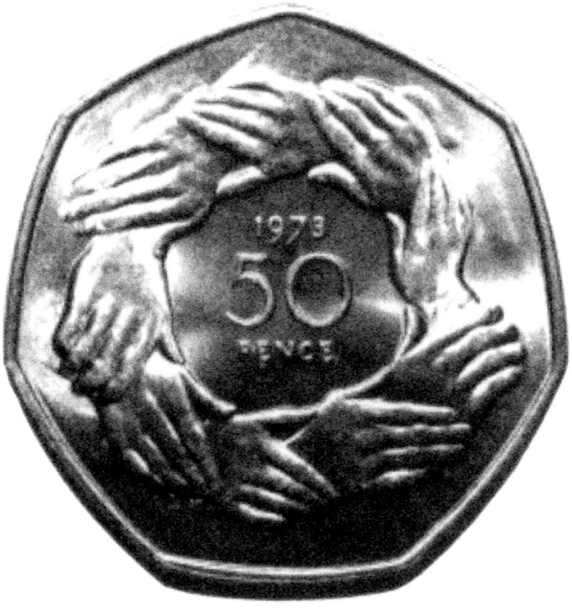

50 pence coin

Arnold Machin and used on all the other coins minted at that time. A departure from tradition was that the date, normally placed on the head of the coin, was, due to David's striking design of the nine linked hands in a circle, placed on the reverse, in the circle's centre. The number of hands symbolised the nine members of the community and David modelled them from his own, Gilli's, his stepson Johnny's and the hands of one of his craftsmen/helpers, Bill Amer. It was a powerful image, though not without its detractors. Letters appeared in newspapers complaining at the loss of Britannia's portrait and the *Sunday Express* thought the design suggested a new horror film, *The Curse of the Creepy Hands*.

David's success with the coin, however, led to a commission to make an effigy of King Hassan for the new Moroccan coinage, which involved a memorable visit to Morocco. On his return he was heard by the *Daily Telegraph* correspondent, 'waxing lyrical about his *Arabian Nights* experience in Morocco . . . particularly about a banquet on a beach draped with cloth of gold where four hundred people dined on legs of beef, roast lamb and lobster piled six feet high and a herd of goats was driven in afterwards to clear the debris.'

As a consequence of his Moroccan assignment, the Royal Mint was able to wrest the contract for striking Morocco's coinage away from the French National Mint, and this probably explained David's receiving a call, early in 1973, to appear before the Coin Committee of England, at St James's Palace. When he was ushered in, he recognised some of the distinguished members, notably HRH Prince Philip and Sir Kenneth Clarke. It was the Duke of Edinburgh who explained the reason for the summons. He asked David to submit a design for a medal to be struck to celebrate the Queen's forthcoming Silver Jubilee. David sensed tension in the room, but expressed his delight at the request, though indicating he would need to be granted some sittings with her majesty to perform his task properly. When some members of the committee expressed disbelief that such a commission could be done in the time available, David realised what the 'atmosphere' was about. When another member of the committee enquired how long it would take him to produce an image, David's reply was precise. 'I could have it done by the day after tomorrow, just as long as I could have the sittings.'

Later that afternoon, now back in Wimbledon, David took a telephone call from an equerry of Prince Philip's. He asked the sculptor if he really could 'do this thing in two days'. When David said he could, he was told to come to Buckingham Palace at 9.50 the next morning. David said he would be there and asked if it would be possible for him to be provided with a selection of recent photographs of the monarch to help him with his task. And with a strong sense of *déjà vu*, the Volkswagen van was again driven through the palace gates, to be parked in the same spot as David had used before.

Carrying a sketch-pad and pencil, he entered the Yellow Drawing Room, where a thick envelope of photographs awaited him. As he looked through them, placing them on a table, he heard a voice outside asking whose van was parked 'in my space'? David was about to go outside and own up, when the Queen entered, waving aside his offer to park in a more suitable place and saying how the van reminded her of one she had been

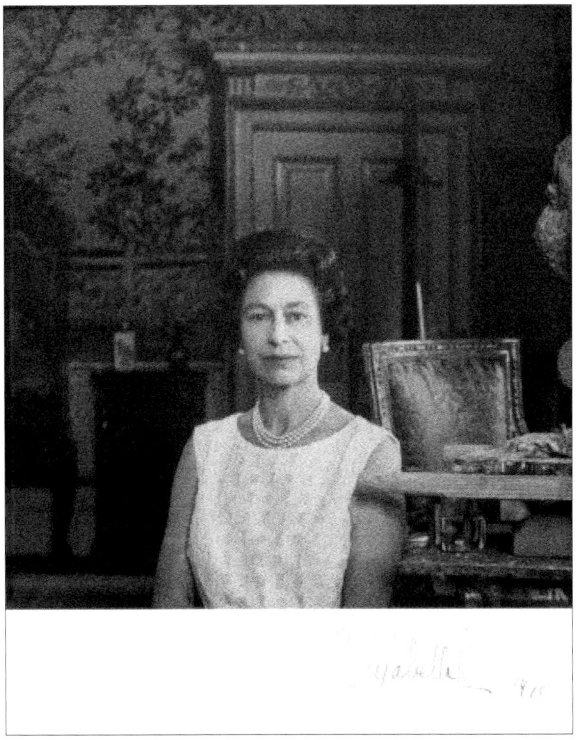

HM The Queen photographed by David during her last sitting for the sculptor

given once to drive in Africa. Standing at the table, where the photographs were spread out, both agreed on a recent portrayal that was harsh in its clarity, but held a hint of amusement in its expression. David began to draw, referring to both the photograph and his sitter, feeling amused by the notion that each occupant of the room was, in a different way, the subject of the other.

That evening, David and Gilli were at a private view of a collection of jewellery by Andrew Grima. Learning of David's morning's engagement, the jeweller suggested that David should sculpt a portrait head of the monarch, but both men suspected the protocol and red tape which would have to be gone through would be tedious and might interfere with the somewhat tight schedule under which David was creating the Silver Jubilee medal.

Next morning the jeweller telephoned David to tell him that he had been making enquiries. It would satisfy all the protocol considerations if Grima was to commission the head and formally present it to the Worshipful Company of Goldsmiths, to which the jeweller belonged. All the extra sittings and liaison work would be discussed with David after the next sitting, that afternoon, at the Palace. The sculptor entered the drawing-room, carrying the circular plate-glass base on which the effigy was taking shape, to find his sitter had arrived before him. David still remembers the Queen's amused remark. 'Mr Wynne, I hear we are to see more of each other,' and his quick reply, 'Yes, Ma'am. I'm just getting used to the idea of being granted such an honour.'

Positioning the chair so the afternoon light would point up the contours of her face, David set to work. Both sculptor and sitter began to chat about the work in hand, but as the sitting progressed, the conversation lightened and turned to holidays, horses, even family life. At one point, David, distracted by a police car driving by, its siren blaring, commented rather flippantly that they were probably late for their tea. Again, the sculptor's memory is precise. 'Do you think so?' queried the Queen. 'Let's see.' She picked up the telephone, spoke for a moment, then said, 'No. There was a genuine reason.' David felt the hairs on his neck bristle. What would have happened if they really had been going for a tea break?

Towards the end of that session, as his confidence grew, he broached an idea he had been considering about depicting the monarch wearing a crown on the medal, though he tempered his suggestion by indicating the time factor might not allow the possibility. The Queen pointed out that her actual Jubilee was not for another three years and she thought it a pity that the medal's quality might be spoilt because of its current time schedule. She was convinced something could be done and David suggested he talk to his associates at the Mint. The sitting over, the Queen departed and David began clearing away his tools. There was a knock on the door. It was the Queen's equerry, Sir William Hazeltine, come to arrange a further six sittings, subject to the Queen's approval, over the next two weeks. Sensing this a good moment, David raised the question of which crown to choose. Sir William said he would consult with the governor of the Tower of London to arrange for David to pay a visit.

Two days later, David presented himself at a side door of the Norman keep, to be met by the governor in person. It was a tense meeting. When David finally saw the magnificent St Edward's Crown, which the Queen had worn at her coronation in 1952, he knew it was the one he wanted. He enquired if it could be lent to the Palace for a couple of days so he could see how it looked. The governor was shocked, insisting the crown could never leave the Tower under any circumstances. On his way home, David decided to contact the Royal Mint and discovered the Coin Committee's sense of urgency was unwarranted. The Mint only needed to know the work was progressing smoothly and the final striking of the medal would not take place for at least a year. When David told them this might allow him time to add St Edwards's Crown, they were not only pleased, but said that, if he brought them the artwork, they would scale the relief down within two days, leaving room for the crown to be in the correct proportions.

The next morning the first of the royal sittings intended for the portrait head took place. The Queen enquired about the visit to the Tower. When David told her that St Edward's Crown was the only one to consider but that there seemed no question of its ever leaving its strongroom, the Queen's response was crisp. 'Indeed, Mr Wynne. We shall have to see about that.' The matter was obviously closed and David settled down to work. At one point, he asked the Queen if he could touch her face, to feel the bone under her eye. After the monarch had agreed, she observed it seemed strange that, though she had sat on many occasions for her portrait, no one had ever asked to touch her face before. She wondered why that was, as it seemed such an obvious thing to do. When David suggested that other artists were perhaps too shy, the Queen laughed. 'Well, that's more than one could say of you, Mr Wynne!'

By the third sitting, the portrait was nearly complete. There is often a moment in the making of any head when the sculptor, being so involved, feels uncertain about his ability to judge the work's overall effect. Feeling this to be so now, he decided to ask his sitter herself what her opinion of it was. The Queen thought it good, but commented how difficult it was to judge when it was a portrait of herself. She enquired if there was anyone else whose opinion David trusted. When David told her about Gilli's crucial role as critic and muse, the Queen suggested the sculptor's wife come at once for tea. Despite Gilli's concerns about what to wear, she presented herself at the Palace, was ushered in, and

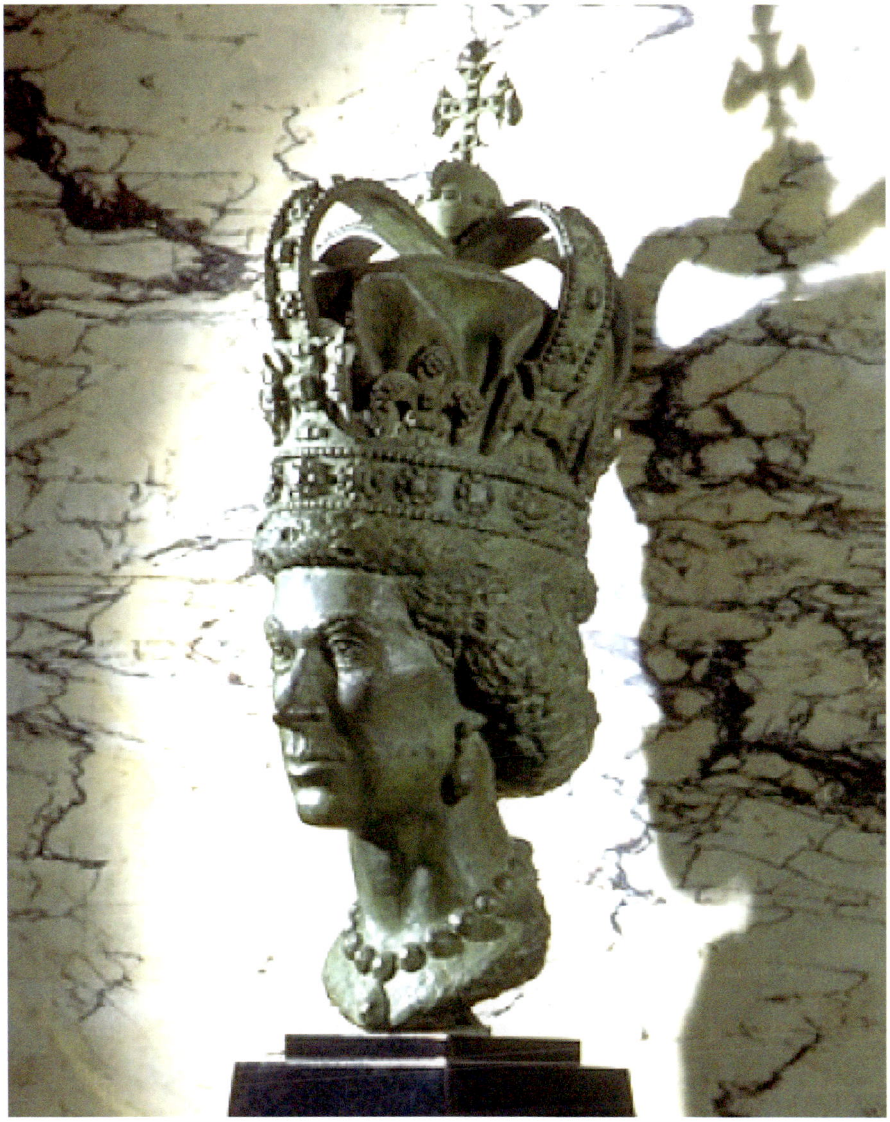

The Queen at Goldsmiths' Hall

Queen and sculptor's wife chatted as David worked. He still remembers overhearing the Queen saying he had rather startled her servants by arriving in plimsolls. Over tea and scones, the Queen asked Gilli for her thoughts on the work in hand. Asking the Queen to return to the chair where she had been posing, Gilli carefully examined the portrait head. She thought it good, apart from the forehead, which could have been higher, and the corner of the left eye, which was a little too low. At the end of the sitting, as the Queen bade them both farewell, she turned to David and said, with, he was sure, a twinkle in her eye, that as the sitting the next day was to be their last, 'it might be prudent to bring a good camera'.

David had not used his battered Rolliflex since the family was on holiday over a year before. On their way back to Wimbledon, David called on the photographer Clive Barda, who was currently engaged in shooting many of David's large public sculptures for a book to be published by

Phaidon Press during the following year. Ignoring Clive's offer to accompany him to Buckingham Palace, he persuaded his friend to lend him his best camera and some lights and to give him a quick lesson in their best use. The next day, when David arrived at the door of the drawing-room, carrying camera, lights and portrait head, he found his way barred by two large guardsmen. They said they were sorry, but David was to await the arrival of the Queen. When David asked why, he was told, most politely, that that information was classified!

He did not have to wait long. The Queen arrived, wearing a stunning necklace of huge diamonds and matching teardrop earrings. The guardsmen saluted and stepped away from the door, and as the Queen entered, she motioned David to follow. In the middle of the table sat St Edward's Crown. It seemed to David it was more glorious in that setting than it had been when he first saw it in its glass case at the Tower. Yet again, David remembers his monarch's words: 'You see, Mr Wynne, there are times when one must exercise one's authority to make sure it is intact.'

She allowed David to spend an hour taking photographs both of the crown on its own and also being modelled by the only person who was legally allowed to wear it. He then took notes of detail and dimensions, certain he would never be given another chance. The finished portrait had been somewhat overshadowed by this remarkable event, but when David showed it, the Queen seemed very pleased and keen to canvass the Duke of Edinburgh's opinion. His comments were equally encouraging.

Over the next two weeks, using lead and plasticene, David painstakingly added St Edward's Crown, the necklace and the earrings, all to the over-life-size scale that he had used for the original portrait head, working from the measurements and photographs he had taken. The sculpture was cast in bronze and unveiled at Goldsmiths' Hall later that year. It still occupies pride of place at the head of the main staircase.

But while the work on the portrait had progressed, David had been neglecting the effigy for the Jubilee medal. The Royal Mint had done their work in reducing the relief, and as he had worked on the crown in three dimensions, he now worked mostly from memory. When it was finished, however, David thought the crown highlighted something amiss with the relief. As Gilli agreed with him, there seemed no alternative but to request one last sitting. He rang the Palace.

It seemed an impossible request. The Queen was in the middle of numerous events celebrating a state visit by the President of Brazil. But, cooperative as ever, the Palace felt fifteen minutes could be wangled into the monarch's hectic schedule if David could come the next morning. He arrived promptly, bearing the relief, and was ushered into a different drawing-room. Eventually the Queen entered and greeted him, but David could tell she was distracted. Her eyes kept straying to a television set in the corner of the room. When David asked if there was something she wished to watch, the Queen told him she had a horse running in a Derby trial at Newmarket, but felt they were too short of time to see it. 'A race only takes three minutes, Ma'am. Let's see how he gets on.'

And so it was that the Queen's equerry, calling in to see if all was going well, discovered monarch and subject, on the edge of their seats, excitedly watching a horse race. The equerry said nothing, but when the leading jockey, wearing the Queen's distinctive racing colours, rode the horse across the line to win, he exclaimed, 'Congratulations, Ma'am.' David, simultaneously, commiserated, 'Oh what bad luck, Ma'am.' The Queen explained to the confused equerry that though it had been a good win, the horse was obviously tiring. She was afraid he would never make the extra two furlongs in the great race itself. As she turned off the television set, David recalls her exact words. 'Anyway, that's enough of that. We have work to do.'

David finished it and the Royal Mint duly struck the Jubilee Medal. There were many worthy recipients, but he was especially delighted that one of those chosen by the votes of local communities was Bill Amer. Bill was a plasterer who had helped David with many of his other sculptures.

In spite of his demanding workload, David had begun regularly to swim with dolphins at a recently opened aquarium in Oxford Street. Peter Moss was an Australian who looked after the place, and it was he who taught David the skills to interact with the dolphins that were kept there. David would come every day before the exhibit was open to the public and swim with two dolphins called Bonnie and Clyde. When the aquarium closed down, the dolphins were 'rehoused'. (Some years later, when David was the subject of a BBC documentary, he and the TV crew travelled to the safari park at Woburn to film him swimming with six dolphins in the aquarium there. He was amazed and moved to find Bonnie and Clyde, his old friends, clearly delighted to see him again, swimming towards him, chattering with joy.)

In connection with his great love for dolphins, he had been commissioned to sculpt a seventeen-foot bronze fountain, *Girl with a Dolphin*, by Taylor Woodrow for their new building, the World Trade Centre, adjacent to Tower Bridge. It was yet another of David's public sculptures in the centre of the great metropolis and there were clear indications that it would not be his last.

Asked to present, with Gilli, the prizes at the twentieth Taylor Woodrow Group's annual distribution of long-service awards, David spoke movingly of his approach to life and success:

> 'We live for seventy years or so, and if we are not bone idle we spend about forty of them working, and if we are not happy working, when are we going to be happy? . . . I think no man or woman can lead a full and dignified and happy life unless their work is something they are conscious of doing well. I think that anyone going into the arts or any profession and not giving an eye to the top is cheating himself.'

In covering the event, the *Taywood News* continued:

> Mr Wynne went on to quote from a letter written by Sir Philip Sidney, the Elizabethan soldier and statesman, a version of which he had put up on the wall of his first studio and taken as his guiding principle: 'He who aims an arrow at the midday sun may be perfectly certain that he will miss his mark, but he may be equally sure that his shaft will fly higher than he who aims at a bush.'

It was clear David still had many more arrows to aim.

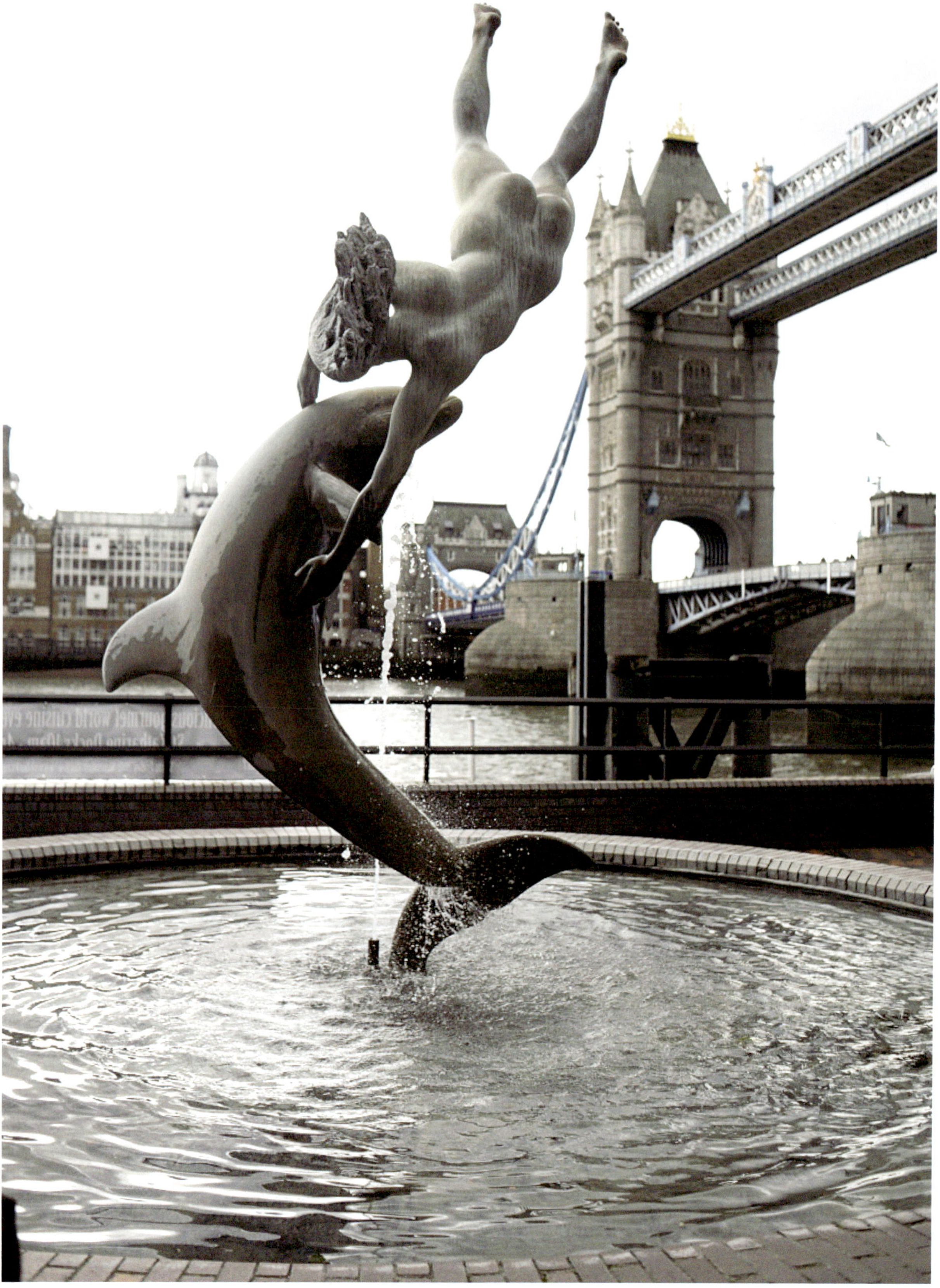

Girl with a Dolphin

11

THERE ARE FEW public sculptures in London as well known as *Boy with a Dolphin*. Londoner s first had the opportunity to see it when David was chosen to contribute to an exhibition of figurative sculpture organised by the *Illustrated London News*, in conjunction with the Greater London Council, in Holland Park in the summer of 1975. More than thirty recent works by eleven leading figurative sculptors were on show and there was much comment in the press about its being the first such exhibition for more than a decade. Given that this was the case, the response from some of the more avant-garde critics did not seem surprising.

> The most disquieting thing about the display [commented the *Guardian*] . . . is that it is like stepping back into the days of open-air sculpture in Battersea Park, and the durability of the bronze-cast fantasy . . . It's disquieting because in the meantime the world and our view of it has changed enough to make much of the work on display curiously anachronistic and bafflingly extravagant . . . David Wynne's boys cantilevered off patient dolphins are best suited to the forecourts of large anonymous modern hotels.

Though a poke at the works on show in Holland Park, this may also have been a sniffy comment on David's recent bronze sculpture of *Four Egrets in Flight*, chosen as a centrepiece for the lounge in the renovated Grosvenor House, which had just recently reopened, with considerable publicity, after a multi-million-pound refit, in fashionable Park Lane.

The crowds who attended the exhibition, however, seemed more than pleased. *The Times* quoted Illtyd Harrington, the deputy leader of the GLC, insisting that 'as a city, we have got to get back to recognising that art is as important as council housing'. The *Daily Mirror* spotted Graham Hill at the private view. He had lent David's *Circling Birds*, 'normally found on the front lawn of his home at Shenley . . . "I have been collecting for three years, but only buy David Wynne's work," he said.' (David would meet another champion racing driver, Jackie Stewart, through Graham Hill, encountering him in St Moritz. As well as being instrumental in the IMG commission to sculpt portrait figures of five of their great

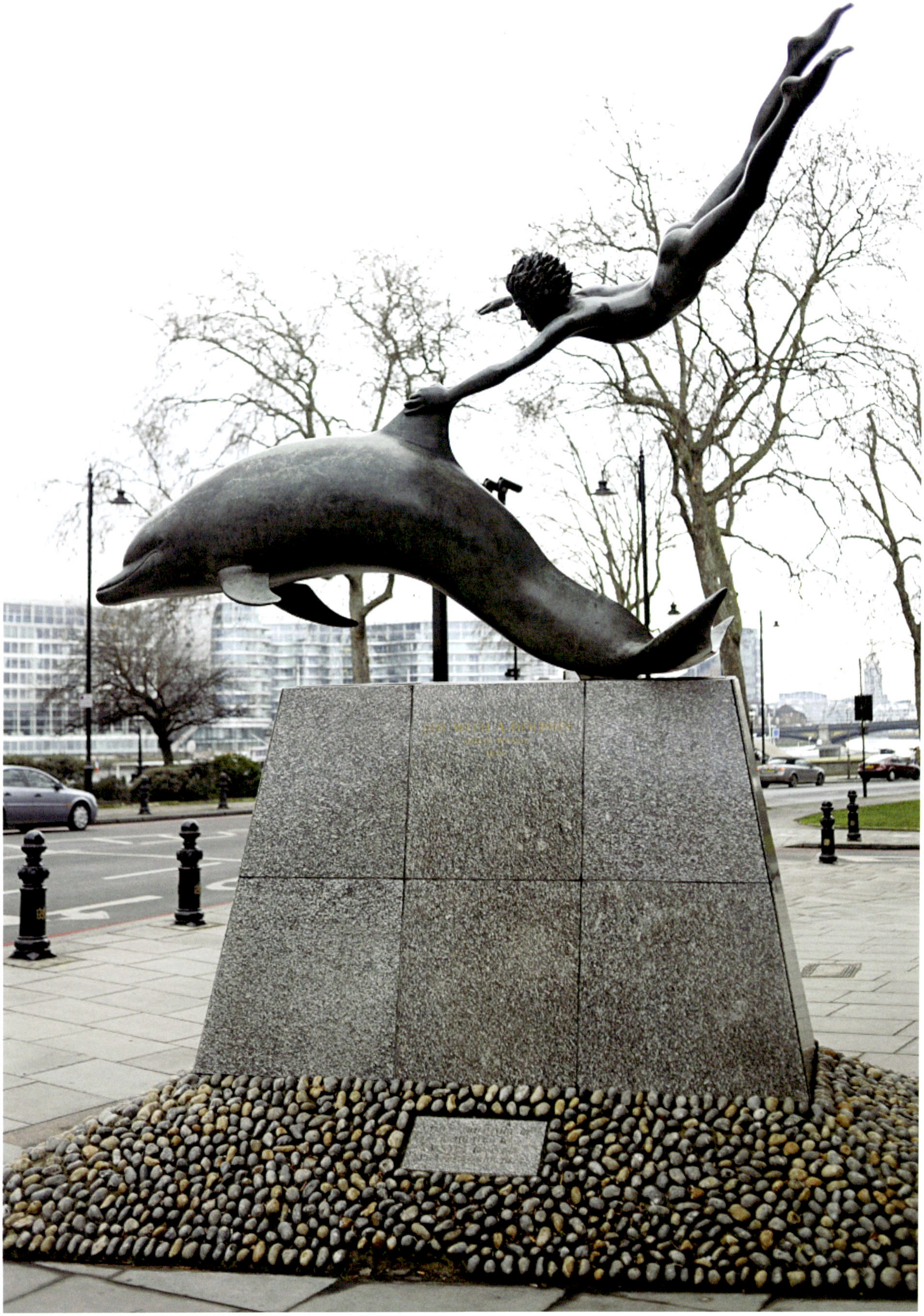

Boy with a Dolphin

sporting clients, Jackie became an important patron of David's work, buying one of the Beatles sculptures and a later work, *Girl with Windblown Hair*, in 2003, for his home in Buckinghamshire.)

It was Frank Taylor who, in 1971, had suggested to the chairman of the First Federal Savings Bank in Worcester, Massachusetts, that David might be a suitable sculptor for a major work to be sited in front of their offices in downtown Worcester. Several proposals had been considered and rejected by the directors and officers of First Federal. Frank Taylor's recommendation had resulted in David's visiting Worcester for a series of conferences and finally, in 1972, he presented a proposal to them for a large water sculpture in bronze. He won the commission.

The idea for the fifteen-foot sculpture, according to the leaflet produced by the Bank in 1974, arose from David's experience of swimming with dolphins:

> Wynne relates: ' . . . Dolphins would actually give one a ride as in the sculpture. Often I thought what fun it would be in the open sea, particularly for a boy such as my younger son Roland, who would be light enough to be towed long distances. Thus the idea was born.'

The work, an edition of four, would also be bought by Grayson's Bank in Sherman, Texas, and the Mayo Clinic in Rochester, Minnesota, presented to them by another patron of David's, Count Rossi di Montelera. Indeed, to highlight the ever increasing interest in Wynne's work in America, the press reported the logistical nightmare of shipping both *Boy with a Dolphin* and *Girl with a Dolphin* in two containers, each weighing a thousand kilos, from the Morris Singer Foundry in Basingstoke to different locations in the USA: *Boy* to Worcester, *Girl* to PepsiCo in New York State.

The Holland Park *Boy* was not placed within a fountain, as in Massachusetts, but was, after the exhibition closed, erected on the corner of Cheyne Walk and Oakley Street, facing Albert Bridge. It had been commissioned by Neil Wates, whose construction company was developing the corner site into a complex of flats and retail showrooms. David's son, Roland, posed for the boy. As the sculpture was modelled directly in plaster, its armature proved one of the most complex that David ever achieved. It was a brilliant piece of engineering, made of steel, lead, wood, aluminium and copper. Its London siting, on one of the busiest intersections along the Embankment, has ensured that thousands of Londoners see it every day. The Embankment is still one of London's main traffic arteries and the statue remains, probably, the best loved of all David's large works in London.

He had another project, however, in mind for PepsiCo. His relationship with Donald M. Kendall, the chairman of PepsiCo, began when David met Kendall with Grant Simmons while he was in New York for his second Findlay Gallery show. An inspirational businessman, Kendall attracted considerable attention when he flamboyantly offered plastic cups of Pepsi to both Nikita Khrushchev and Richard Nixon at their infamous 'kitchen debate' in Moscow. It had been Kendall's vision which created one of the finest collections of large sculptures in the world, at the new PepsiCo

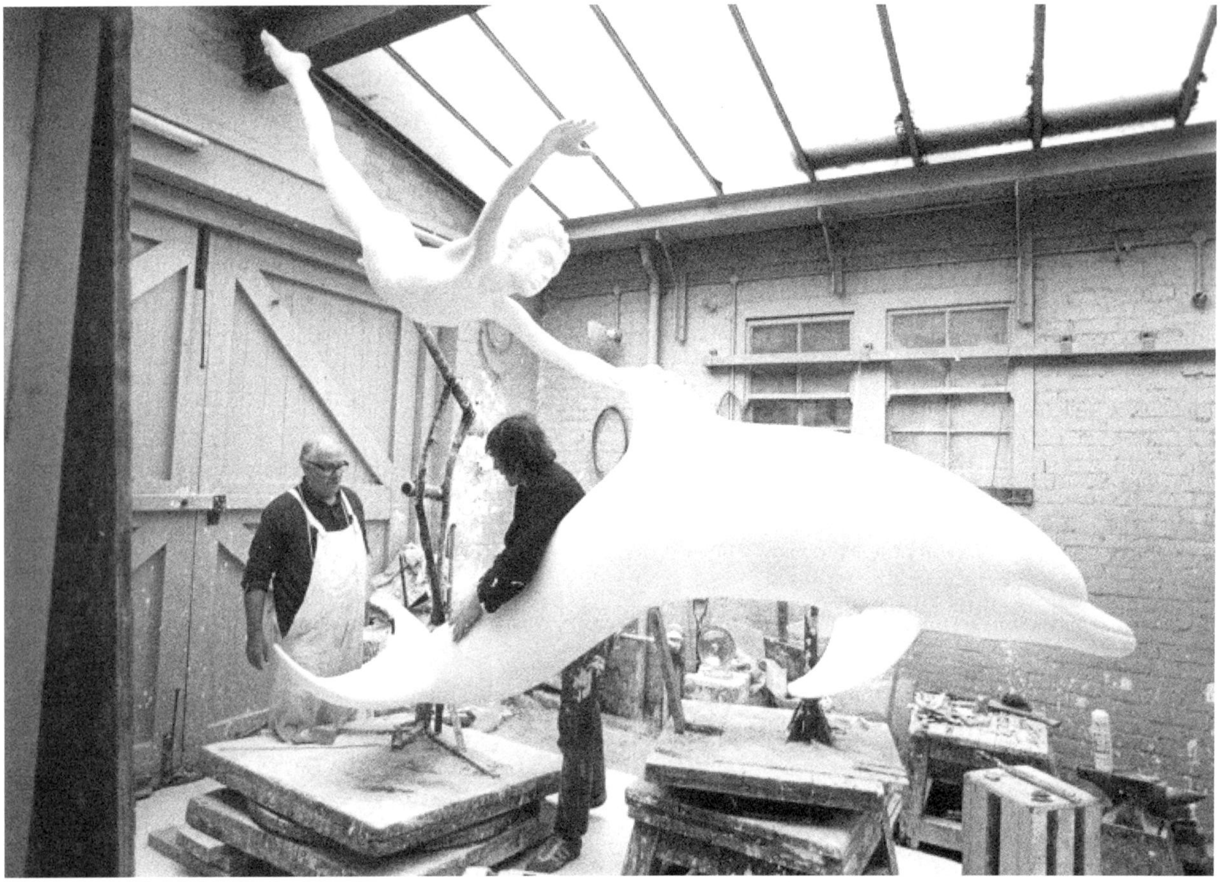

David with Bill Amer discussing the uniting of the two figures

headquarters in Purchase, New York. Alexander Calder, Henry Moore, Alberto Giacometti, David Smith, Jacques Lipchitz and Arnaldo Pomodoro were just some of the artists with whom David's work would now be placed, among the rolling lawns and gardens of the building's impressive grounds. Donald Kendall had taken David for a drive around the sculpture garden and had asked him if he were commissioned to make a sizeable sculpture where he would like it put. With little hesitation, David said right in front of the main building, and suggested the businessman come and see the maquette for *Girl with a Dolphin* then on show at Findlay's. Kendall, pleased with the sculpture, and agreeing it belonged on the site David had selected, asked if there was anything unique which he would like to sculpt but whose cost might be prohibitive for other organisations.

Back in Wimbledon, having breakfast with the family, David told them about his visit to the PepsiCo sculpture park and Donald Kendall's question. Johnny said, 'Grizzly bears. You've always loved them.' That day, David started work on a maquette.

According to the *Banff Crag & Canyon*, the local newspaper of the Banff National Park in Alberta, Canada, recording David's expedition to see the grizzly bear in its natural setting in September 1974: 'Wynne asked Kendall how they might like a 52,000-

pound grizzly bear in black marble . . . ' David has a more vivid memory. At the conclusion of a discussion with Donald Kendall, negotiating his fee and sorting out the daunting logistics involved in the creation of the bear, Kendall's parting remark went straight to the point: 'It'd better be some fucking bear!'

According to the *Calgary Herald* on 6 September, David was formally presented with Alberta, one of Calgary Zoo's Rockie Mountain grizzlies. David, with Gilli's help, had arranged for the bear, abandoned by her mother, to journey to the Loch Lomond Bear Park, where 'Mr Wynne will study Alberta's habits, then take a year to complete his work'. And more excitement was still to come. The *Reader's Digest* for June 1975 printed an article, purportedly written by David, called 'Four Legs and a Bunch of Claws', bearing the dramatic by-line: 'The enraged grizzly charged, a perfect killing machine. In her path the young artist stood, waiting.'

In fact, the article was compiled by a staff writer on the magazine from David's dictated tapes of his experiences. The transcribed account went on to tell of his expedition, in the company of park warden Bill Vroom, high up into the mountains of the Banff National Park:

> I had come from England late in August 1974 . . . to observe grizzlies in the wild. I am a sculptor, and I had been commissioned to do a grizzly in stone. A 36-ton block of black marble would soon be waiting in England. I had studied the photographs, read the books, been to the zoos . . . . I learned that the few grizzlies that had survived the white man's obsession with killing had sought sanctuary in the last total wilderness, the desolate mountains of the far West.

David then described the long trek up into the mountains and the waiting that was rewarded when a mother and her cubs were sighted; after two weeks, they disappeared, however, disturbed by some wolves.

> They say bears do strange things to people. I know they completely captivated my imagination. [During the next two days Bill and David followed the family of silvertips, until their last evening – the most beautiful of all] Nothing disturbed the beauty of those high and lonely peaks which burned red and gold in the sunset. No sound but the far-off yelp of a coyote, no movement but the shadows creeping up the slope where we stood. One reads about mystical experiences. One reads about exaltation. It wasn't just the big-horn sheep, the elk and the grizzly bears that were alive, but the grass, too, the mountains, the clouds. The whole planet burst like a rainbow, and the only word for it was glory.

Then the bears came, this time from another direction, and the mother 'began to rear up on her hind legs, snorting and gnashing her teeth. Bill glanced quickly at his rifle, checking its position against the log. He spoke quietly: "The old girl's real mad tonight . . . We're between the youngsters and their supper." ' When the young cubs started loping towards the two men, from less than two hundred yards away, the mother charged:

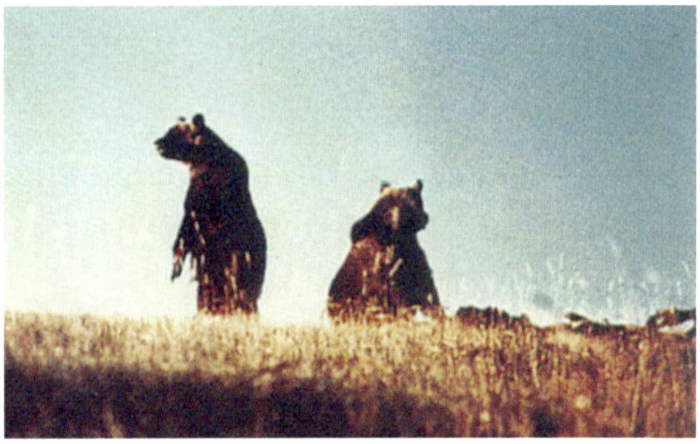

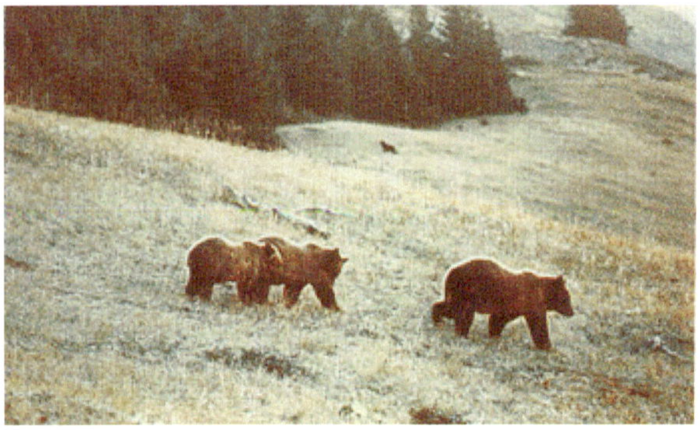

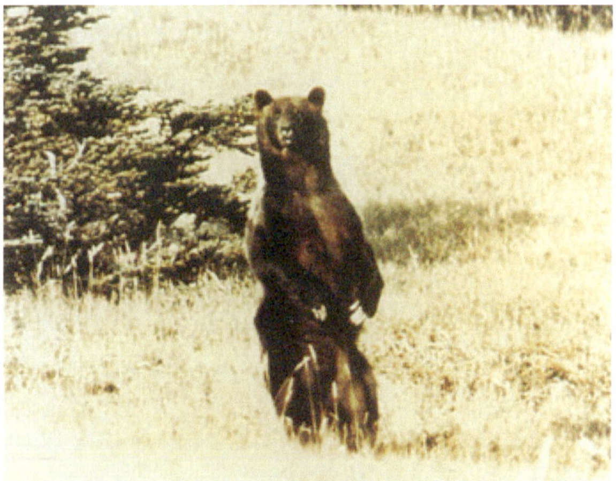

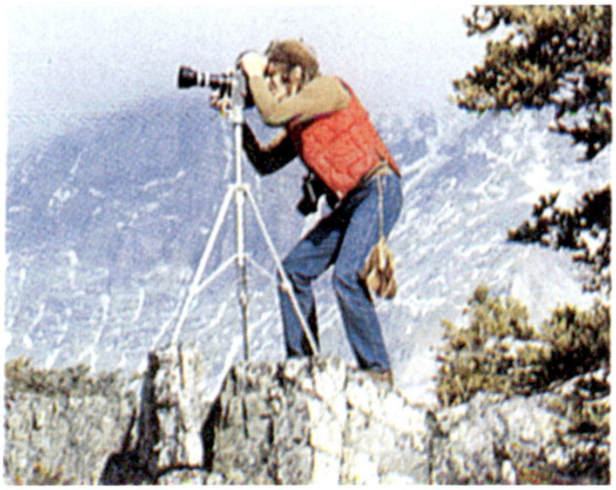

Confronted by bears in the high Rockies

I watched her through the viewfinder of my movie camera, clicking away as she came straight at me. Her mouth was wide open, and she was running flat and low to the ground – 450 pounds of frothing fury coming at 30 miles an hour . . . Bill did not fire. He stepped forward, waved his hat in the air and shouted at the top of his lungs, 'Get away!' Incredibly, she skidded to a halt, barely 40 feet from me, whirled off and ran back up the hill. I went on taking pictures . . .

The *Reader's Digest* article was headed with three of David's photographs showing the mother grizzly charging ahead of her cubs, coming flat out and then turning away. The last two photographs are a little blurred, but as the commentary points out: 'Understandably, the camera was a bit shaky.' David concluded his tape with a prescient plea for conservation: this was many years before the peril that so many wild creatures face had become widely appreciated.

At dinner, chief park warden Andy Anderson listened to our account of the charge. Then, over coffee, he said something I will never forget: ' . . . for a long time man has been trying to dominate nature, to tame the wilderness. Some of us are beginning to realise that it's time to stop, if we want any wilderness left . . . [when] the last grizzly crouches in his cage in some city zoo waiting to be fed, may not our children ask: "Where is the wilderness that was to be preserved for all generations . . . and where is the grizzly bear, who was king of these mountains?" '
Beneath my breath, I could only add: 'God save the king!'

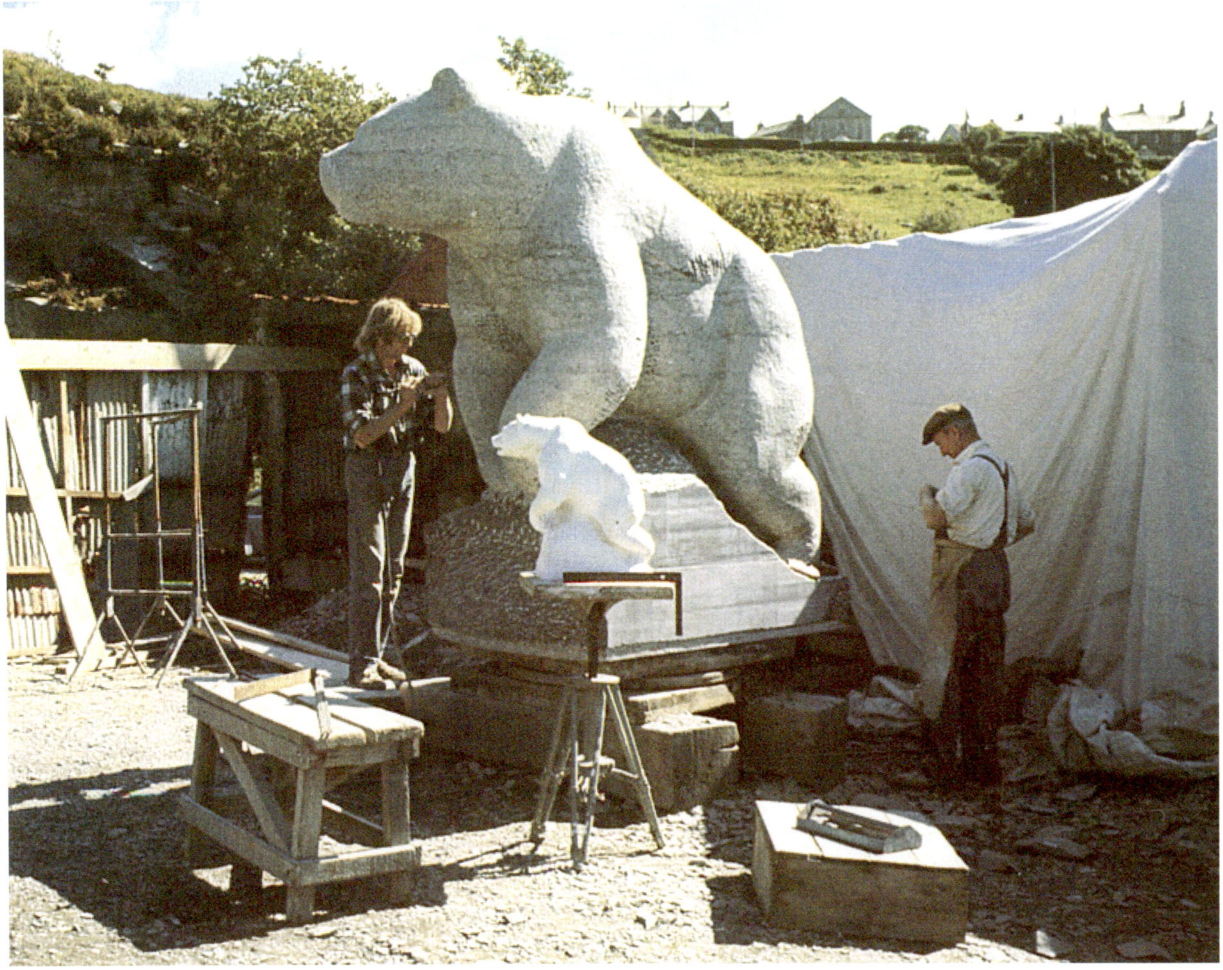

The block of marble being carved on Bodmin Moor

David returned to England to model the maquette, and an enormous block of Belgian fossil marble was sent to the quarry on Bodmin Moor in Cornwall. The quarry was owned by Peter Throssell and it was here that David met the owner's daughter, Robin, then aged eighteen. Their friendship was to be one of the most important relationships in David's life.

Robin became, and still remains, a crucial partner in the evolution of all David's work. Now an accomplished sculptor in her own right, Robin's vital role as his assistant began in 1975, and their developing trust, mutual dependency and, eventually, love have been central to David's life. If Gilli was David's guiding light, Robin has been his passionately dedicated apprentice.

On site in Cornwall, he also had the help of two granite masons, Les Williams and Peter Nottle, and after nine months' work, the bear slowly emerged. 'The pose chosen for the bear,' David wrote later, 'is a strange one. Grizzly bears are being shot out of their last stronghold in the high wilderness. Once they roamed from Florida all the way to Alaska. Now there is no place on earth where grizzlies can live in peace. So he is standing on the edge of a cliff, on the precipice of extinction.'

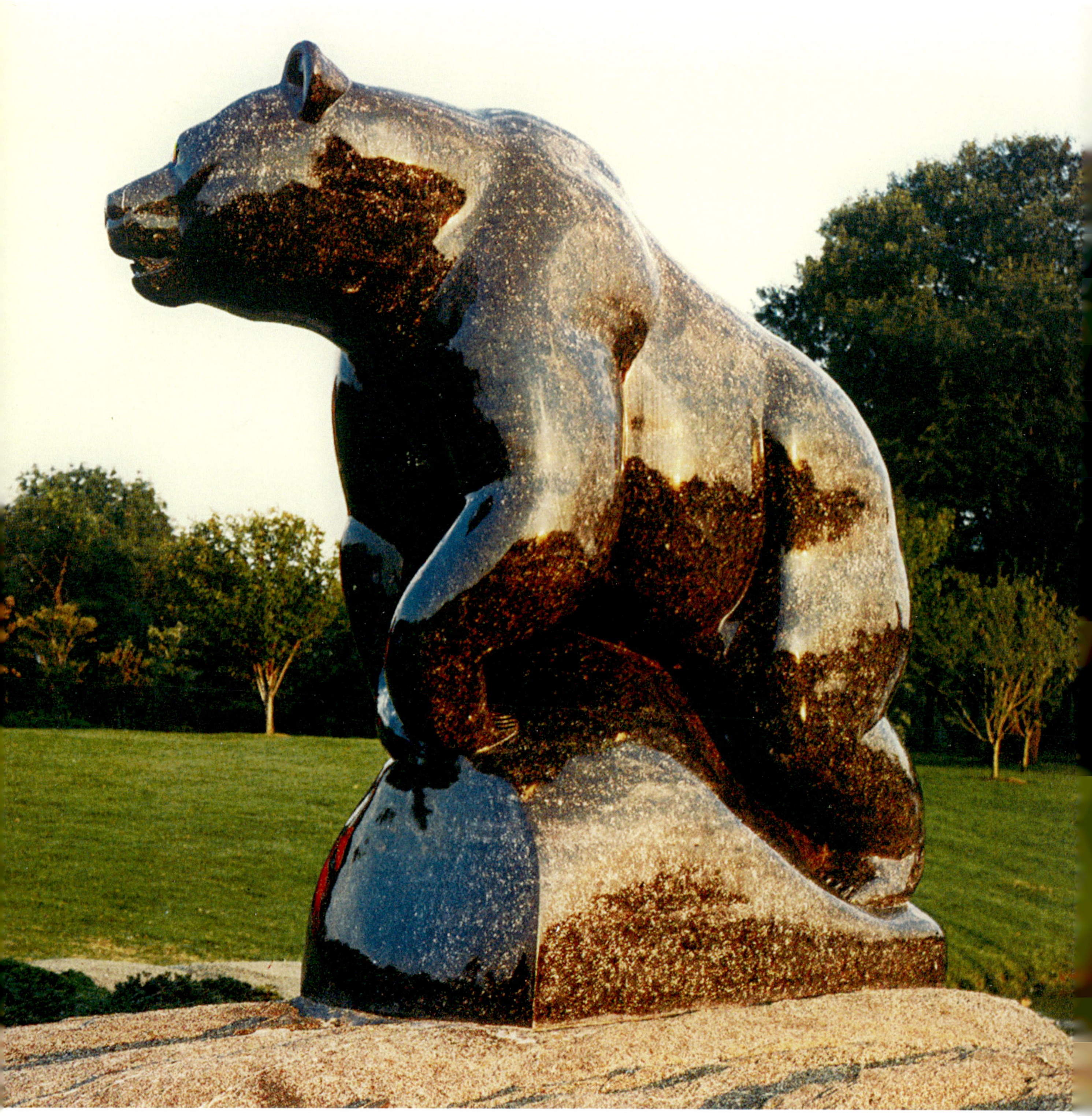

Grizzly Bear

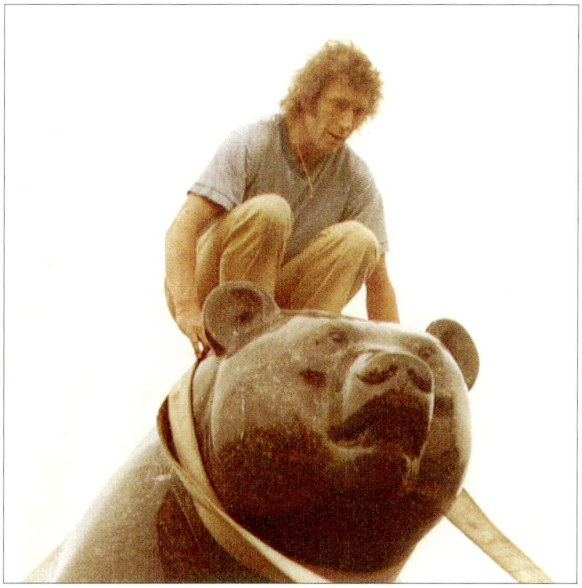

David placing the carving in position.

Dramatic photographs of David directing operations during installation, upright on the bear as it dangled from the arm of a 45-ton crane, appeared in the press. Ken Witburn and Charlie Edwards, master craftsmen who often worked with David, had travelled to America with him to help fix the statue in the sculpture park. They employed a technique borrowed from antiquity to lower the sculpture the last few inches. A large bag of sugar was placed on each corner of the plinth (though the ancient Egyptians used other substances) and as the huge weight descended, David and his craftsmen-crew shouted instructions to each other, ensuring the sculpture came down as accurately as possible on to the sugar. This left enough space between the sculpture and the plinth to allow the slings from the crane to be slipped from under the sculpture's base. Once the straps and slings had been cleared, buckets of water, poured simultaneously, dissolved the sugar and the sculpture came finally to rest in its desired position. The company's house magazine, *Pepsicola*, for June 1976, erroneously informed its readers that: 'Wynne needs to be right on the piece as it's positioned, to provide proper balance.'

To celebrate its arrival, an exhibition of David's work was held inside the main building. Over six thousand visitors saw a retrospective, consisting of sixty of his pieces, which ran for eight weeks. NBC television, the house journal proudly boasted, aired a four-minute piece – '(by the television clock, just short of an eternity)' – on their 21 June prime-time national newscast. At a huge dinner to celebrate the opening, David made a speech. It was the year of the American Bicentennial, and David congratulated the USA on its very special birthday, but he had one question to ask: 'So it's a bicentenary, but where are all the bison?' *Grizzly Bear* was David's most massive work yet and not only stood as a monument to the cause of conservation but also marked his own half-century. He turned fifty just as the bear was undergoing its final polish.

12

IN JUNE 1977, David was the subject of a BBC2 documentary, narrated by Humphrey Burton, *One Pair of Hands*. It was screened on the same day that his portrait head of Lord Hailsham was unveiled in the Law Library at Christ Church, Oxford. It was the third of his bronze portraits for the college; Lord Home's and Lord Salisbury's were already in place there. The television programme portrayed David engaged in a variety of projects. Footage from his expedition to the Rockies allowed the programme to show David at home in Wimbledon screening his adventure to Gilli and the children. A group of councillors and businessmen from Sheffield are observed rather nervously discussing with David the cost of their commission for a stainless-steel equestrian statue, *Horse and Rider*, twelve feet high.

Nancy Banks-Smith, the legendary television critic of the *Guardian*, was diverted by David's comments as he worked on the sculpture commissioned for Bowood House – 'I've never made a reclining woman.'

> Sculptors [she wrote] must find their public a heavy cross . . . Mr Wynne's attitude to this trait is exemplary. On the day his first big commission – four fellas heaving on a rope – was to be unveiled, Taylor Woodrow rang to say, 'Someone has painted the private parts. What shall we do?' 'Wait till I get there,' said Wynne, 'in case it's an improvement.'

Ronald Hastings in the *Daily Telegraph* was equally beguiled:

> . . . it seems a lonely occupation as he travels the world gathering ideas and commissions . . . but he described it as 'the most privileged existence you could possibly have. All I have ever done is to experiment, to practise.' . . . Recently the good people of Sheffield, having seen Mr Wynne's model of a proposed tall and skinny horse, suggested that children might climb up it to the detriment of both. He replied: 'I've got thirty-four public sculptures around the world and not one has ever been damaged.' He then artfully recommended stainless steel as the best material. I suspect that Mr Wynne is not a sculptor because he is good at it, though he undoubtedly is, but because he really loves children, animals and beautiful girls, and wants to scatter them permanently all

over the world, preferably with a personal message. For example . . . he spent three weeks in the Rocky Mountains and came up with a grizzly bear out of a 36-ton block of marble, 'rather sadly and royally, standing on the edge of the world, for grizzly bears, you know, have nowhere to go'. This romantic truthfulness applies equally to human models. 'I try to tell the truth lovingly, not to caricature or to belittle but to show what the person's mother saw in him as a little boy or girl. To distil the good out of them.' A sort of Mozart in stone, or a Chekhov who hears the axes falling.

When *Horse and Rider* was finally unveiled in May 1978, the tabloid press picked up on the suggestion that the naked rider's face was that of Princess Anne. David's inspiration had been the White Horse of Uffington, a huge Celtic chalk figure on the Marlborough Downs. The work was commissioned by Jonathan Stone

Sheffield was then a manufacturing town and David chose to create the sculpture from stainless steel – invented in Sheffield, 'so [it] was appropriate. It is very strong, so that thin and tenuous forms could be used. [I] strove to make something wild and wonderful, a glimpse of freedom and joy.' The model for the rider was Edward, David's sixteen-year-old son. Amused by the press furore, David told the *Sun*; 'It has given me a bit of a laugh . . . I really wouldn't dream of doing a naked sculpture of the princess.' Edward, a pop-group guitarist, said: 'It's the first time anybody has mistaken me for Princess Anne. I don't really know which way to take it. I don't think I was looking very regal when I posed for the statue and I think it looks like me.' His comments were printed beside his photograph, underneath a picture of the sculpture. 'Well,' teased the *Sun*'s copywriter, 'is it Anne?' The *Daily Mail* interviewed Sheffield's Steel Castings Research and Trade Association's assistant director (*Horse and Rider* had been assembled by six of their welders). 'Mr Keith Robertson,' wrote the paper's reporter, 'said yesterday: "There have been a lot of pretty choice remarks about this statue by the lads, but this suggestion is the best yet." ' The newspaper's headline was more considered: 'Princess Anne? No it's my son' – and their photograph of Edward clearly showed what frothy nonsense the whole fuss had been.

Another fuss was to erupt when it was suggested that David carve a white horse on Butser Hill in Hampshire to mark the Queen's Silver Jubilee. It was, according to an interview with David in the *Sunday Telegraph* in September 1977, when he was 'skiing last winter in Switzerland with Prince Michael of Kent that we had what we thought was a brilliant idea'. Prince Michael discovered the perfect location, sought the agreement of the county council and David prepared a design. Then 'it became a controversy of Concorde-like dimensions . . . even spilling into the correspondence columns of *The Times*. It will cause a landslide said some. Scarce orchids will be uprooted, said others . . . ' David's scheme was on an heroic scale. The carving was to be 360 feet long and 60 feet high. He even arranged for a helicopter to be employed in the removal of the top soil. David also intended to use ten agricultural students from Oxford and Cambridge to help him and his son Johnny cut the turf. But the project was never approved. The protestors won.

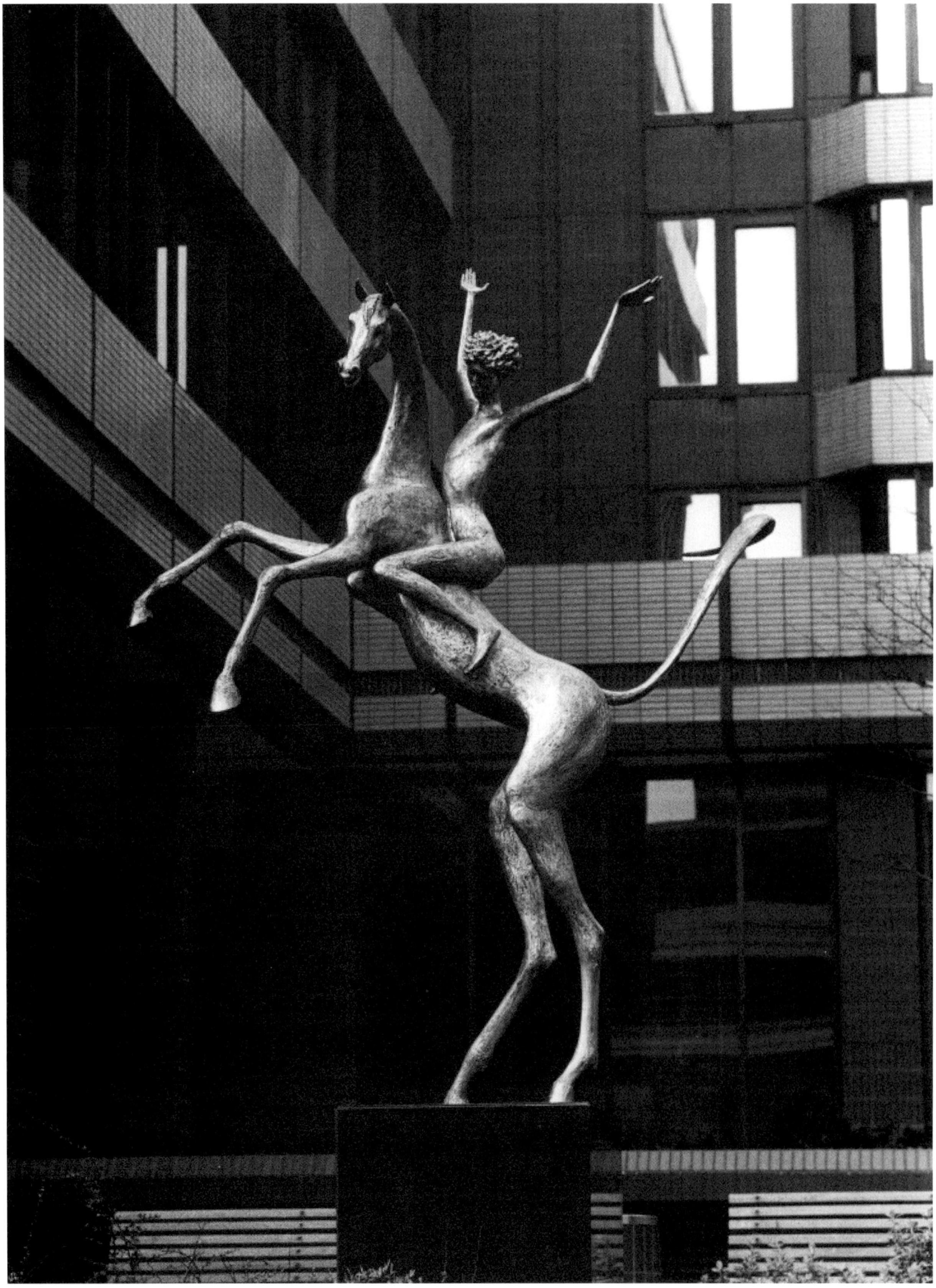

Horse and Rider

13

DAVID'S LOVE of the Cresta Run propelled him not only down the mountainside at frightening speed, but also hurtled him into the cream of European high society. His regular trips to Switzerland helped him forge lasting friendships with the mega-rich and famous. It was Susan Autgarten who first invited David to ride the Cresta. Her god-daughter, Virginia Wade, was a good friend of his. David had made her portrait head in 1972 and the tennis player had been his model for *Girl with a Dolphin* in 1973. The Cresta is an ice run, rebuilt each year, winding down for a mile from St Moritz through a steep gully and round ten hair-raising corners. Speeds can range from fifty to eighty miles an hour, depending on the skills of the rider, and its attraction can be addictive. Lord Brabazon of Tara, an early devotee, compared the Cresta to a woman, but 'with this cynical difference – to love her once is to love her always'. And David certainly did love her.

Riding the Cresta, which is owned by the St Moritz Tobogganing Club, is more than just an extreme sport, however. The social life which occupies the nine short weeks that the run is open attracts a remarkable array of royalty, aristocracy, business tycoons, film stars, sportsmen and what we now describe as 'international celebrities'. The Corvilia Club is the most exclusive of venues. It nestles high up in the mountains above St Moritz and it was here that David got to know many of his future patrons.

One of them was Count Rossi di Montelera, who became a great friend. The count once asked David which guests he would like to sit on either side of him at a dinner party the count was about to throw in the sculptor's honour. When David said he didn't know who was staying at the resort, the count replied his choice could be not only from those in St Moritz but of anyone who might be in Europe. David suggested 'the two most beautiful women in the world': Audrey Hepburn on one side and the Begum Aga Khan on the other. Princess Salimah Aga Khan would later recollect:

> We met at a dinner [in St Moritz in 1973] and as I was expecting my third child at any moment we talked about having babies. In those days men were not encouraged as they are now to participate at births, but David had already done so, and what he said about the delivery of his

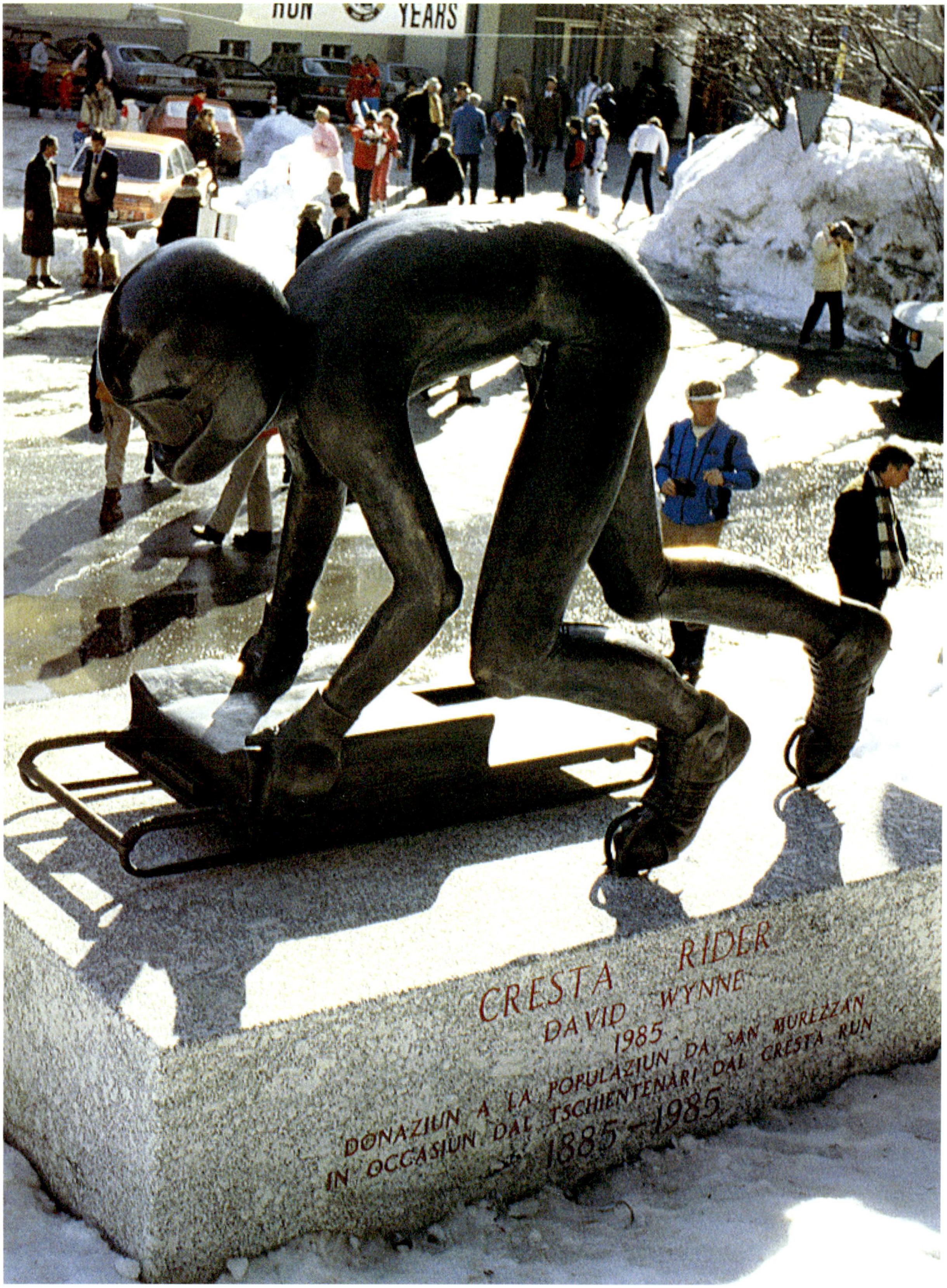

Cresta Rider

first son Edward was so touching it will remain etched on my heart for ever.

David recollects dancing that night with Audrey Hepburn. When he suggested, reluctantly, they should go back to their table and change partners – for everyone wanted to dance with her – the film star insisted she only wished to dance with him and draped a string of pearls over his head to reinforce her request.

One night at the Corvilia Club, the Shah of Persia allowed no other man but David to escort his wife around the dance floor. At dinner on another night, the wife of Herbert von Karajan suggested they have an affair. The great conductor seemed amused to hear his beautiful wife whisper, 'Come and see me, David. I only show my paintings when I'm in bed.' 'That's good,' replied David. 'I only look at paintings when I'm in bed.'

One of David's most vivid memories is of seeing Graham Hill fly his small plane high up over the mountain range to reach St Moritz, nestled in the valley beyond. It was a spectacular and dangerous feat yet somehow evidence of the sheer exuberance and fun with which the Cresta was invested by its devotees. In 1985, when the club wanted to commemorate its hundredth anniversary in some fitting way, David sculpted *Cresta Rider*, a six-foot bronze showing a rider at the top of the run, about to plunge down the mile-long tunnel of ice.

It was in St Moritz that David first met Lord Shelbourne. According to *The Times* Diary, 29 June 1978:

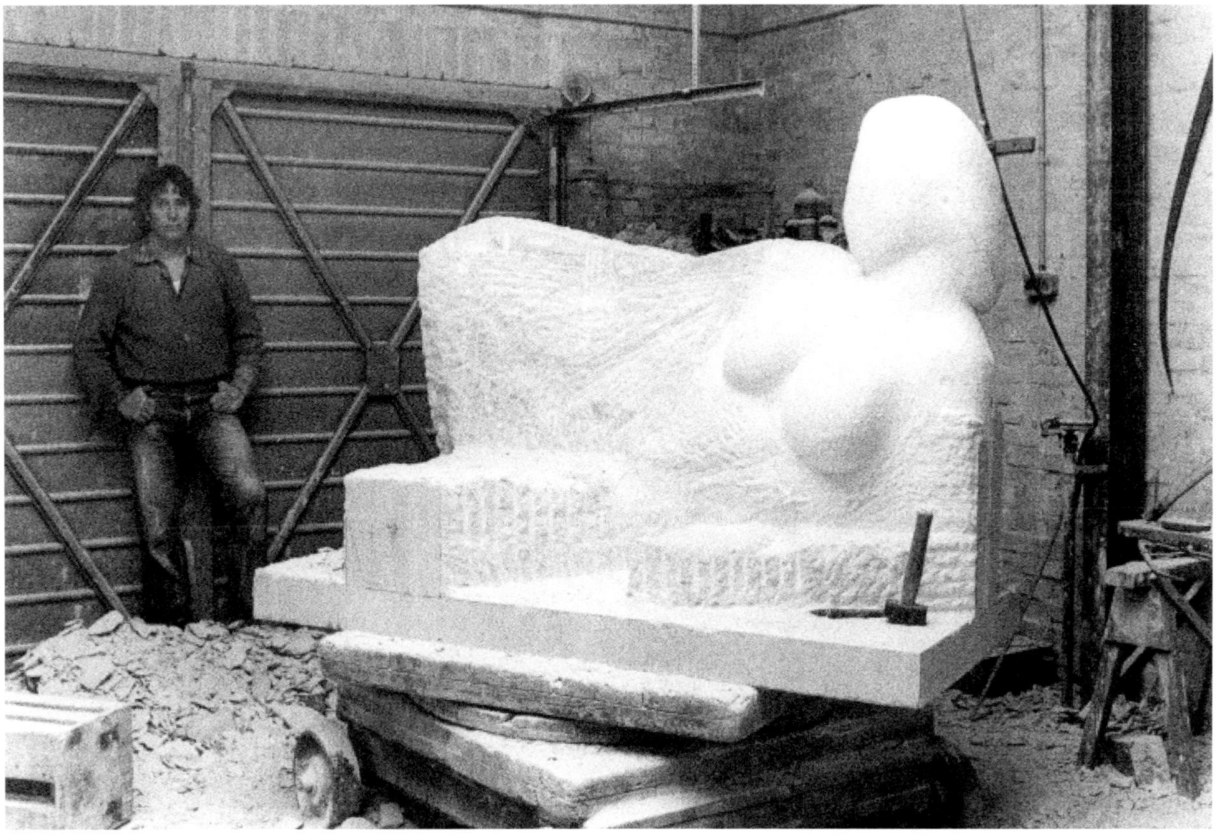

Bowood Figure, work in progress

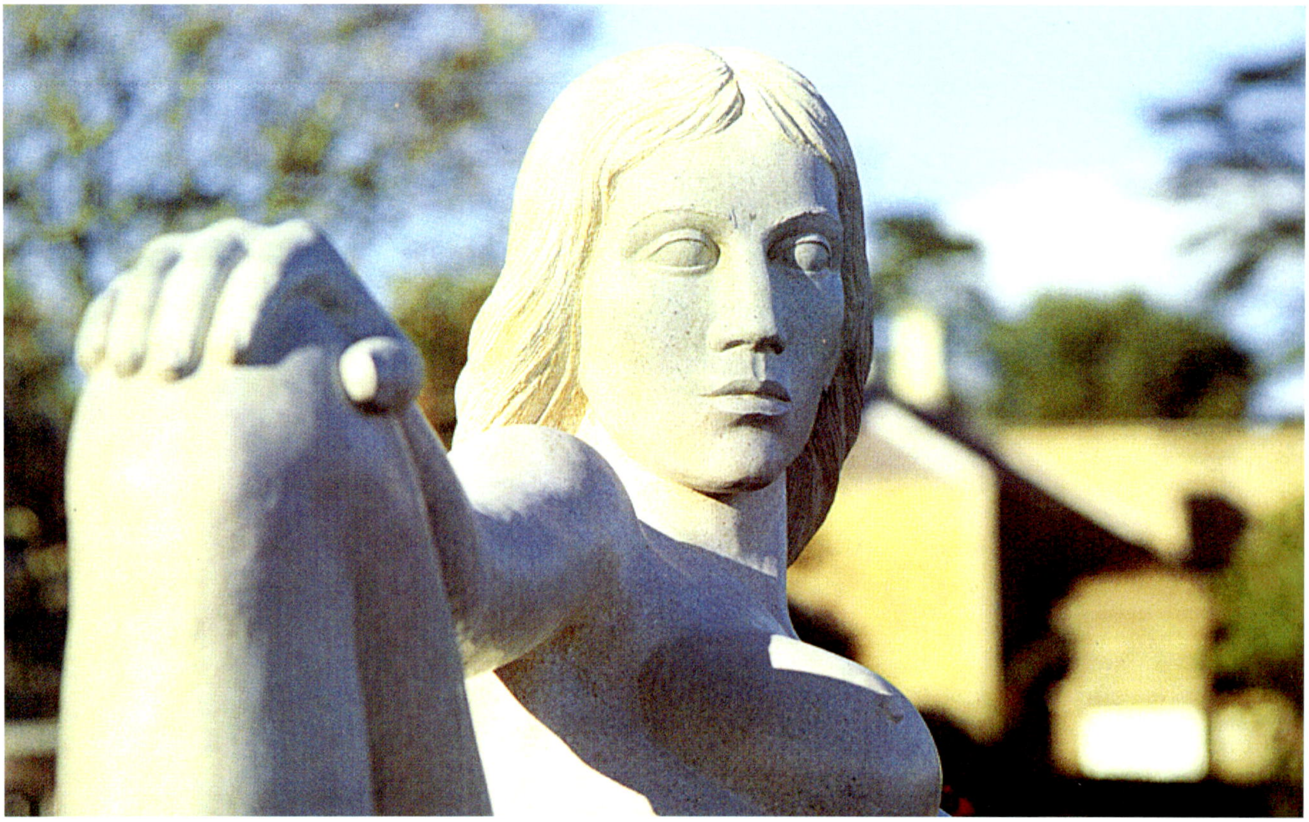

Bowood Figure

. . . surely one of the most remarkable private commissions this century . . . came from Lord Shelbourne, who has been delighted by Wynne's work for many years and wanted to replace a classical sculpture which had disintegrated in his Borghese-style gardens at Bowood in Wiltshire. Wynne told me: 'I wanted to create something utterly tranquil to fit in with the Capability Brown landscaped park.' Measuring six foot by four it is the first larger-than-life naturalistic figure 52-year-old Wynne has carved out of stone . . . 'It took me six months just to get the mass of the weight off, and I lost some myself,' he told me. Wynne is not surprised there aren't more sculptors tackling great blocks and the reason is not for lack of patrons. 'There is plenty of money around – it costs no more than the staff Rolls-Royce – but it is hard work.'

Carved from an eight-ton monolith of honey-coloured Nebrasina marble, *Bowood Figure* was worked with the help of another of David's assistants, Derek Carr. Nicola, David's stepdaughter, was its model. Positioned on a plinth at the top of a great flowing sweep of baroque stone steps at the front of the house, she sits, said David, 'like a calm goddess gazing over the rich English landscape'. According to the *Wiltshire Gazette*, 'One of the fifty-odd guests at the unveiling party suggested it might be regarded as pornographic by some visitors. "Certainly not," said Lady Shelbourne. "I think her face is her saving grace." ' *House and Garden*, in November 1979, called the work:

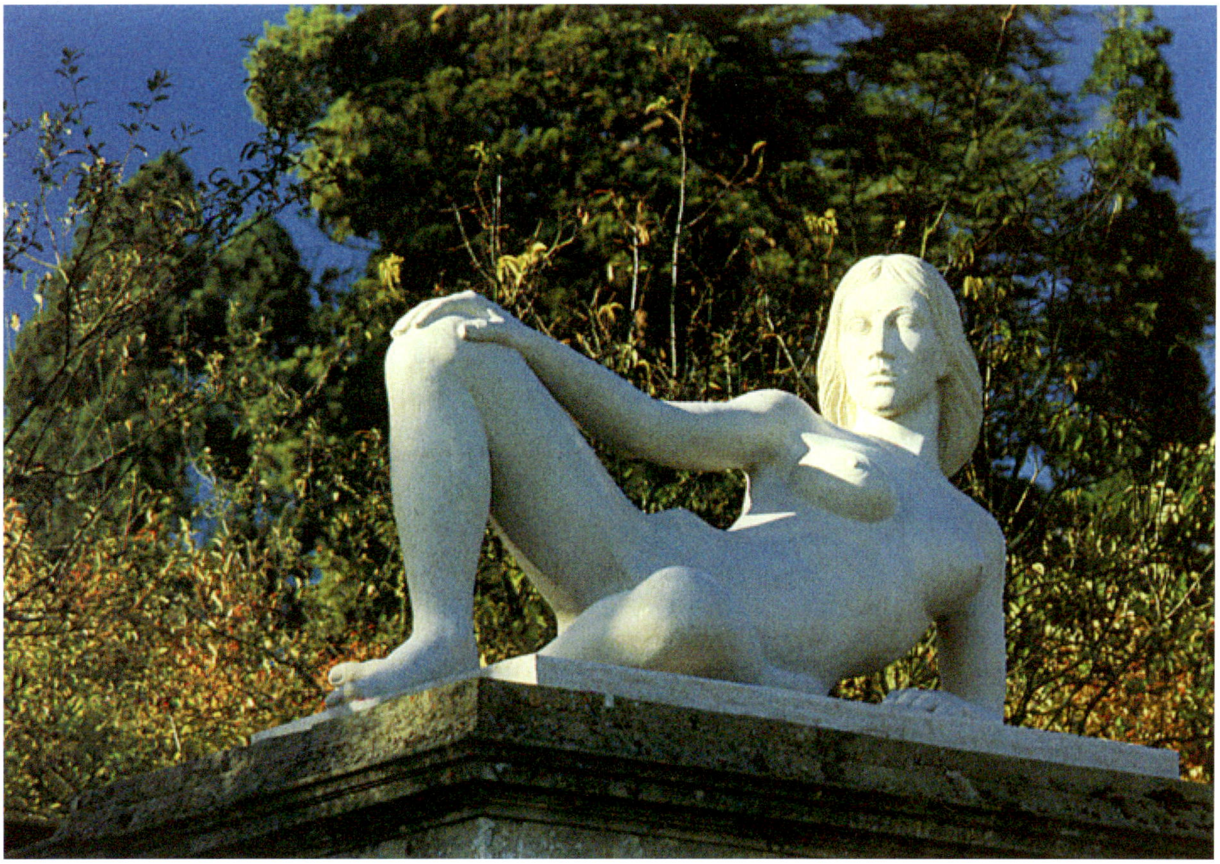

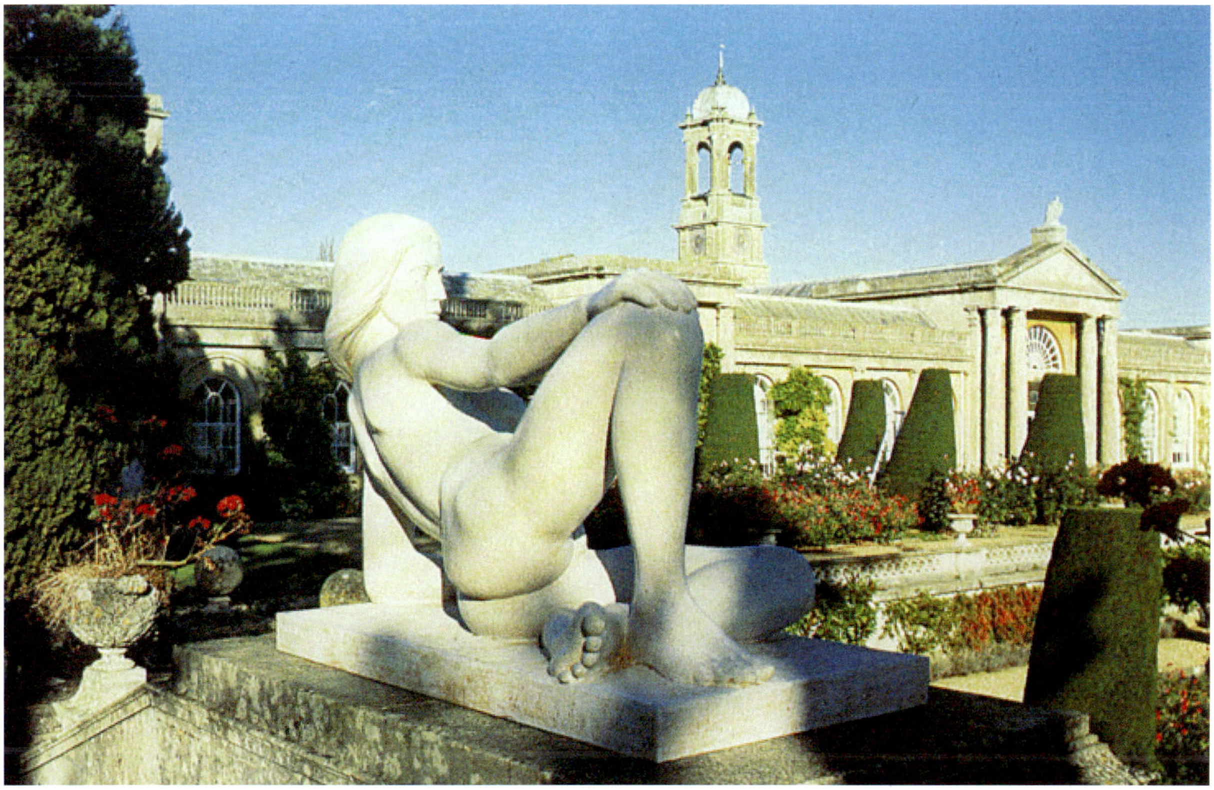

> the largest and most courageous commission this century, in Britain, for a garden sculpture . . . Wynne knew that he wanted 'to create something beautiful and peaceful – nothing to disturb the tranquillity of the setting'. He has made a strikingly modern, yet classical nude . . . Wynne . . . unashamedly derives his inspiration from nature and equally unashamedly tries to capture a sheer love of life in his sculpture.

The article ends: 'His work starts at £5,000.'

Another important patron for David came as a result of a five-part television series, screened on BBC2 during May 1978. John Hickman, a property developer, was asked by the planning department of Kingston-upon-Thames if he would consider commissioning a large sculpture to stand in front of his latest development in the centre of the Royal Borough. He thought immediately of David. The officials had suggested the theme of Kingston's Coat of Arms, granted in 1572. Hickman would later recall that someone piped up , ' "What about the three salmon of Kingston?" "Wonderful!" I exclaimed. "I promise to do it, and David Wynne will be the sculptor." Thus started a warm and amusing friendship and the first of several sculptures I happily commissioned from him.'

John Hickman had 'recently seen a documentary series on television – *Taking Shape* – about a sculptor who had done a major piece for the centre of Sheffield, and I was so impressed that I made a note of his name.' Not all were so impressed. *Arts Review*'s Frances Spalding was outraged. 'Why this work merits five BBC television programmes on the history of its making needs some explanation. Even Henry Moore has never enjoyed such publicity at the expense of public money.' But not all the critics felt so strongly. The *Sunday Telegraph* thought 'it had a touch of magic', and though the *Daily Mail* thought five episodes rather too many, it considered David 'as fluent with his vocal chords as he is with a chisel and [he] produces beautiful things'.

With his usual regard for absolute and authentic creation of the form he planned to represent, David spent time studying the salmon run in Galway and Connemara. 'He even dissected a number of large fish to make sure the sculpture was accurate in every detail,' reported the *Surrey Comet*, as though this was a remarkable fact. But like his great hero, the painter George Stubbs, David would always take endless pains to ensure his sculptures were as anatomically precise as he could possibly make them. And this was achieved by long hours of study, observation and drawing.

The *Leaping Salmon* fountain sculpture captured a dramatic moment. The big male threatens the smaller cock fish, and the hen turns away. John Hickman remembers:

> David is keen that his patrons inspect progress from time to time. In the case of *Leaping Salmon*, he invited me to examine the six-foot plaster, after I had agreed the design in an eight-inch maquette. Once finished I was allowed to comment, but not before! . . . As a developer I have the opportunity to commission sculptures from time to time, not only to enhance the related building but also for the enjoyment of the passer-by. David Wynne has contributed enormously in both these aims.

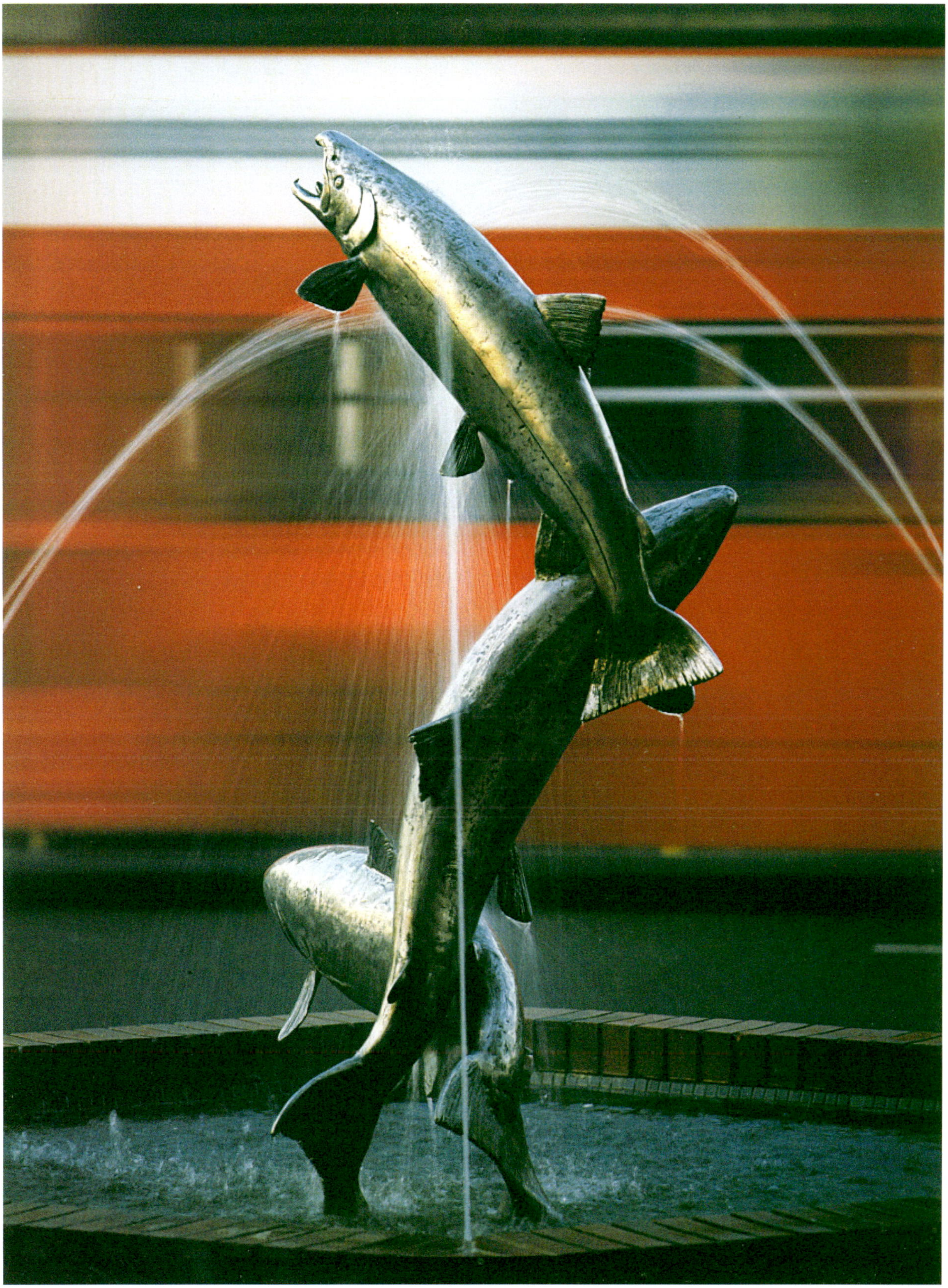

Leaping Salmon

14

IN THE *Daily Telegraph* for 29 September 1979, the newspaper's diary reported that Mappin and Webb, the Royal jewellers, had just announced the sale of 250 silver replicas of *Boy with a Dolphin*. 'They say,' wrote the diarist, 'that at £995 the replica is going cheap, since the price was fixed last year before silver began its latest dramatic rise.' He continued:

> The sculptor's studio . . . has no newspapers, radio or television, so I was surprised to hear [David] air his political views with some vehemence. Senator Edward Kennedy, for instance, is his *bête noire*. When, at a dinner party in California, the Senator began to 'disparage the British Crown and constitution', David Wynne decided that one of them would have to leave. 'And,' he said with satisfaction, 'since the dinner party was being given in my honour, I did.'

Quite why the journalist thought an artist's studio should accommodate the paraphernalia of the media, though, no doubt, a good way to preface the story, is a mystery, but the small piece is further indication of David's growing fame and reputation. Gilli and he had decided, after the media frenzy over the Beatles' portraits, that though the growing demand for David to appear on chat shows or discussion programmes on radio and TV was flattering, what mattered most was David getting on with his work. In the end, that was the *sine qua non*. Mappin & Webb, in their sales brochure, acknowledged the sculpture's popularity with the public, but noted that David insisted on having complete control over the work, and he 'designed the replica not only for the smaller size, but also specifically for the different medium of silver'. He supervised the casting 'at every stage, and only when he was completely happy with the result, did Mappin & Webb's skilled silversmiths start to work on the final cleaning and polishing.' Each piece was mounted on marble and the brochure urges the silversmith's clients to order as soon as possible. In a brief biographical paragraph about David, the Queen's jeweller had no hesitation in stating that David 'is acknowledged to be the leading representational sculptor of his generation'. The entire edition sold out.

But there were times when David's decision to ignore the media circus would prove impossible to abide by. Victor Lownes was an associate of Hugh Hefner's who ran the English side of the various *Playboy* enterprises, including the sometimes notorious club in London's Mayfair. One day, ill in bed, he had watched the BBC film about David's work and decided to recommend him to Hefner for a commission to create a large fountain sculpture to serve as a focal point for *Playboy*'s new Atlantic City club-and-casino complex. David flew to the infamous mansion in Los Angeles by Concorde and private plane to discuss the matter with Hefner. He decided to sculpt 'a complicated and subtle group'. *Two Swimmers* was created to rotate slowly as a fountain played on the two forms. The girl swims by the boy, eyes closed and totally self-absorbed. He turns and strains to let her pass. David explained: 'He is like a bow, her arms the string, and her body the arrow. In one sense he is breaking himself to let her fly free . . . '

The many weeks, spent in study and thought, that were necessary before the large plasters were made were not of great concern to the popular press, however. They were preoccupied with other matters. When David requested that *Playboy* centrefold Victoria Cooke, chosen by Hefner himself to be the female model, be sent over to Wimbledon to be drawn and studied for the extraordinarily difficult task of creating a figure as though it were in water, the press was agog. She flew, reported the *Evening Standard*, in March 1981, on Concorde, to ' "sit in my studios . . . ," said David. "Then I worked mainly from drawings, watching her swimming." '

The finished sculpture was a large piece, 138 inches high, and the bronze weighed fifteen hundredweight. Stainless-steel bars inside reinforced both figures in their circular movement, for David's remarkable composition pivots imperceptibly on the toe

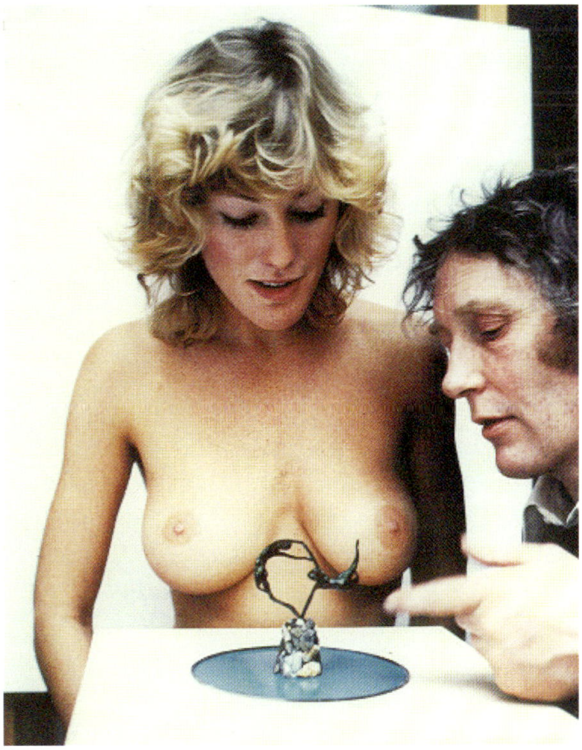

Victoria Cooke

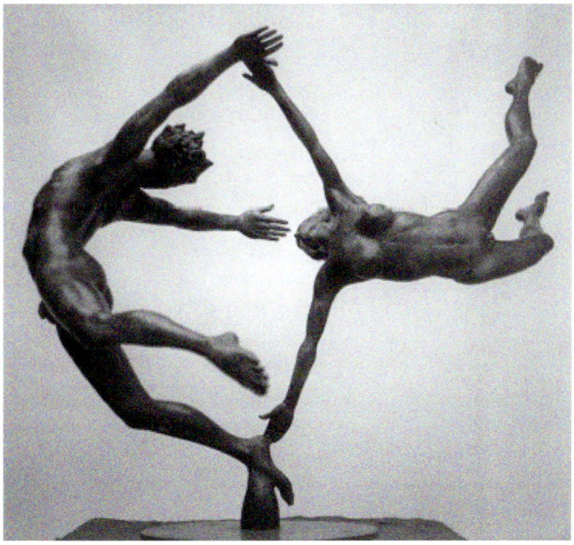

Two Swimmers maquette

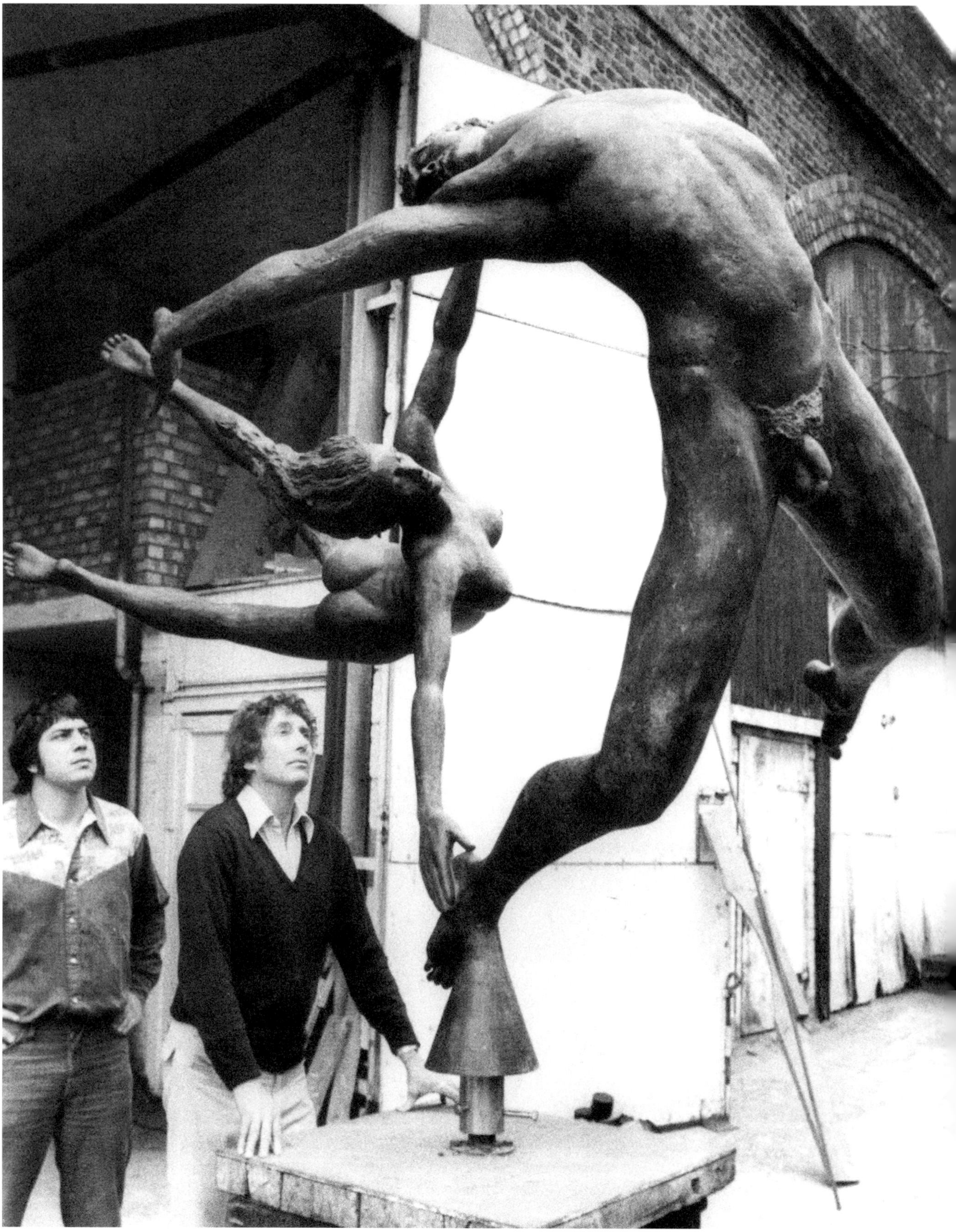

Two Swimmers

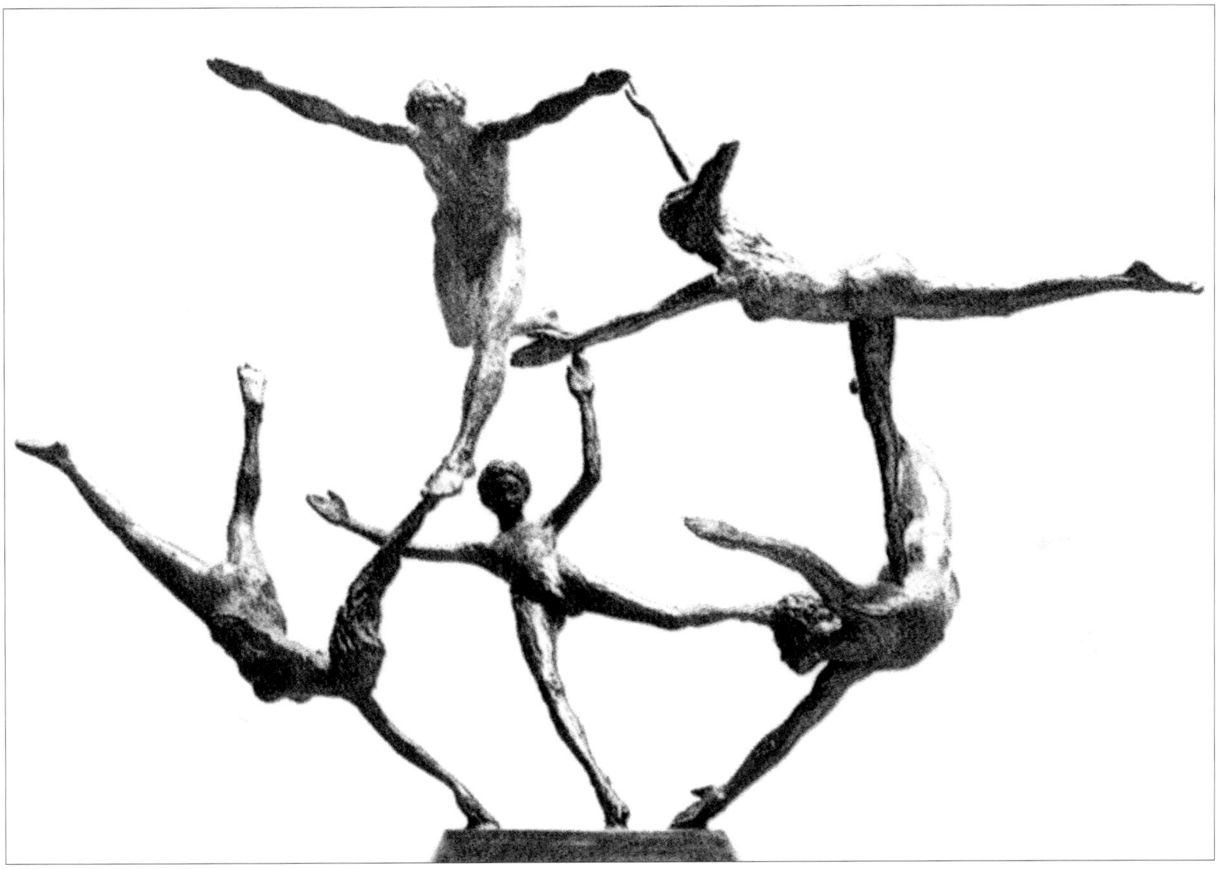

Five Swimmers

point of the male figure. Johnny was the model for the boy, but as he ruefully informed the *Standard*'s reporter, 'there was a lot of imagination in it . . . I certainly can't bend over that far.' The newspaper's headline was somewhat dramatic: 'Sculptor's son joined for ever to naked beauty he's never met.'

Figures swimming had long captivated David's imagination. The Grosvenor Estate commissioned *Five Swimmers* for their fountain in a new shopping centre in Staines, and though smaller in conception than the Atlantic City fountain, the logistics involved were equally complex: this time, the water moved within the sculpture, with jets shooting from the open mouths of the five cavorting figures. The sculpture's maquette was shown, along with eighty-seven other pieces, at a retrospective exhibition held at Cannizaro House on Wimbledon Common in May 1980 and opened by HRH Prince Michael of Kent just as Merton Council announced the sale of the historic mansion, only yards down from Rushmere. David reluctantly became involved in a local political fracas about how the proposed sale should be completed. Merton burghers wanted an office development; its citizens an art complex. The council fudged a compromise with part of the beautiful ground floor retained for 'cultural and recreational pastimes' and the remaining two floors sold off to Mammon.

Prince Michael had been made president of the RAC Club in Pall Mall following the death of Lord Mountbatten, the club's president from 1943 until his assassination by the IRA. David was commissioned by the club to sculpt a posthumous bronze bust of Lord Mountbatten and this he did, working with the help of video film and the admiral's dress-uniform coat, lent him by the family. It was said that Mountbatten was the most decorated officer of his generation: 'almost a shirtfront of medals and [more] on his dress coat,' David remembers. 'I took it up to London when I modelled the head . . . and I had this thing set up on the table as a dummy and I modelled every single one of those medals . . . '

David had become friends with Mountbatten's daughter and her film-producer husband, John Brabourne. He wanted David to sculpt his portrait head as a surprise Christmas gift. Deciding to cast the sculpture in green bronze, David advised Lord Brabourne that he should be careful just how he planned to surprise his wife. It's a very strange thing, the sculptor told his patron, to see an over-life-size head of a family member for the first time. Lady Brabourne would later tell David it had almost given her a heart attack when her husband, having put the bust at the end of their bed, suddenly whipped the cloth off.

The Messenger unveiled in 1982, was commissioned by a large publishing conglomerate, IPC, to adorn their new headquarters in Sutton. The idea for a 150-inch equestrian statue was born, David later wrote, from:

> the brief ['communication'] given to the sculptor. To him this meant the passing of a message, an urgent call from one to another, the eternal cry of our inmost being. 'Wake up, remember!' There is another reality, a place that children know, but one that we turn from when the material world seems so real to us. Then we forget it altogether. But still in dreams the horseman comes. He pauses for a moment, his wild horse pawing the ground, soon to plunge on, and the boy calls to the reapers in the valley, 'Remember! Now, before it is too late!'

David and Robin travelled to Rome and Venice to see the equestrian statue of Marcus Aurelius and the Four Horses of St Mark, to draw inspiration from the past, and they also spent time studying the Arabian horses at the Milla Lauquen Stud. Johnny was the model once again, though the creation of the figure was to prove difficult. Sir Keith Skinner, the chairman of IPC, authorised the publication of a small illustrated book celebrating the evolution and completion of the sculpture. There are numerous photographs of the boy's body being worked and reworked until it was as perfect as David could make it. 'It seems,' he wrote, 'sometimes that a sculptor's ideas and his vision have to be made and destroyed many times before the work is complete.'

An hour after Shergar had won the Derby in 1981, the Begum Aga Khan telephoned David to ask if he could sculpt a portrait of the great horse as a surprise birthday gift for her husband, Shergar's owner. Robin and David went to Newmarket where the horse's trainer, Michael Stoute, lent them a room near the stables in which to begin a minute study of the horse. They measured:

> every bone, the size of the hooves, the thickness of his hocks, the length of his

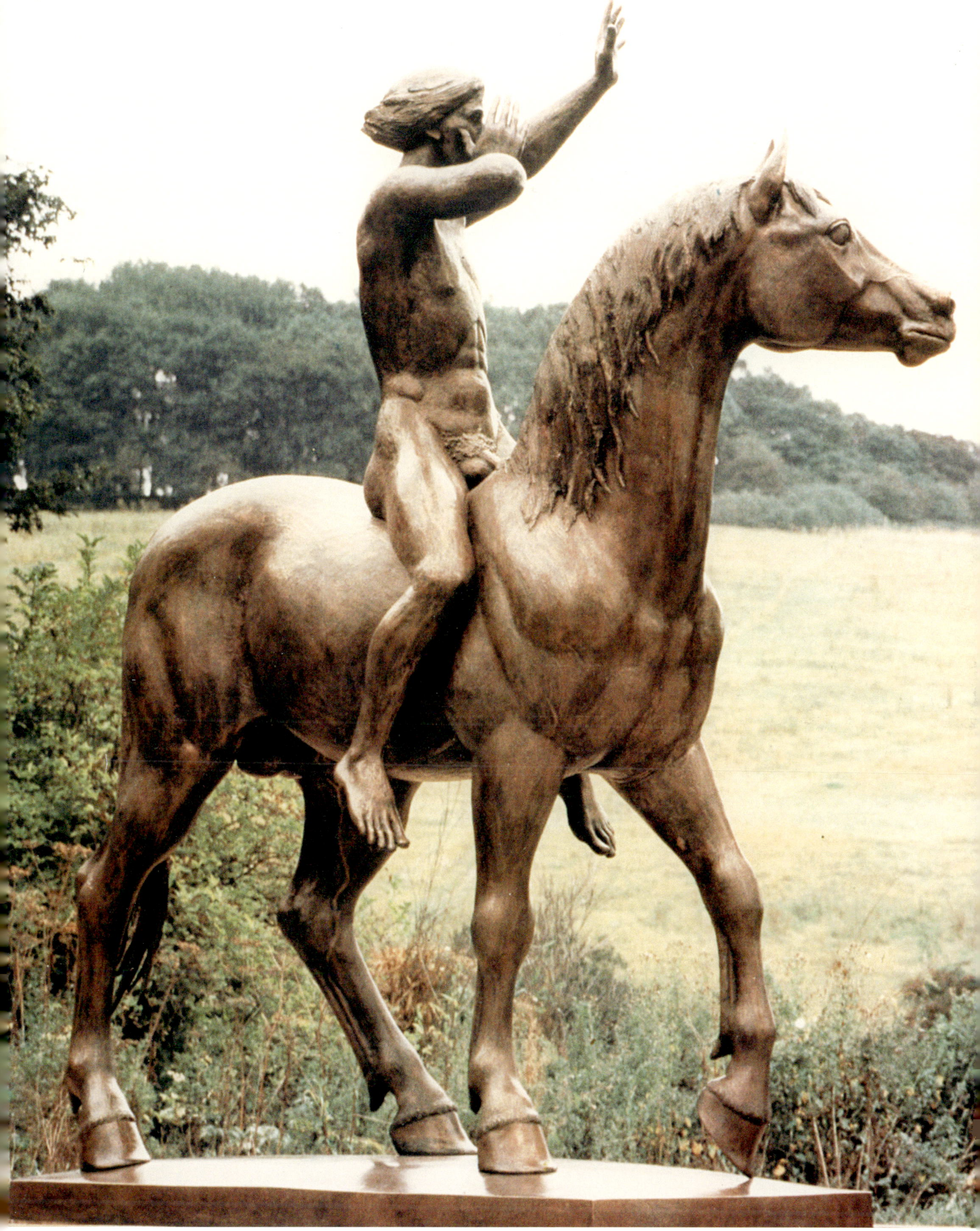

The Messenger

tail, eye to nose, every measurement you could think of. And at the same time they turned out the horse for us into a little private paddock and we watched him go round. We watched him galloping through the mist in the early morning, on the Gallops, up towards us and we really immersed ourselves in that horse.

Robin remembers the horse's 'wonderful temperament. We were holding his tongue and he'd let you do anything.' They were helped in all this endeavour by the stable's staff and by one man in particular, who would become vital in the creation of all David's equestrian work from then on. The head stable lad, Andy Andrews, had an eye for a horse that was, according to David, 'just unbelievable. He'd say, "You haven't got him right, David," or, "No, the eyes are in the wrong place," and I moved the eye by a millimetre and Andy said, "That's more like it. That's more like the horse." ' David gave an emotional address at Andy's Newmarket funeral service, remembering the times they spent together, around the world, creating a series of life-size sculptures of the legendary horses owned by the Aga Khan and others, as David's reputation as one of the finest sculptors of thoroughbreds in the world gathered momentum.

To complete the Shergar portrait, David managed to sculpt the actual jockey who had ridden the gallant horse to its Derby victory, Wally Swinburne. There remained the problem of transporting the secret birthday gift to Aiglemont, the Aga Khan's chateau in Chantilly. Johnny made a travelling box for the sculpture, with a base more than four feet long, and David blagged his way, with the box, on to a flight to Charles de Gaulle. Customs stopped him in Paris and informed him a decision would be made the following day about whether or not the statue could be imported. By then, the Aga Khan's chauffeur had met David, as arranged. Aeroport Charles de Gaulle is cylindrical in shape and as the two men pushed the statue around the glass ring to consider their options they noticed some doors which were unlocked. Skidding through them to a lift, the two desperados went straight to the basement and David kept watch while the chauffeur fetched a huge Mercedes. With the box half in and half out of the car, they tore away from the airport and along the back lanes to the chateau. When they thought they were safe, the chauffeur stopped the car, mopped his forehead and told David, 'Monsieur, le crime c'est fatigant [crime is tiring],' to which David replied, 'Bien sur!' They arrived as the Aga Khan was dressing for dinner and the Begum got various footmen to help David push the sculpture into position and give it a final polish. 'My husband's delight,' she later recalled, 'was a joy to behold and made all our efforts worthwhile.' David's memory is vivid:

I'll never forget it. He stopped, tiptoed up to it and he looked at it and he looked at it, turned to his wife and said, 'There's nothing on earth you could have given me which would have given me as much pleasure as this.' . . . He kept on getting up from dinner, going in and looking at it again.

Three months later, the glorious horse was kidnapped.

Two years later, in 1983, David won the commission to create a great figure of Christ

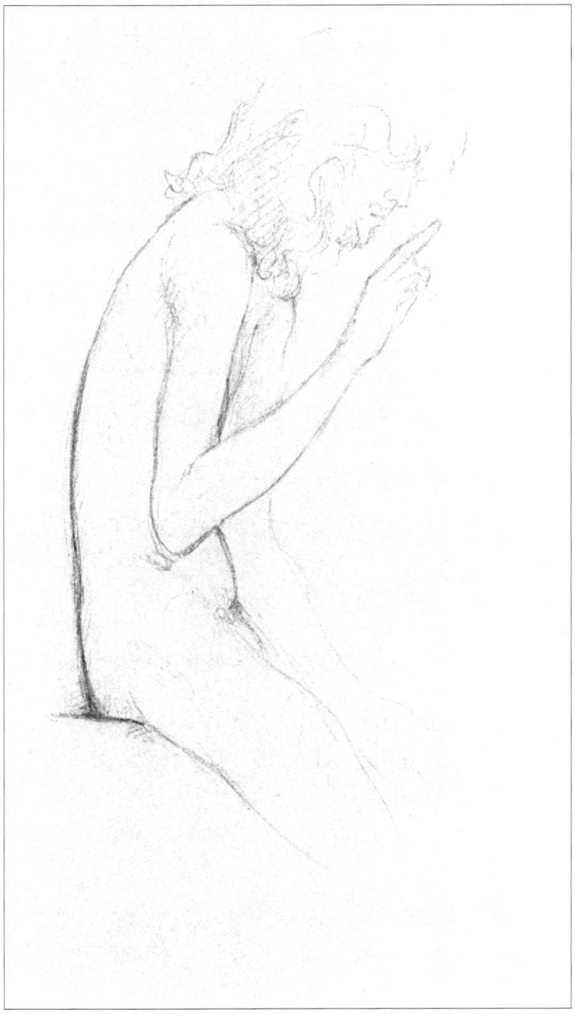

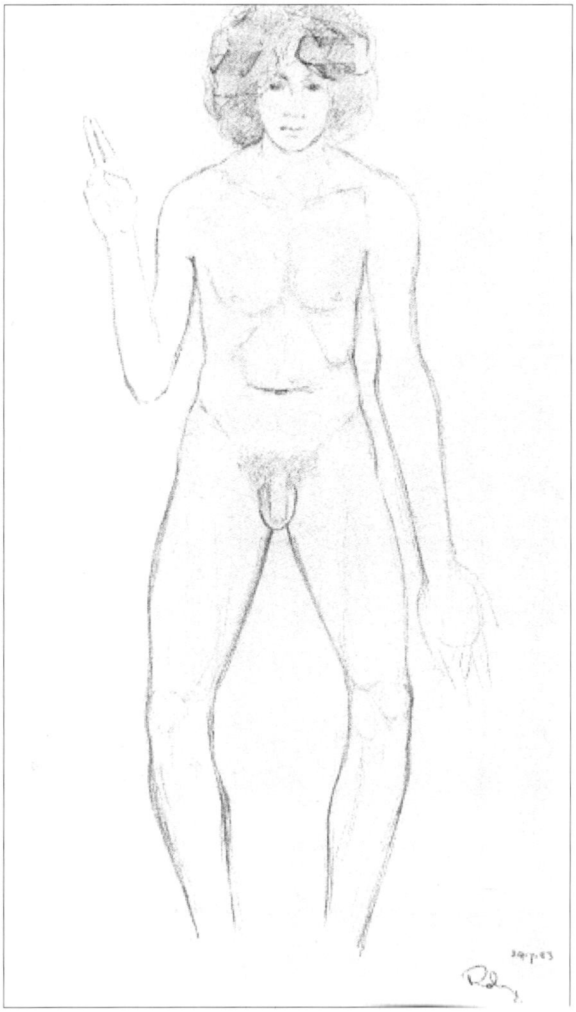

Edward and Roly as models for *Christ*

to replace medieval fragments at the apex of the massive west front at Wells Cathedral. In a vast composition, known as the Chivalry of Heaven, a huge Christ figure sits aloft above his saints, angels and disciples. It was David's most important commission to date and may well be the most significant of all his works. The Gothic facade, begun in the thirteenth century, had fallen victim to the ravages of nature and the abuses of religious intolerance. Weather damage and Puritan destruction had left of the Christ figure, ninety feet above the green in front of the cathedral, only fragments of its knees. After the commission had been won, these fragments were transported to Wimbledon for David to begin work. The politicking and back-room shenanigans had been extreme. Six other sculptors had been in the running and the competition had been intense. David travelled down to Wells and insisted on meeting the Dean, Patrick Mitchell. Later Dean of Windsor, he wrote a memoir of the eighteen months it took to complete the great figure. It was, he remembered, 'one of the great privileges of my life'. He continues:

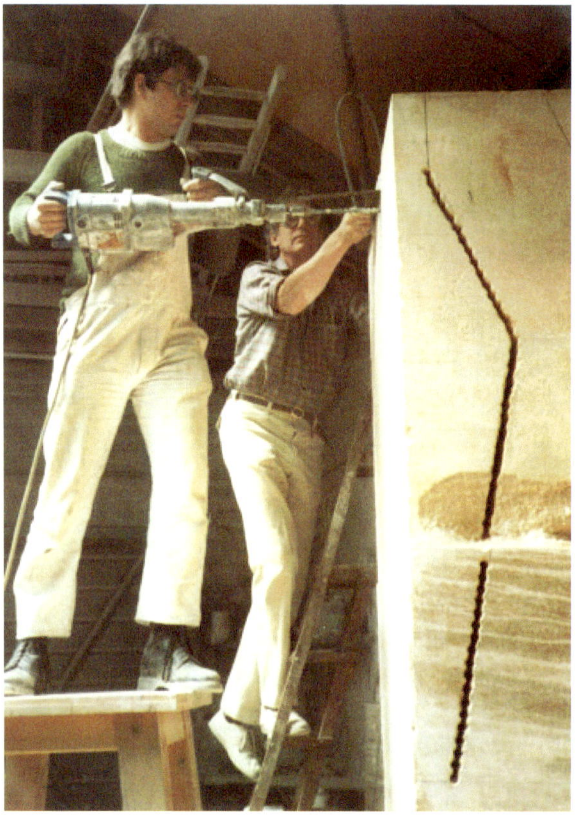

Johnny helped with the initial drilling of the block

It is now so much a part of its architectural setting that it is hard to think of the West Front without it. Yet the project was a daunting one, involving harmony with nearly three hundred medieval figures of high calibre; and the spiritual challenge was immense . . . We met frequently in Wells, where David was determined to absorb the surroundings and to learn wisdom from craftsmen like Peter Cooley, the Superintendent of Works, and David Rice, the Master Mason.

We also met periodically in David's studio in Wimbledon, where Gilli prepared unforgettable dinners in their former farmhouse overlooking the Common; but before dinner we worked hard (and laughed a lot) in the studio. David perched me on an old stool covered in stone-dust, with a strong whisky in my hand, while taped classical music was played. During my early visits, we contemplated two huge blocks of Clipsham stone specially selected from Rutland . . . Like other great sculptors, David could 'feel' or 'see' the figure which would emerge from the blocks. During my later visits, I would be looking up to the developing figure in its various stages, because it was hoisted high in the tall studio in order to give the right impression from below, since the figure was to be almost a hundred feet up.

Together we worked out the Theology of the Christ for Wells. David [undertook] a spiritual pilgrimage to

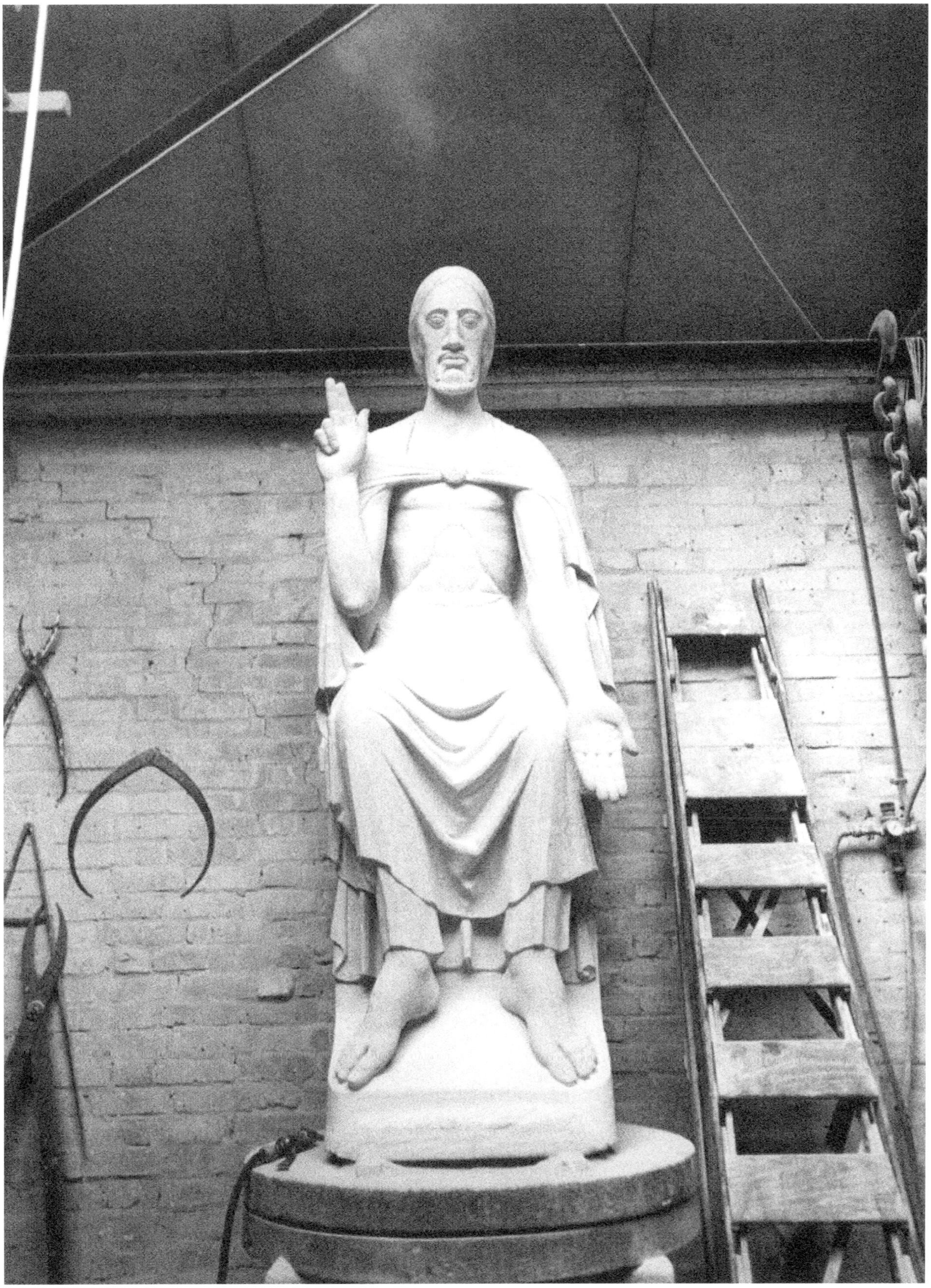

Christ for Wells – work in progress

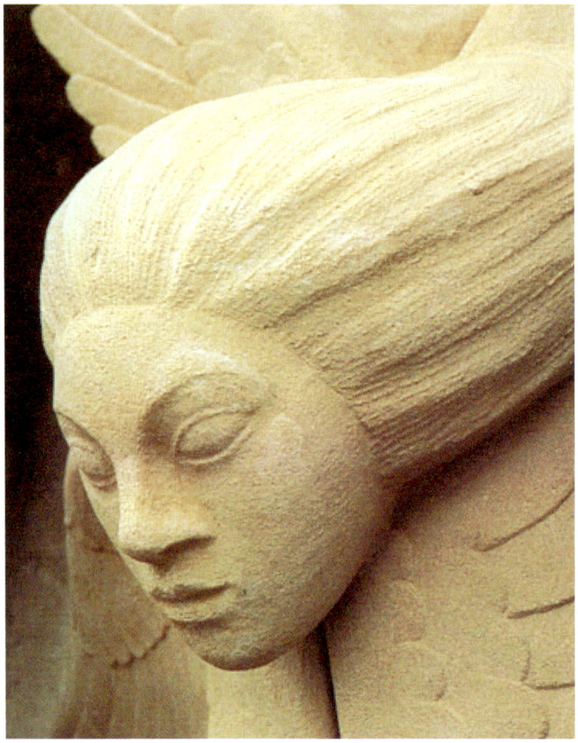 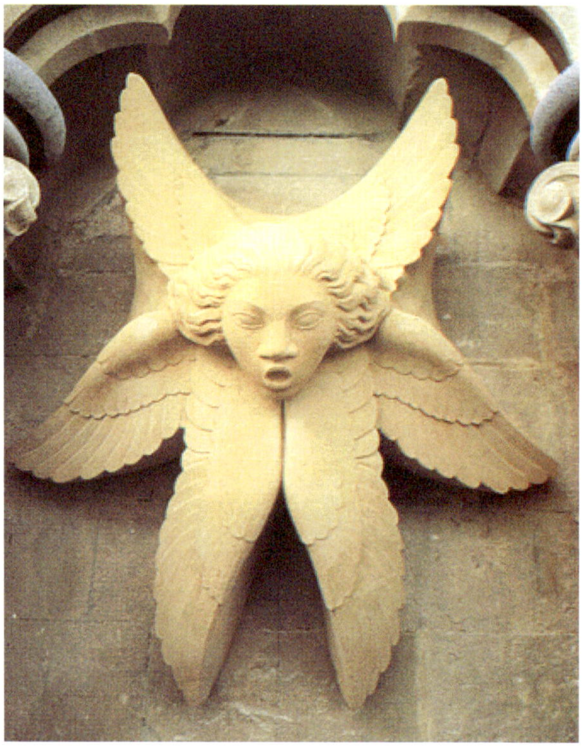

The seraphim

France to look at great sculptures of the Redeemer, such as the one at Vezelay; but the design for Wells could not be a slavish copy or a mere pastiche of medieval types from elsewhere: it had to be a creative work which would fit the context and also be reasonably faithful to the evidence of the medieval fragment.

So the Christ for Wells took shape gradually . . . I am convinced that the medieval gravitas of the thirteenth-century figures has been wonderfully matched by the sculptor . . . In February 1973 a fierce controversy had broken out in the national press about the whole idea of replacing or completing any of the figure sculpture at Wells . . . The dispute simmered on until 1985, when HRH The Prince of Wales unveiled the new figure and its two supporting seraphim. From that moment mercifully all criticism ceased, and today the redeeming and reconciling Christ reigns supreme over the Chivalry of Heaven at the Mother Church of the Diocese of Bath and Wells.

David retains a less spiritual memory. He

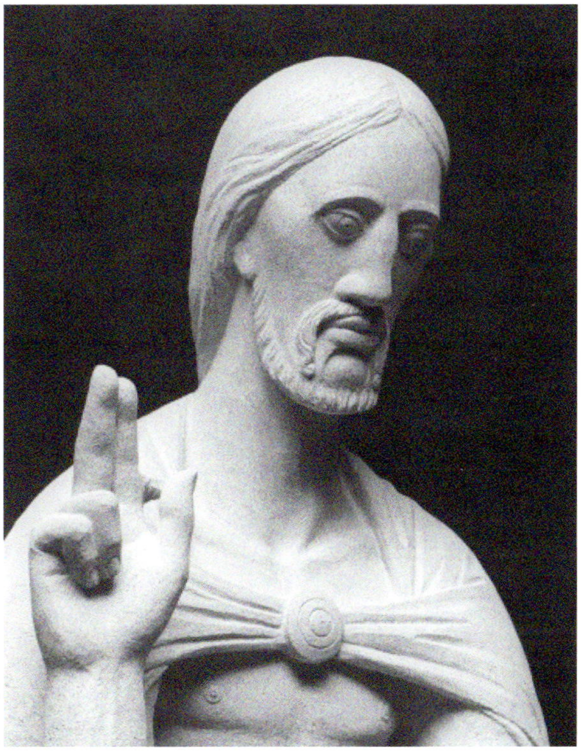

Christ

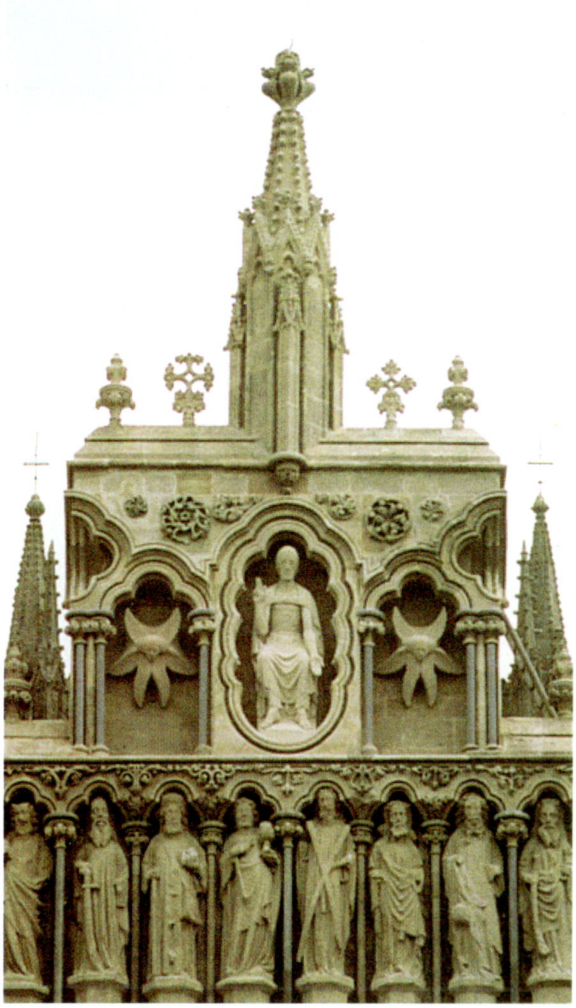

Risen Christ in place at Wells

had been the only contender for the job to request that he go to the top of the scaffolding to see where the actual figure was to be sited. He was taken up by Peter Cooley, the clerk of works, and it was Cooley who telephoned him three days later to let David know that there was to be a meeting where the other contenders would be showing their maquettes. David had not been informed. He entered the meeting, having been told at the door that he could not go in, and placed his maquette on the table. It was clear David had been the only sculptor concerned enough actually to inspect the siting; 146 life-size sculptures adorn the west front; David's *Christ* was the only one which respected the style of the original. But the battle was still not won. David made his big maquette next, to be shown, as he remembers, to 'a very, very august group of swells': the Cathedral Committee of England.

David had now been preoccupied with the Wells Christ for over six months. He had often spent time quietly perched in the apex where the figure would be placed, feeling he could just chuck a stone and hit the tor at Glastonbury. He and the Dean

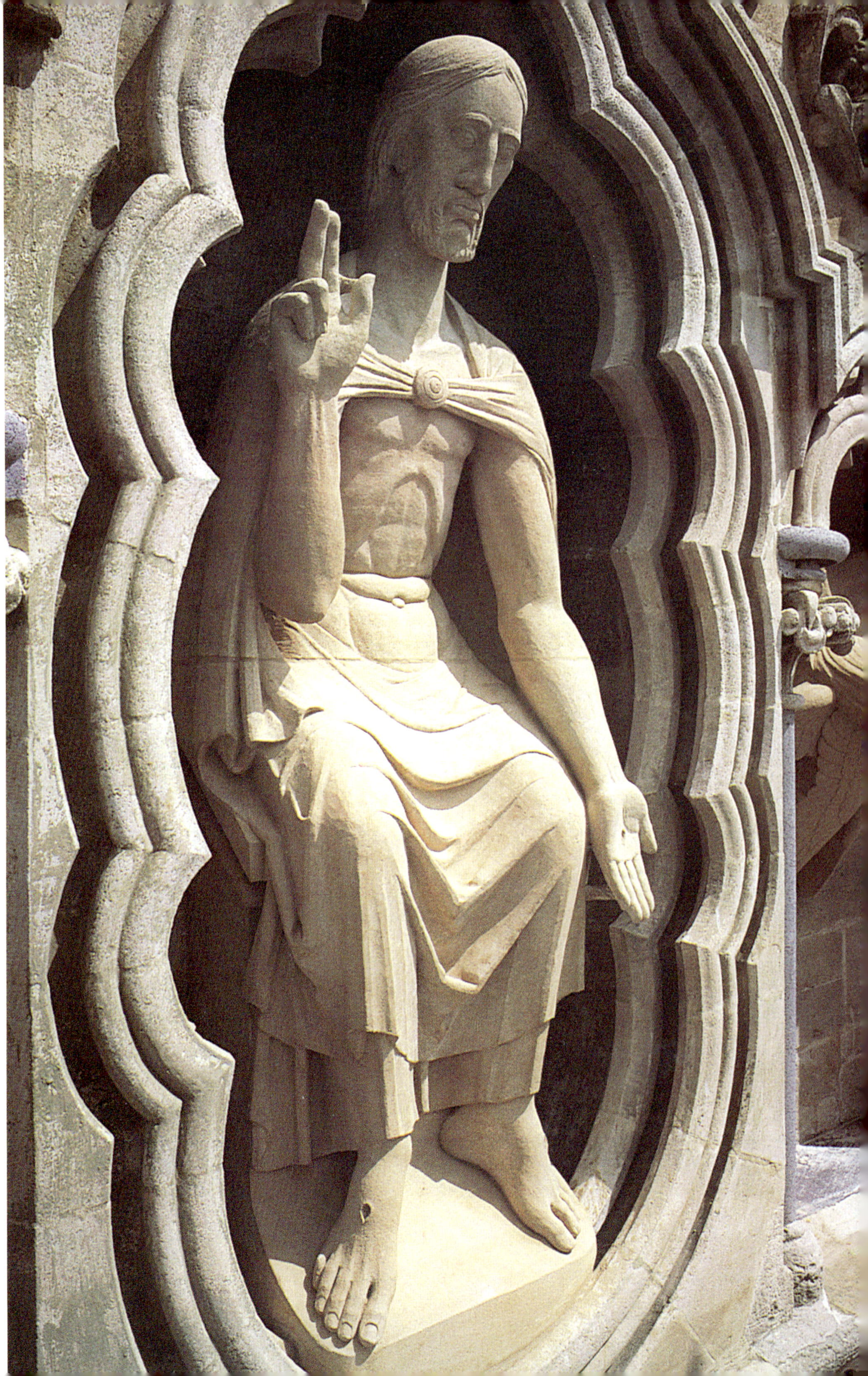

would often sit on the green opposite the west front, talking about the evolving sculpture as the sun set across the cathedral's magnificent facade and supping port while tourists drifted by.

As if the pressures at Wells were not enough, David and Robin were working on a life-size statue of Fred Perry, commissioned by the All England Club to stand before the entrance to the Centre Court at Wimbledon, and had also commenced an extensive commission from the IMG organisation to create portrait figures of the agency's sporting stars: Jackie Stewart, Pelé, Arnold Palmer, Jean Claude Killi and Bjōrn Borg. An astonishing workload! Moreover, there was another large exhibition to be organised at Thomas Agnew, in Old Bond Street, planned for the autumn of 1983. It was just at this time that David began to show signs of a potentially crippling illness now called bi-polar syndrome but at that time known more cruelly as manic depression. Against this frenzy arrived the august committee to see the Wells Christ maquette. By then, David felt he had made the best figure he could, using his sons, Edward and Roly as models. His main preoccupation had been the problem of the height and angle against which the figure would actually be seen from the ground. An anatomical distortion – the femur had to be shorter than the shin – was necessary to allow the top part of the Christ figure to be correctly sited, slightly looking down. It had been a long, tiring process. About fifteen dignitaries arrived and after 'stalking around', one of them said to David: 'You know, Mr Wynne, I think you should think again.' David recalls:

> I had a big hammer in my hand and I turned to him and said, 'Think again? I've been working on this, praying and living this thing for six months and you ponce into the bloody studio and you tell me I should think again!' and, unwittingly, I raised this hammer and he really thought I was going to strike him. Think of it, I'd been months in the deepest meditation, talking again and again to Patrick Mitchell, working out all the feelings of the other figures, everything like that, and this bloody young whippersnapper . . . Then they said, 'Well, Mr Wynne, we can't come to any decision now, because our Chairman hasn't seen it.'

David then played his trump card. 'He has, you know. I took it to show the Prince of Wales yesterday at Kensington Palace. He said it was wonderful.' And the final flourish was still to come.

> With that they all filed out and one of them said, 'I think that's all.' I said, 'No. It's not all. You haven't thanked my wife yet for the tea.' It was then they looked sheepish, filed out, got in their cars and away they went. That was the last time I saw the bloody committee.

Risen Christ, carved from limestone, is ninety-six inches high. The starting point was the fragment of the original Christ. Two huge blocks had to be employed and in the initial drilling of the blocks, Johnny helped. The replacement Christ had to blend with the apostles, saints and kings which for hundreds of years had adorned the west front, perhaps the most beautiful facade in all Romanesque art. Having won the battle

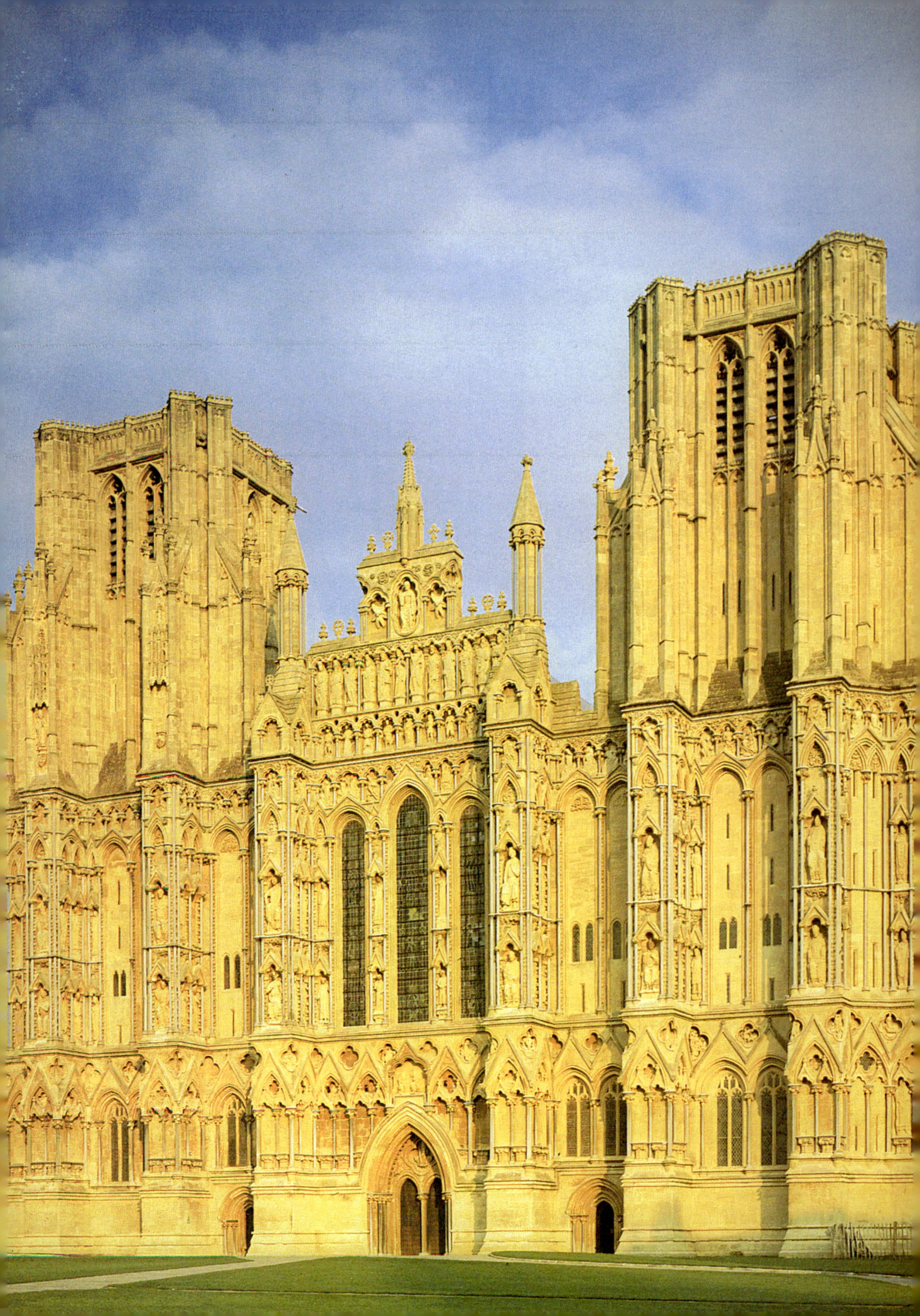

at last, David took a solitary three-week break sailing down the Nile, studying the great remains of Egyptian antiquity, and also spent some weeks at Findhorn, seeking solace away from the mounting pressure. A film crew had been engaged to make a documenatry of the whole undertaking. Channel 4 screened the result on the night of 28 June 1985, when the sculpture was unveiled by HRH Prince Charles. It is still an extraordinary documentary to see, showing each stage of the sculpture's evolution. Remarkably, the figure is made in two pieces, the top half simply resting on the bottom half, dead flat. Right up on top with nothing holding it. No pins, nothing. Just resting there, as indeed the other figures have for centuries. Achieving this was made even more difficult by the disparity in the separate blocks' density. The upper block was softer than the lower. Perhaps the finest accolade *Risen Christ* can be given is that few people seem able to tell what is old on the huge facade and what has been restored.

David was unable to resolve everything for himself, however. Yet again, his craftsmen colleagues rallied round. Derek Carr carved the folds of Christ's robe, in a remarkable homage to those medieval stonemasons whose craft had created the original. (David always readily admits the significant debt he owes to the craftsmen who have worked with him throughout his creative life – like Charlie Edwards, mentioned already for his work on *Grizzly Bear*. Derek Carr was a wonderful stonemason who beside his contribution to the Wells *Christ* helped with the Ely *Madonna* and many other works and was fundamental to their completion. Harry Murphy was an extraordinary plaster-caster who was working with David at the time his son Edward was born and became very fond of the boy. David has a vivid memory of Edward standing in his cot weeping, saying, 'The man's gone . . . ', the night before Harry died. And Bill Waldren is a metal chaser at the foundry David still uses. His unique feature is his beard, turned green from years spent in the foundry.) David also had to sculpt the archangels around the *Risen Christ*. There were almost no records of what had originally stood there. Even the Bible was unhelpful. Six winged seraphim are fiendishly difficult to make, given that the original craftsmen were so literal. The cathedral's archives did list two, but there were no visual aids to go by. David finally decided on carving just two, their faces protruding from six feathered wings, one mouth open, one mouth closed, looking 'sort of windswept as if they had come down from the clouds'. Giving a talk at the cathedral about the whole endeavour, David was asked by an old priest where he was going for his inspiration for the face of Christ:

> I just pointed upwards, like that [he says]. The priest smiled and sat down. It reminded me of the story of the schoolgirl drawing a picture and the teacher saying, 'Who's that meant to be?' When the little girl answers, 'Jesus,' the teacher tells her nobody actually knows what Jesus looks like. The child replies, 'Well. They will when I've finished, won't they!'

The Agnew exhibition had forty-six sculptures on show. The most spectacular was called simply *Kneeling Girl*. It was carved in Kudu marble, a rare South African stone, bought for him as a birthday present some eleven years earlier by George Harrison.

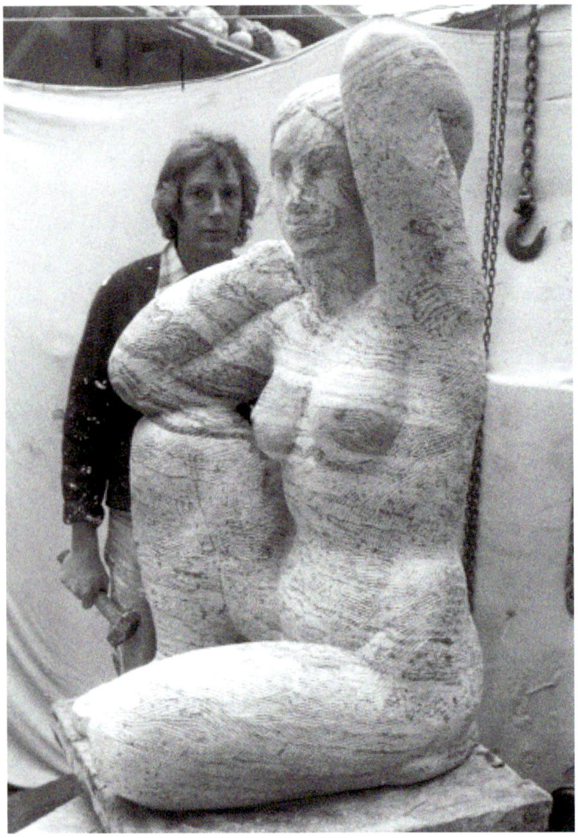

Gaia in progress

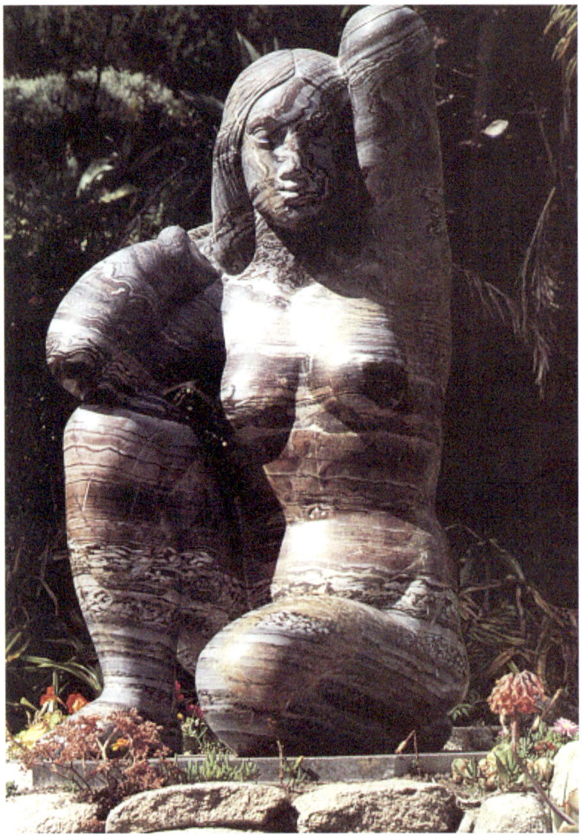

Gaia in situ

David and George had been visiting a mason's yard which used to be just by Putney Bridge, looking for stone suitable for the Hindu temple the Beatle was building for Hare Krishna. The mason had told George the magnificent green marble block would be almost impossible to work. So George bought it for David and the huge block had stood in his studio while the sculptor pondered its destiny. After four years' contemplation – two small maquettes of kneeling girls were in the Agnew show – David decided on the best pose to fit the grain within the stone itself. Gilli was the model. The figure did not reach its spectacular island site until four years later, when it travelled to Tresco, one of David's magic places. By then the work had evolved into *Gaia*, the goddess of the earth. The marble's varying hardness made the work exacting to carve. The figure grew out of the block over several years and David determined the form of the figure by the colours as they appeared in the sculpting. *Gaia* is the work of David's which will define his artistic legacy. It had preoccupied him for more than a decade – as an almost constant presence in his furiously intense working life. Fred Perry's statue would be a little easier.

15

WHEN THE ALL ENGLAND Club decided to honour the achievements of Fred Perry by commissioning a statue of the tennis champion to be erected at Wimbledon, it was David's friend and long-time tennis partner, Charles Huw Williams, who was instrumental in ensuring David would be the chosen sculptor. Williams was a member of the club's committee.

David and Fred made a good team. In many ways, their chosen careers had both followed controversial and fiercely independent paths. Perry shared David's uncompromising disregard for most Establishment mores. The traditional attitude that the professional sportsman would never quite match up to the gentleman player in matters of taste and conduct had echoes in the art establishment's attitude to David's work and opinions. They also got on very well together.

David and Gilli visited Fred in Jamaica, where Perry managed a golf resort. He lived modestly, but arranged for David and Gilli to stay in a villa above the resort, near to Kingston, where even a butler was provided to ensure their time there was as pleasant as it could be. David decided to sculpt the great man in action, about to sweep a ball back over the net towards an imaginary opponent. He finished the head and was about to return to Wimbledon to complete the sculpture when he and Gilli realised their children would be furious with them both if they did not visit Bob Marley's grave as a token of the whole family's love and respect for the great musician. When the butler found out what they planned, he insisted he drive them in his car and even supplied provisions for the journey.

It was a very hot day. They made their way to the grave, paid their respects, left and were about to enjoy the food and drink, brought out from the car's boot by the butler, when David remarked how wonderful it would be if the beer were ice cold. The man disappeared and returned a few moments later with a battered pail, full of ice. It seemed amazing to David that here, by a remote graveyard, high in the hills, the butler could find the means to serve ice-cold beers. It was simple, he told David. An old lady in a nearby building had just died, and the corpse was surrounded with ice to keep it cool until the embalmers arrived.

David and Fred became great friends, with Fred even advising David on his game, and

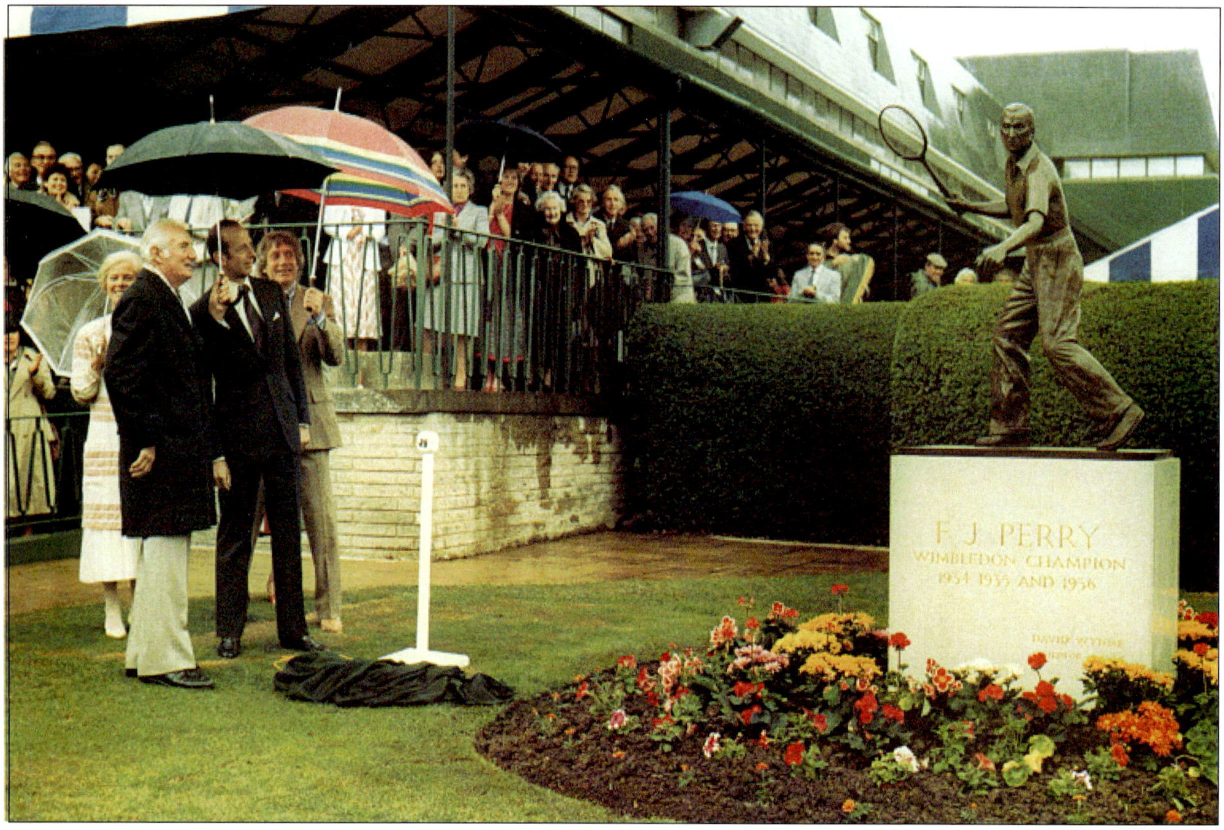

The unveiling ceremony for Fred Perry's sculpture at Wimbledon

on one occasion insisting that David thrash an arrogant tennis pro whom Fred thought needed to be taken down a peg or two. The sixty-inch figure was unveiled in 1984, by HRH The Duke of Kent, outside Centre Court. It was Wimbledon fortnight, and it was raining. The great player adored his statue, and after his death his widow arranged for his ashes to be interred beneath it.

David had first begun to show signs of his bi-polar condition when he went to the Rocky Mountains to study the grizzly bears. He would get what he described as 'the most fantastic buzz . . . you start to speed, but you don't know you are. Other people can tell.' Certainly those close to him could. David's stepson, Johnny, who, with Robin, would often work closely alongside him, suggested it was David's intensity that triggered the episodes which now began to manifest themselves. Johnny thought David's passion to draw and sculpt the great bears faced with extinction, or to render into solid form the agony and passion of the Risen Christ, 'somehow triggers the chemicals that trigger the highness [mania]'. Johnny compared David's intensity to the electrical energy of a pop concert: ' . . . in electrical terms it's like positive feedback which we always try to avoid because positive feedback is what leads to the screaming microphone on the stage'.

Robin describes what it was like:

> . . . . some people did find it frightening. It was great, [David] could go into places and [he] could make the world as [he]

> wanted and it was great sport. And [he] came in and it was like a whirlwind coming in and it was fantastic. But nobody could reach [him]. [He] couldn't hear anything anybody else said or see anybody else.

The worst episode began one evening at the Garrick Club. The club's staff were concerned about his behaviour from the start. He had brought into the club, as his guest, a pregnant woman he had befriended in the street and insisted she be given a grand meal. This done, he set off towards the Mall having decided to see the son of his great friend from Cambridge days, George Knaggs, whose regiment was on sentry duty at Buckingham Palace. Peter, one of the Garrick's porters, followed him. After shouting through the Palace railings and being told to go away by the police on duty, David began to clamber up the Victoria Memorial, determined to hail his friend's son. Despite the best efforts of Peter and two policemen to calm him, David finally had to be pulled down from the top of the statue and taken, in a police van, into custody at the nearest police station. Handcuffed, he continued to cause a fracas and was finally sectioned, under the Mental Health Act, and taken to the Maudsley Hospital, one of London's leading psychiatric institutions; there he was to spend probably the worst few weeks of his life.

He still remembers being forcibly held down and injected, but after that he knew nothing until he came round some days later to find Gilli bending over him. For the next four months David remained in hospital, though he was moved to Beckenham for some of that time. For David now:

> it's a blur. I thought I was going to die and it felt like dying . . . I remember saying to myself I'm in a black, black hole underground and I don't know which way is up so it's no good trying to get out, and then just when people came to see me, a little tiny shaft of love came in and that sort of made you realise that you were still actually in the world.

It would, in the end, be his work that saved him. That, and the support of his family. The treatment was predictable. Again, Johnny remembers:

> The drugs themselves that they give you, [cause] the most horrific shakes. It's basically the same stuff that they put small doses of in travel-sickness pills. It's called Tamazapan. And then they give you drugs to stop the shakes, which compound the whole nastiness of it, and it's a vicious circle that you sort of slowly climb out of, and if you happen to see the specialist on a good day then they'll reduce the drugs, otherwise they'll slap you on the same stuff for another month.

David was once asked if he saw a relationship between the two states – the extreme high and the extreme low.

> I've just no idea in the wide world. I've thought about it and thought about it. You go up when you're happy, when you're doing well and you're doing things, and you suddenly go over the top and you suddenly find yourself speeding in your head and they say it's chemical. I don't know whether it is or not . . . you think you're better than you are. You think you can do anything and you're God's own gift to everybody but you're not, but you

think you are. And that's the danger of the whole thing . . .

His recovery was slow. Realising the extraordinary pressure his illness was putting on his family, he accepted a course of lithium to stabilise his behaviour and he returned to Wimbledon, calmer but unable to work.

I was at home, doing nothing and sitting there and George Knaggs, for instance, came round to see me and I said, 'I'm sorry, George, but I can't see you,' and he'd say, 'Well. I'm coming anyway.' And I said, 'Look, I can't sit still,' and George said, 'That's fine. I don't like sitting still. We'll walk about.'

It was the positivity of great friends and loving family, such as this fragment of memory relates, which slowly brought David back from the abyss. But it was Gilli's insistence that he undertake a commission to create a sculpture for a hospice for the dying that finally ended David's brutal period of black despair.

Sister Mary Perpetua, the principal of St Raphael Hospice in Cheam, had written to see if David would consider making a sculpture of St Raphael, the angel who accompanies the dead on their journey from this world to the next. David was convinced he could not work again. He decided to decline the commission, but Gilli insisted he at least try. To please her, he arranged an appointment to visit the hospice. It had been many months since he had donned the obligatory elegant suit, required dress code for any initial commission-related interview. Their meeting was recorded by both of them.

For David:

A car took me to this hospice and there was this wonderful old lady . . . and she said, 'Come in, darling,' as if she knew all about it. I don't think she did, I don't think Gilli told her, but she said, 'You've been very ill, haven't you?' and I said, 'Well yes, I have,' but she said, 'This is going to cure you because you'll be doing this with these people here who are all dying.' And no way was I going to say no, so I looked at the place and we talked about it and I suddenly began to have creative thoughts again.

Sister Mary's account takes over:

David and I discussed our vision of the finished work. We did not want it to excite the patients as a work of art or to puzzle or to worry them. We were not after a 'clever piece' which was difficult to understand. There had to be immediate recognition of a simple and direct message.

A study of the sculpture shows how successfully that shared vision was implemented. It can be seen from every angle and the message is crystal clear: 'Do not be afraid – I will guide you for I know the way well.'

David claims, and he ought to know, that the actual posture of the angel, which is the essence of its success, was the inspiration of his wife Gilli. When she saw the courtyard into which it was to be placed . . . she suggested that the figure should make a hundred-and-eighty-degree turn so that from whatever angle it was viewed, the message of hope and reassurance would be plainly visible . . . Though angelic, the figure is not turned fully towards heaven. This was precisely the intuition for which we and David are

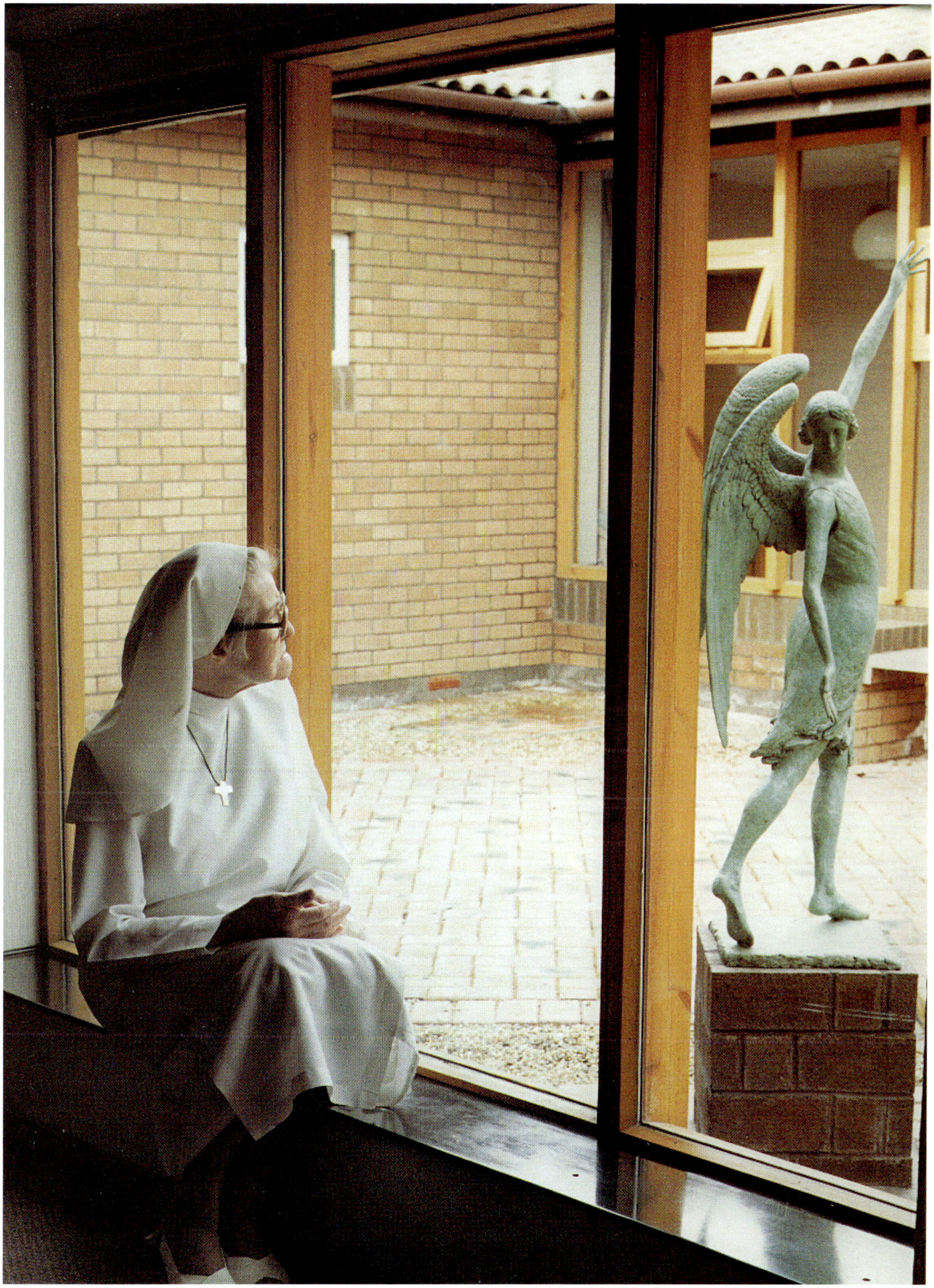

Sister Mary Perpetua and *St Raphael*

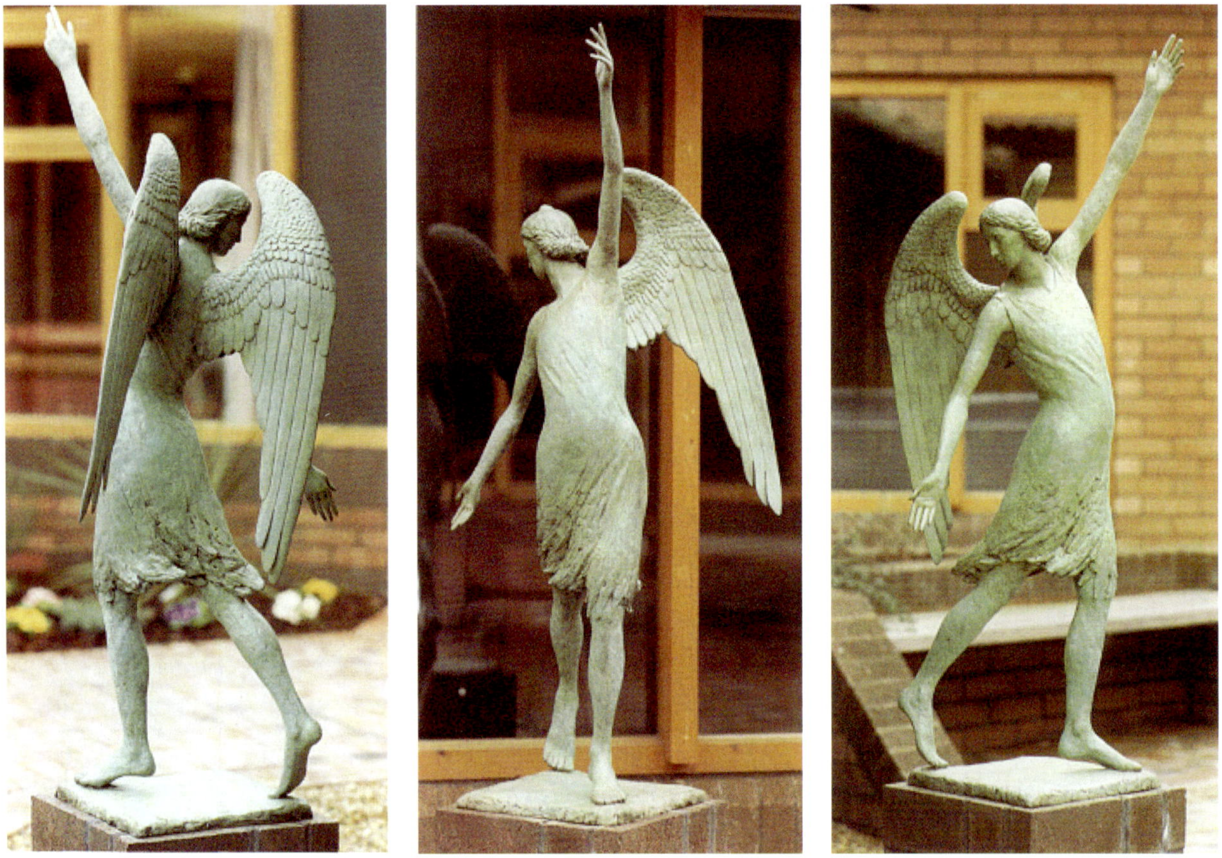

St Raphael

indebted to Gilli . . . We did not know it was to be the setting for such a striking impression of the philosophy of the Hospice Movement. David assured us that the sculpture is 'a small piece of my work and it was made with love'. Indeed it expressed love; and its incredible beauty is proof that love lasts for ever.

The figure of St Raphael was modelled in clay, whereas the wings were constructed in plaster, with Robin's help. It was a complicated endeavour. Gilli's hands and feet were the models for those of the angel, but David changed the proportions to make them slenderer and longer, so that the figure almost seems to float, aided by the remarkable sculpting of the dress. When a journalist suggested to David that the headline for an article he had written about the *St Raphael* should be, 'A Prayer in Bronze', David simply replied, 'That is what it is meant to be.' It had been a healing and rewarding time for David. One day, he took his fox terrier, Bunter, to the hospice. Ever playful, the small dog jumped up on the bed of an old man. As David went to retrieve the wayward animal, he noticed the man was crying. 'I thought I'd never see a dog again,' the old man told him. The process of creating *St Raphael* had brought about the rebirth of David's spirit. It seemed the therapy had worked.

In order, given the nature of the institution, that the installation of the sculpture should be as low-key as possible, a small lunch had been organised to follow

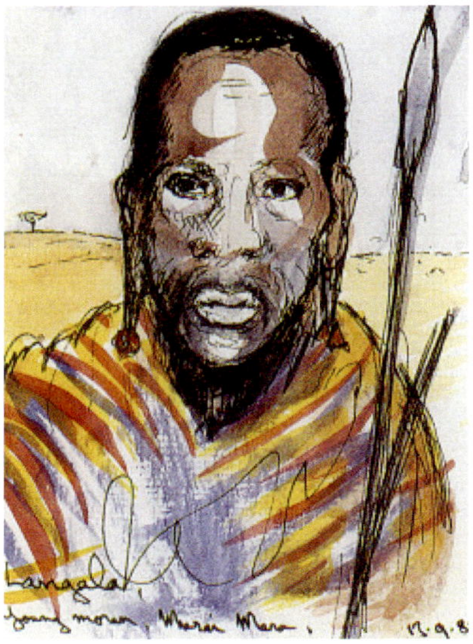

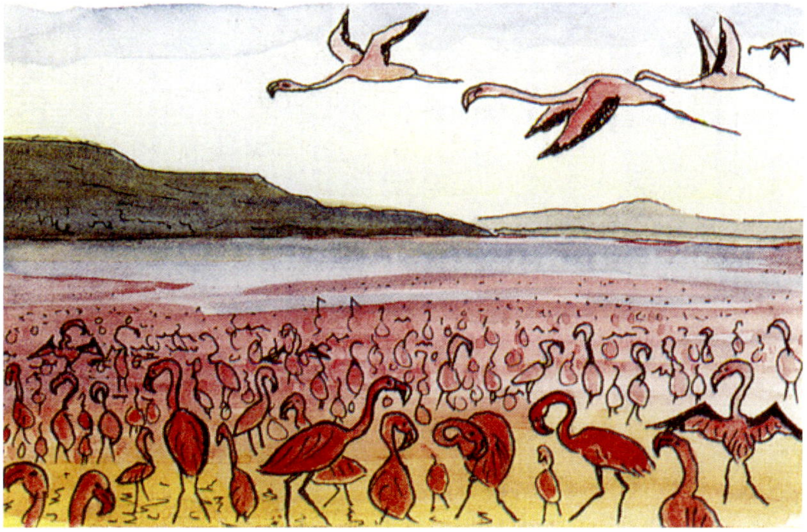

From the African notebooks

the statue's homecoming. When David had overseen the operation, Sister Mary Perpetua suggested they go to look at it from the chapel. *Province*, the hospice's international newsletter, can describe the rest:

> [David] tells of his dismay when he realised he had entered the chapel still smoking his cigar. Nonplussed, he asked Sister Mary Perpetua if it was all right. He was amused and reassured by her forthright response: 'I'm sure God won't mind but some of His friends might.' However, one of His friends, Father Sheridan, imitating his Divine Master who changed water into wine, jokingly transformed the cigar smoke into incense . . .

In 1986, and after the completion of *St Raphael*, David made his first journey to the African bush to study animals in the wild. His friend, the merchant banker, David Scholey, offered David the chance to join him and his family on a safari to Kenya. When David told his friend he couldn't afford it, Scholey laughed that all he needed was his cab fare to the airport. His life seemed his again. As Robin wrote:

> Less comfortable for those around him is his lack of consistency as he follows where his instincts lead. David's ability to recognise and appreciate the source of inspiration, whatever the field, is reflected in the wide range of his loves. He may one day be carving a huge marble block and the next day have flown unheralded to Africa to make models of some strange animals in the bush.

David's first sight of Africa, from the window, as their small plane landed, was of a Grant's gazelle. It seemed to him that here, indeed, was Eden. It was the beginning of a profound love affair with the continent, its animals and people, and his trips, which became frequent, produced some of his finest small sculptures. Over the years he would visit, many times, Kenya, Tanzania, Namibia and Botswana.

In Africa, he mastered the technique of capturing the essence of the living animal, observing the antelopes, baboons, elephants and leopards in their natural habitats.

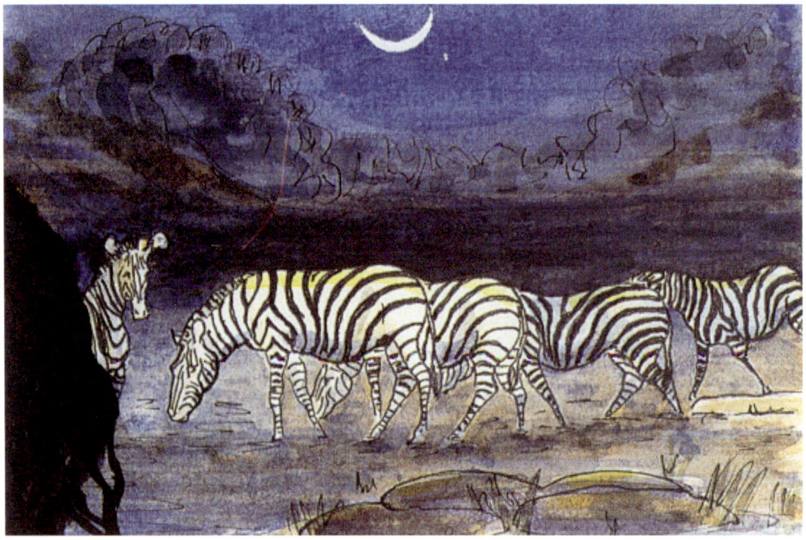

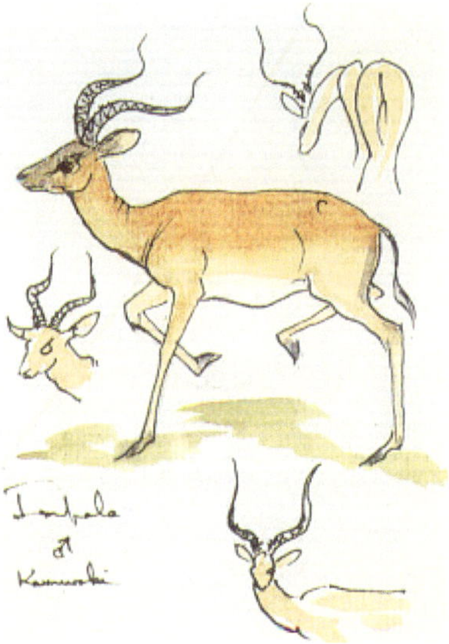

From the African notebooks

He constructed, before each trip, small armatures of the animals he wished to sculpt. He would hide in the bush, attempting to get as close as he could to the particular animal he was studying. In Savuti, in Botswana, he modelled bull elephants from a tent which was erected by a waterhole where the animals came to drink. He stayed for two weeks, until the great animals were no longer concerned by his presence as he drew and studied them. Then, with plasticine, he would begin the sculpture.

David's African subjects are perhaps his principal claim to sculptural greatness. It is thought by many that they will come to be regarded as among the most skilful representative artefacts of wild animals ever made. But this sculptural legacy was not achieved without mishap, and often, real danger. In Namibia, with Robin, David went in search of a Black Rhino, having been asked by the World Wildlife Fund to sculpt an animal facing extinction. Accompanied by two native trackers, they climbed up into the hills, stumbling over the rocks and wild brush of the Kalahari, the oldest desert in the world. The Black Rhino will often move to the top of the hills during the day, as it is cooler there, and they were lucky enough to find one. David stood below the animal and began to draw it, while the others stayed farther down so as not to disturb it.

Presently, the animal began to amble down the hillside, and knowing he must hurry, David tried to finish his drawing. But when he looked up again he saw the rhino had begun to canter towards him. Suddenly, the beast broke into a gallop and David realised he now had nowhere to escape to. He could not outrun the rhino and the desert hillside was rocky and overgrown. Waiting until the animal was almost on him, David leapt to his left, in between the rocks. The rhino thundered past, so close he could smell it. Robin and the trackers were able to scare the animal by throwing rocks at it until it cantered off. David, with a badly scored leg and what he later discovered were two cracked ribs, walked the nine miles or so back to camp. The next day, he began to create his *Black Rhino Charging* – in the safety of his tent.

Not all his animal encounters were so fraught. On one occasion, in Kenya, David was drawing a bull giraffe munching leaves. The animal suddenly leant down and licked him on his head. The next day, the cook at their camp, in great agitation, told David that some Maasai tribesmen were at the camp's entrance wanting to talk to the 'man who speaks Giraffe'. David spent a great deal of time with the Maasai, drawing them and eventually becoming very close to one in particular, Langala, a seven-foot warrior (*moran*). When it was time for David to leave, Langala asked him if he would like the gift of a spear, to ward off the lions in his own country. When the Maasai was told there were no lions in England, the warrior said nothing, bent down, kissed David full on the mouth and simply walked away.

Sometimes David's African encounters had more comic aspects to them. Looking for lions near the Zambezi, after a hectic, bumpy journey in a rackety jeep, his friend was following tracks which David could not see. When he asked where the lions were, he saw an ear protruding from some long grass. To his amazement, he discovered that he and his companion were in the centre of a circle of lions – it was as if they had been catapulted into the middle of a cricket pitch with a dozen or so lions acting as the fieldsmen. David asked what they should do next. Lloyd, the main tracker, was not fazed. 'Do what I do,' he said, and proceeded to march out of the circle, whistling loudly. David followed him, step by step, and the lions, some snarling, moved aside. It must have looked, David said, like a moment from some slapstick silent film.

Another expedition into the bush afforded an unusual bonus. Spotting a broken-down truck, David got Kuria to stop their jeep to see if there was any help they could offer the stranded passengers, one with a tiny baby. Against his companion's advice, who thought it dangerous to stop, David approached them and discovered that the truck had run out of petrol and the driver had no money. When David gave him money, the man took him to the rear of the truck and produced a bottle of Moet & Chandon in return. Asking if this was good and being assured that it was, the driver fetched out a whole case. David gave him some more money. For the next few weeks, David and his Kikuyu friends could be seen sitting outside his hut, in the dusk, smoking large Havana cigars and drinking the finest champagne, probably looted from an embassy in Ruanda.

And one of David's most magical animal sculptures came about through another chance encounter. Visiting Kenya, he had been walking in the forest with his Kikuyu companion, Kuria. It was nearly daybreak when they saw a male leopard resting on a tree branch. As they watched, the dawn began to break, sending shafts of sharp, clear light though the dense forest trees. The leopard stretched and jumped to the ground, almost in front of them, and rolled over in the grass. As he did so, a cloud of butterflies flew up from underneath him, and just as a kitten will toy with a moth, the leopard lay on his back and played with them. Kuria looked at David and said, 'You make this one!' *Leopard with a Butterfly* was created in 1966.

Heidi Almendinger, who lived in Botswana and came to know David well, once described his technique as he created three elephant sculptures:

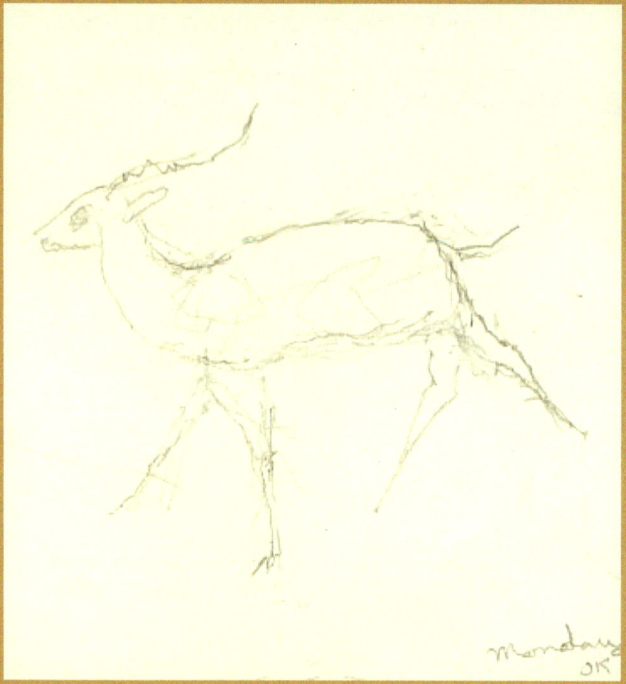

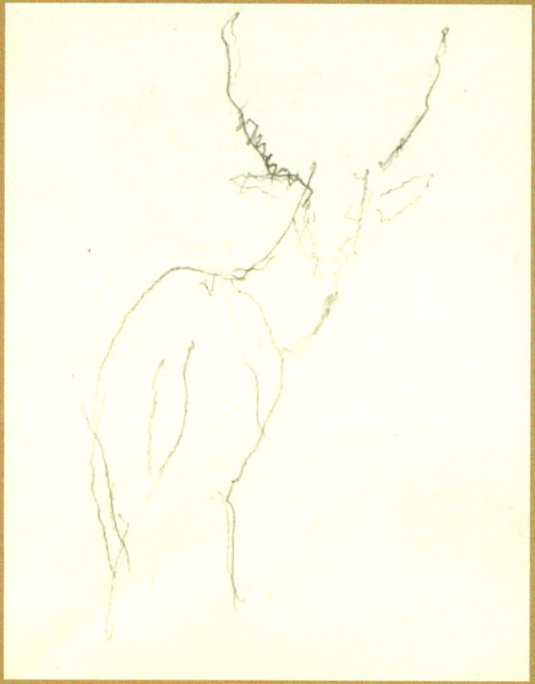

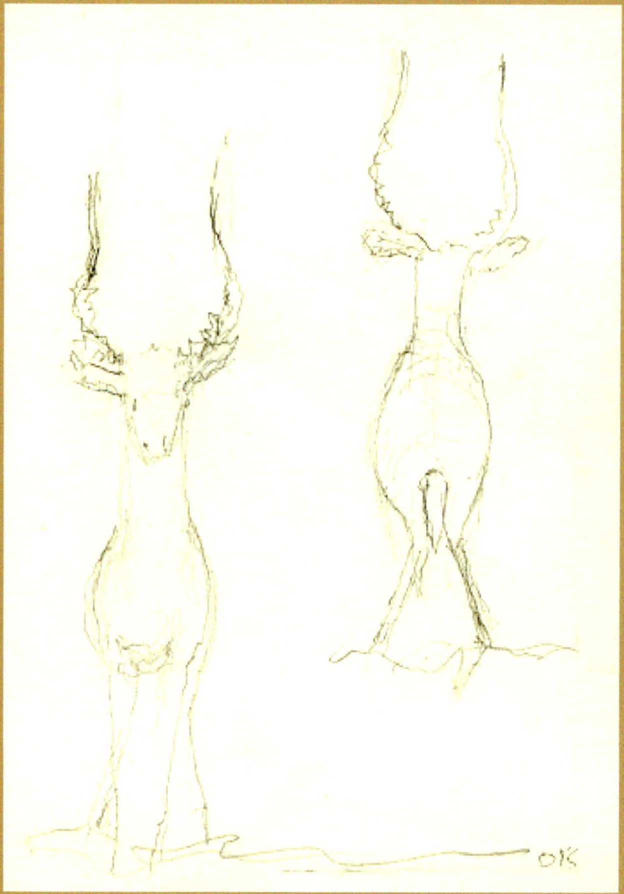

David's sketches drawn during his recent trip (2010) to Africa. They were executed at great speed and will aid in the completion of a future work – a sculpture of three impala.

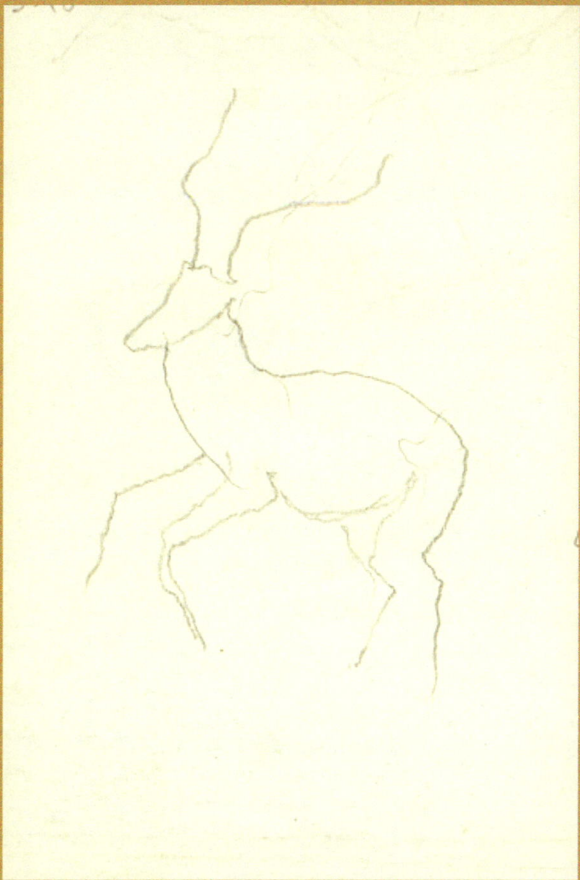
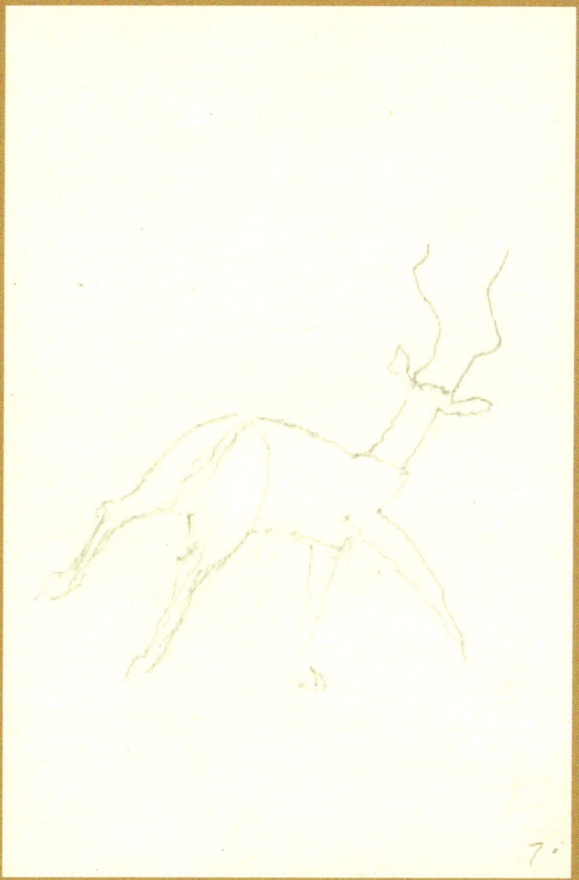
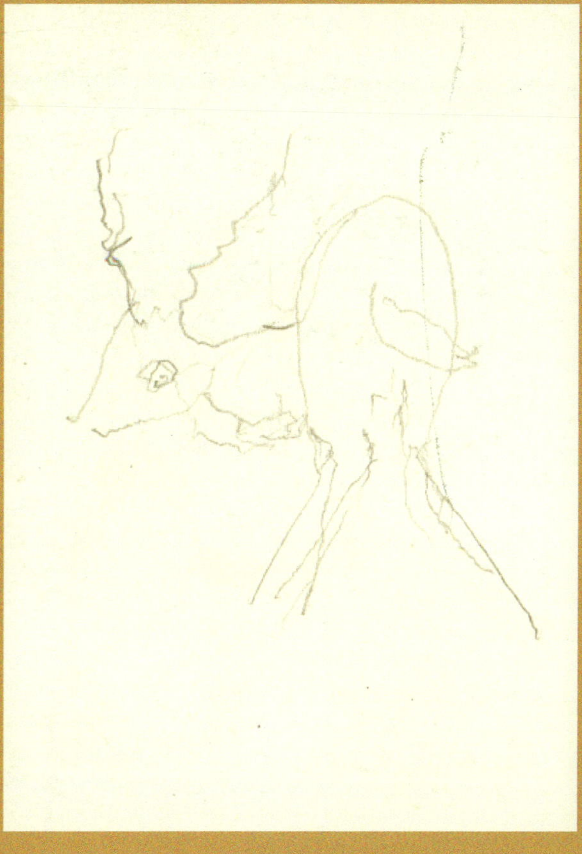
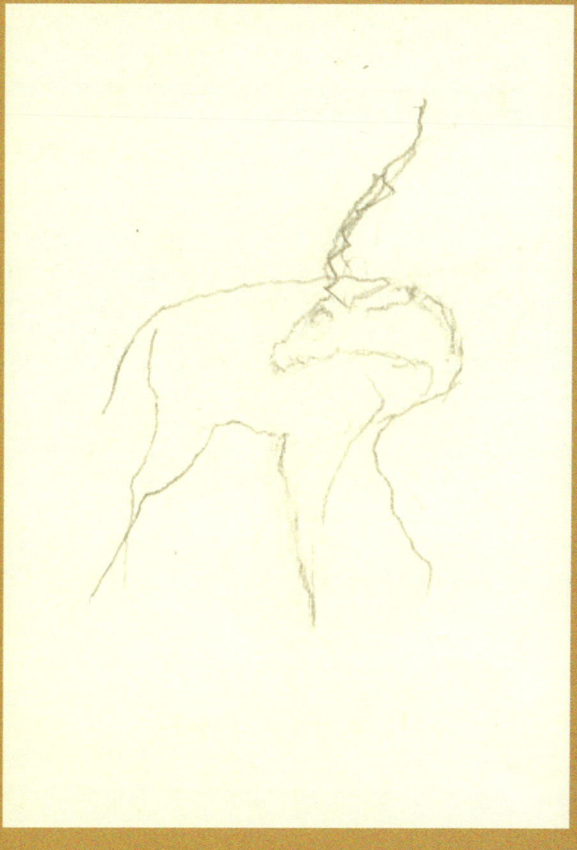

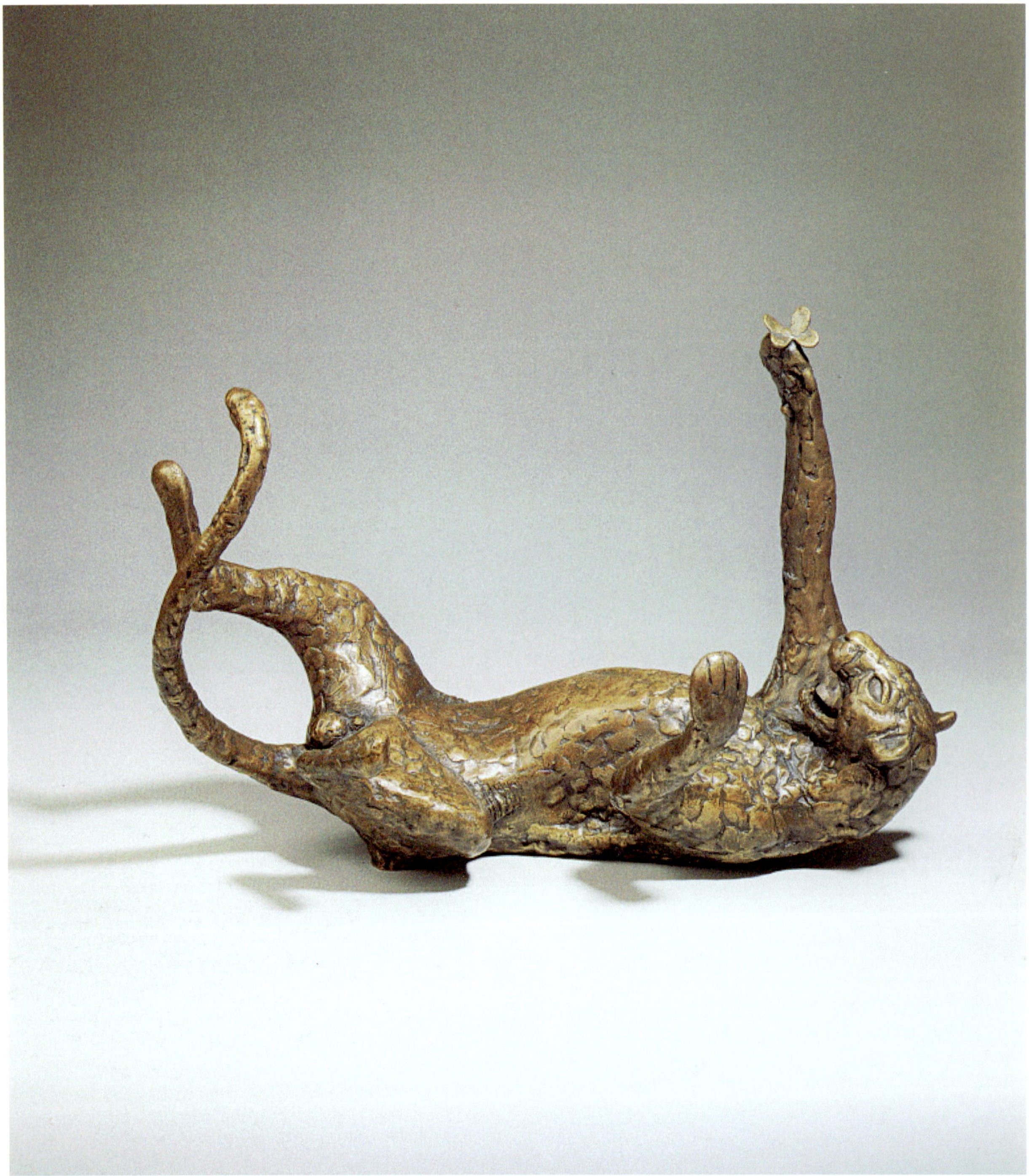

Leopard with a butterfly

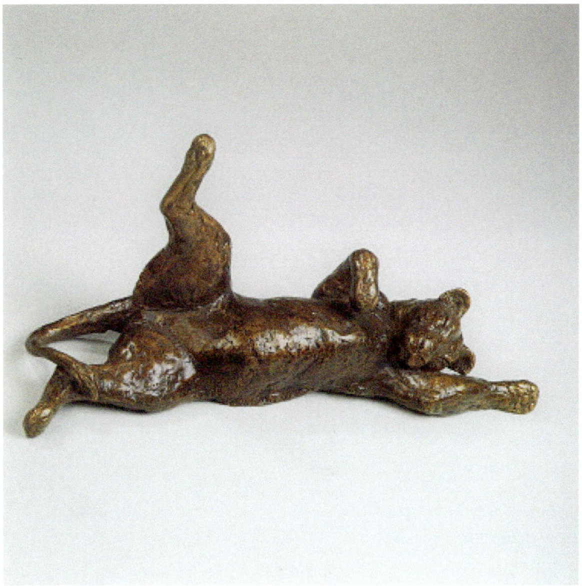

Lioness asleep

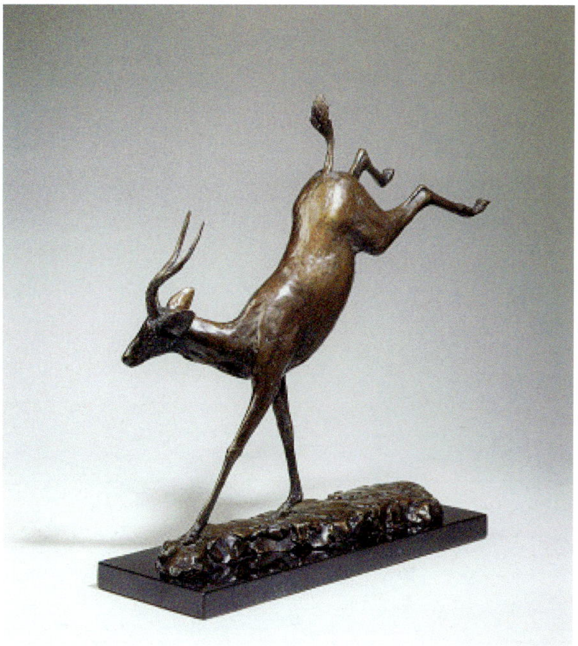

Jumping impala

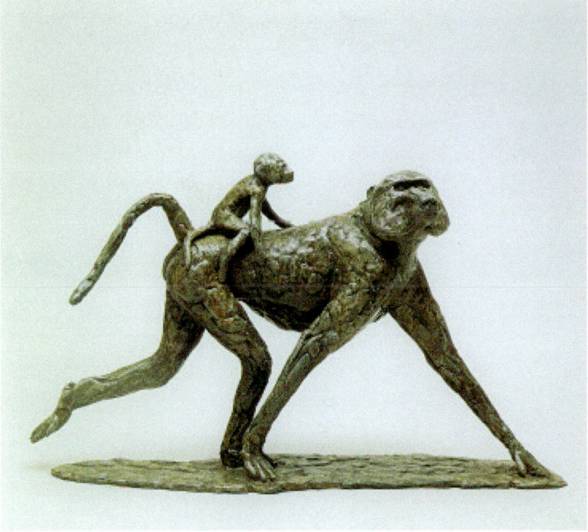

Baboon with baby

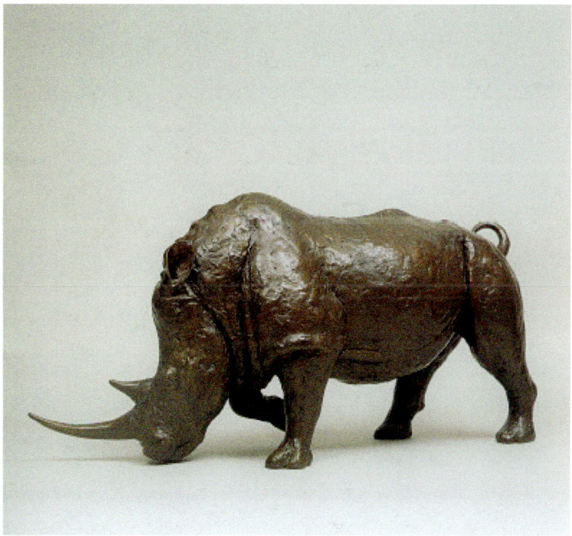

Bull rhino

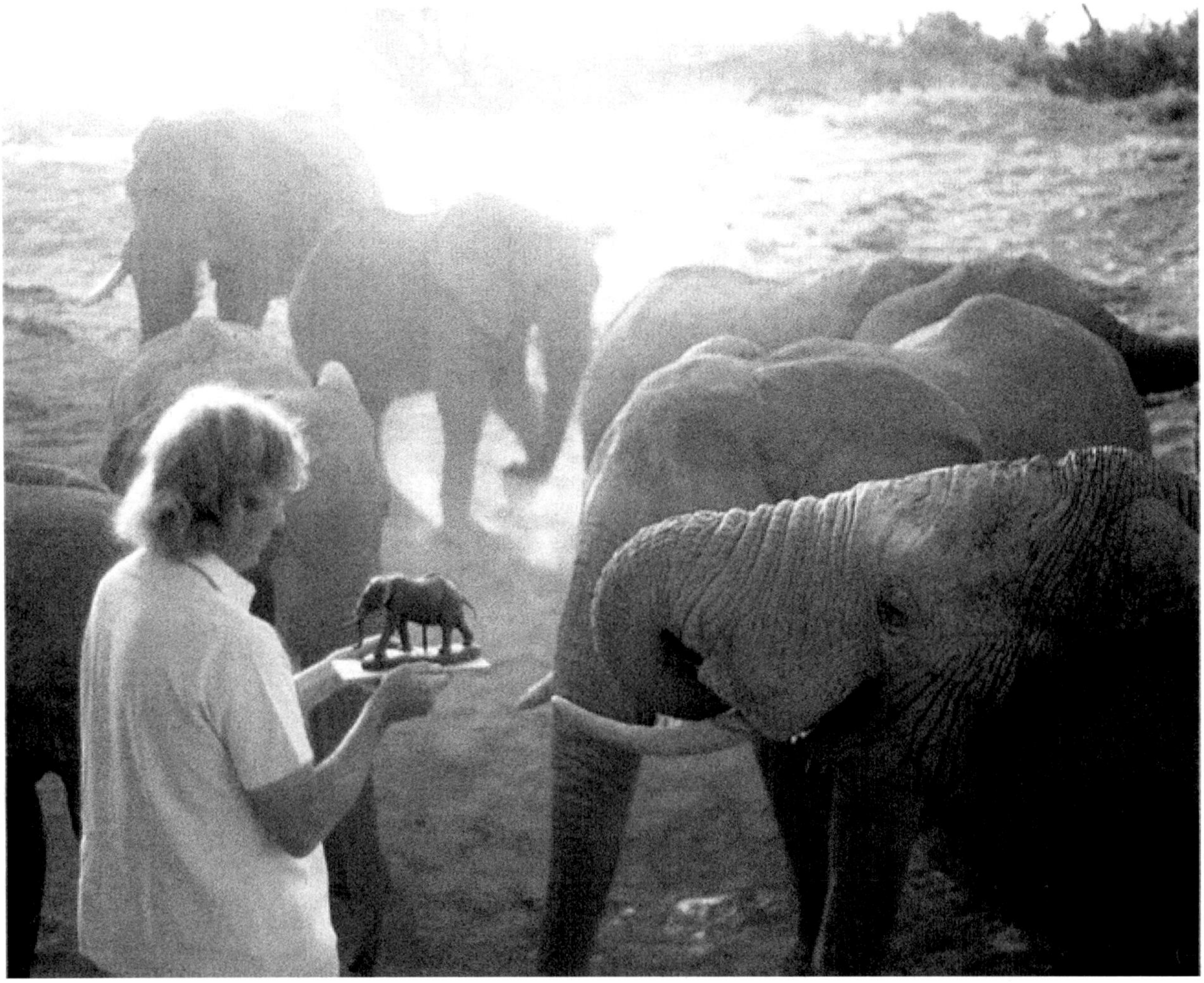

David working in Botswana

The ground is too hot for the human foot but the slowly passing elephants have adapted over eons to the harsh conditions of the continent. Quietly they follow their track to the waterhole and have recently become accustomed to see a grey-haired man outside his khaki tent. Sometimes they stop in silence to watch him, sometimes they flap their large ears and wave their trunks, sometimes they pass quietly by . . . After a first visit of two short days he has now returned with his tools. Daily for three weeks this spare, tall figure stands bending over his tripod making elephant sculptures . . . the artist is lost, oblivious to the heat of the day . . . He stands back, lights a cigar, gazes long and carefully, unhurriedly picks up the spatula again, takes off plasticine or adds it, moves a leg, alters the tail, bends and rebinds the trunk.

He asks for criticism from his new-found friends who share the deep love and understanding of these mighty creatures, and there are lengthy discussions . . . He returns with new enthusiasm and again

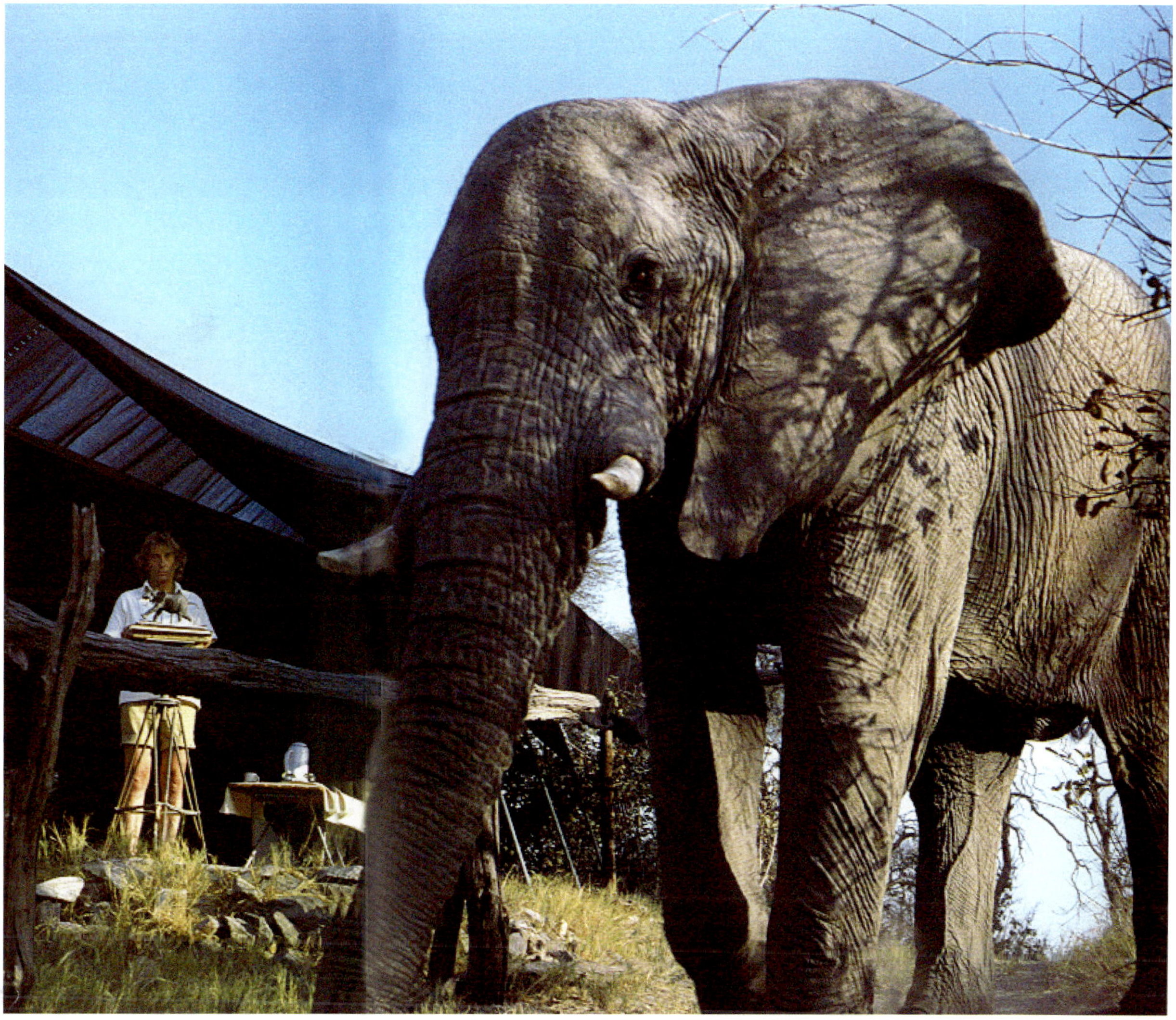

David sculpting a blind elephant

reshapes the head . . . He has given birth to two bulls, both beautiful, each in a different but typical pose . . . The last elephant will be charging, a difficult movement to capture. David disappears for a day and when we see him again he has found new energy and inspiration . . . Again he wants our comments and as so often we find ourselves having to look first at the live models. We learn to see with David's eyes . . . The days pass and the sculpture gets its wrinkles, its toenails, the trunk is moved closer to the tusk, the lifted feet get pads and the tail is swung up just right.

. . . David never tires of watching the elephants at the waterhole and always finds new details. He is meticulous . . . Here, then, they stand before us . . . Soon the sky is turning pink and the sculptures become silhouettes. We must bid farewell to the sculptures and to the man we have grown to love . . . David belongs here; he understands Africa, it has touched his soul and no doubt he will be back.

16

A FEW MONTHS BEFORE David's breakdown, he had gone out in a little fishing boat, off the coast of Wales, to swim with a dolphin. David had heard of a fisherman who claimed a dolphin would always come up to see him whenever he took his boat out. It was a very rough sea, but that did not prevent David from jumping in to play when the dolphin did present itself.

Some time later, David happened to pick up a book, the *Awakening Earth*, by Peter Russell. One of the very first modern ecological tracts, it propounded the concept of our world as a living being. David was intrigued by its argument and delighted to discover, by chance, that Russell had been a member of the crew that had taken him out to find the dolphin that day. They became good friends and the book inspired David to create a tangible representation of the book's core belief. When the Swiss merchant bank CBI required a sculpture to be placed in the square in front of their new headquarters in Geneva, David took them a maquette which, in homage to Russell's work, he named after the book. On 30 August 1987, he wrote, under the heading 'Night Thoughts on the Awakening Earth': 'The small maquette is superb, in that it works all over from everywhere!' His thoughts are a fine example of how he approaches the completion of any final sculpture:

> *Don't lose this whatever else comes out in the larger maquette.*
>
> *Its only shortcomings so far as it goes, are:*
>
> *the inner cavity slopes collect water*
> *the right arm is too mean*
> *the left hip is 'arthritic'*
> *the facial expression is not resolved*
>
> *And the left hand is coarse. The flow of the hair, the relationship of the masses, the small sphere, and the amount of abstraction, all do convey a planet swimming in space.*
>
> *I'm still not sure (though Gilli is) that it should not turn.*
>
> *It [the little maquette] looks wonderful floating on a wine glass on the kitchen table with a lily behind it.*

Edgar de Picciotto, an associate of David Scholey's, and the banker who commissioned the large work recalls:

> We met David Wynne and our meeting with him sparked it all. We had already been seduced by his sculptures, and we understood each other immediately.

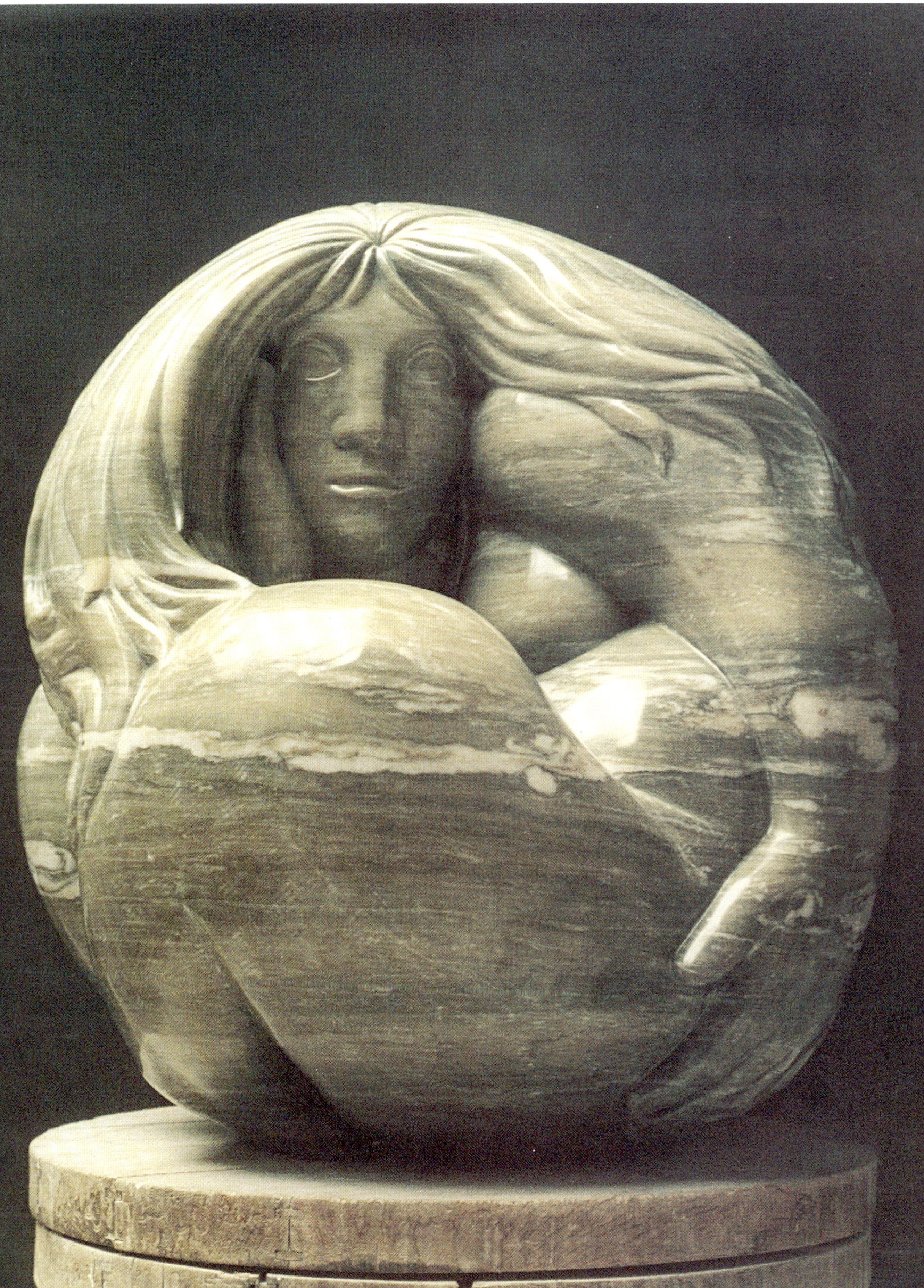

Thinking of the unity of our world, of the interdependence of all the elements of our universe, of the current means of communication which instantly change our globe, David started looking for an expression of the creation of this brand new world. When he came back to us he proposed the theme 'The Awakening Earth', which refers not only to this new state of the planet, but also to the spring of new hope. A human shape emerges from the sphere and shows that mankind always draws strength from itself. Ultimately, hope rises from the spontaneous generation of energy and from a state of permanent awakedness. For David Wynne the selection of his raw material is vitally important, as he shapes that material to give it expression. [The sculpture] manifests a particular gravity, which conveys an earthly nature, thus evoking the deep origins of those new forces sought by man, which witness the birth of hope for all mankind. The relationship between the original conception, the shape and the material was thus achieved . . .

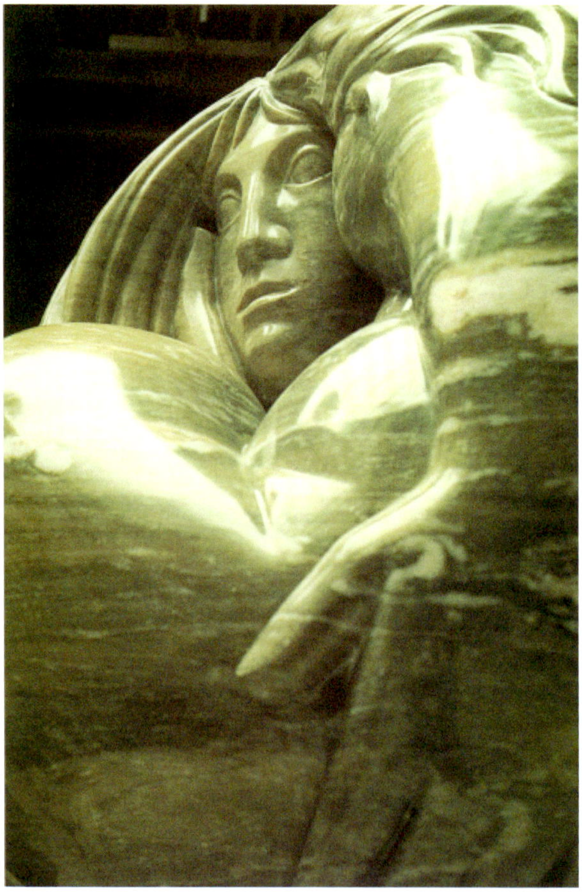

Awakening Earth detail

Carved in green-and-white Turkish marble, *The Awakening Earth* stands forty-two inches high. Gilli's advice, as ever, was taken and though the work weighs several tons, the piece can be turned on its pedestal by a touch of the hand, but not mechanically. It is no surprise that David is drawn to work grounded by a sense of the spiritual. One of the best accounts of this dimension to his art was written by Robin. She wrote an Introduction to David's third monograph, published in 1993 by Lund Humphries. It is worth reprinting here the part which deals with David's profound belief in art's inherent religiosity:

David Wynne is now sixty-six years old. So often during the middle years of an artist's life the joy and naivety of youth fade. It is a time when their work can become repetitive and lacking in vibrancy, when success can lead to a loss of that goal which forces the risking of all and the willingness to suffer the agonies of creation. Not so with David. Consider the awesome task of carving a *Christ* for the west front of Wells Cathedral, the vitality of the Sheffield *Horseman*, the tension of the *Two Swimmers* and the serenity and power of the five large *Goddess* carvings. [David] believes as did the Ancient Greeks that real art, together with real philosophy, real science and real religion, are the four pillars of civilisation, raising us from the slough of materialism. He tries to hold his subject up to the light of God. To model for David [Robin was his model for a number of remarkable sculptures] is to feel that one has been seen truly and that one's body has been celebrated as a part of the planet, a vessel for bringing harmony out of chaos and a new object of beauty into the world. David has never sought the assurance of keeping something in reserve, nor has he conformed to the platitudes of social convention. In this he was encouraged by his wife Gilli, whose great maturity and compassion, whose understanding and eye for art were David's guiding light until her death in 1990 . . . When first working as his assistant, on *The Messenger*, I found it difficult to accept the paradox that we were making both a horse and a symbol of the essence of the horse to convey a message. That message is best put in David's own words: 'The object of art is praise. It is to communicate emotion, to remind us of another order, where all is harmony.

'It is as though a traveller returning from a voyage to another world was asked what it was like and what he had seen. He cannot say. But he smiles and says, "I brought this back." All who see it say, "Surely I have seen that before. It reminds me of what I felt when I was a child."

'Artists of every generation help us to remember why we came and where we are. For the real world is not about politics, or newspapers, or money, or prisons, or evil. Evil does not exist, except as a mirage, the shadow of good.

'If one reads the great magic books – the Koran, the Upanishads, the Bible – a word that so often appears is "praise". To praise creation is the object of art and the object of life for man. The animals and the plants do it naturally; we have to be constantly reminded. To listen to music, to hear poetry, to see beautiful buildings, or paintings, or sculpture reminds us why we are here, for these are in praise of the creation.

'When I decide to make a sculpture of a beautiful girl or a rare animal, I am striving to worship that creature, and thus to worship nature. I try to love it as the creator loves it and to see it through his eyes. When I make a portrait head I try to tell the truth lovingly; never to belittle, nor ridicule, nor caricature. Find what is most perfect, most beautiful, and most essential; that is the core of what I am trying to do.'

17

TRESCO, one of the Isles of Scilly, has a special place in David's story. A wealthy merchant banker, Augustus Smith, bought the islands of Tresco and Bryher in 1834, from the Duchy of Cornwall. He was a plant collector and botanist, and created gardens based on sub-tropical and temperate-climate plants, collected from around the world. The island, some twenty-nine miles south-west of Land's End, benefits from the warmth of the Gulf Stream. The Abbey Garden came to be one of the great botanical sites of Europe and, over four generations, the Dorrien Smith family created a small community of just over a hundred and fifty people, who now assist them in running the island as a unique holiday attraction. No cars are allowed, apart from those vehicles needed to run the estate and its tourist business. The only way to get there is by small plane, helicopter or steamer. David, Gilli and the children went there often for idyllic holidays and became friendly with the island's owners. Indeed, the great-grandchild-in-law of Augustus often expressed the hope that if the holiday business ever became successful enough, the family would commission David to create some special sculpture for the place.

Her son, Robert Dorrien Smith, had known David since his childhood, when the Wynnes stayed there. He remembers:

> The Abbey Garden is a most magical place and for many years I had a particular site in mind for a sculpture to add another dimension to the botanists' paradise, although much of the formal architecture of the original 1830s' garden was buried under rare and exotic plants from all over the world . . . In 1987 we experienced frost and snow on the island – a phenomenon unknown for a generation. The garden was devastated – huge trees and thousands of plants and shrubs were killed . . . In one sense, it was a disaster, but it was above all an opportunity . . . to replan and replant this amazing place of beauty.
>
> It was a complete coincidence that took me to David's studio one day in January 1989. I had not seen him for years but I still harboured the desire for a Wynne bronze at Tresco and I had a number of preconceptions about what it might be and where it might go. While walking and talking in David's studio after lunch that day, I remember asking David

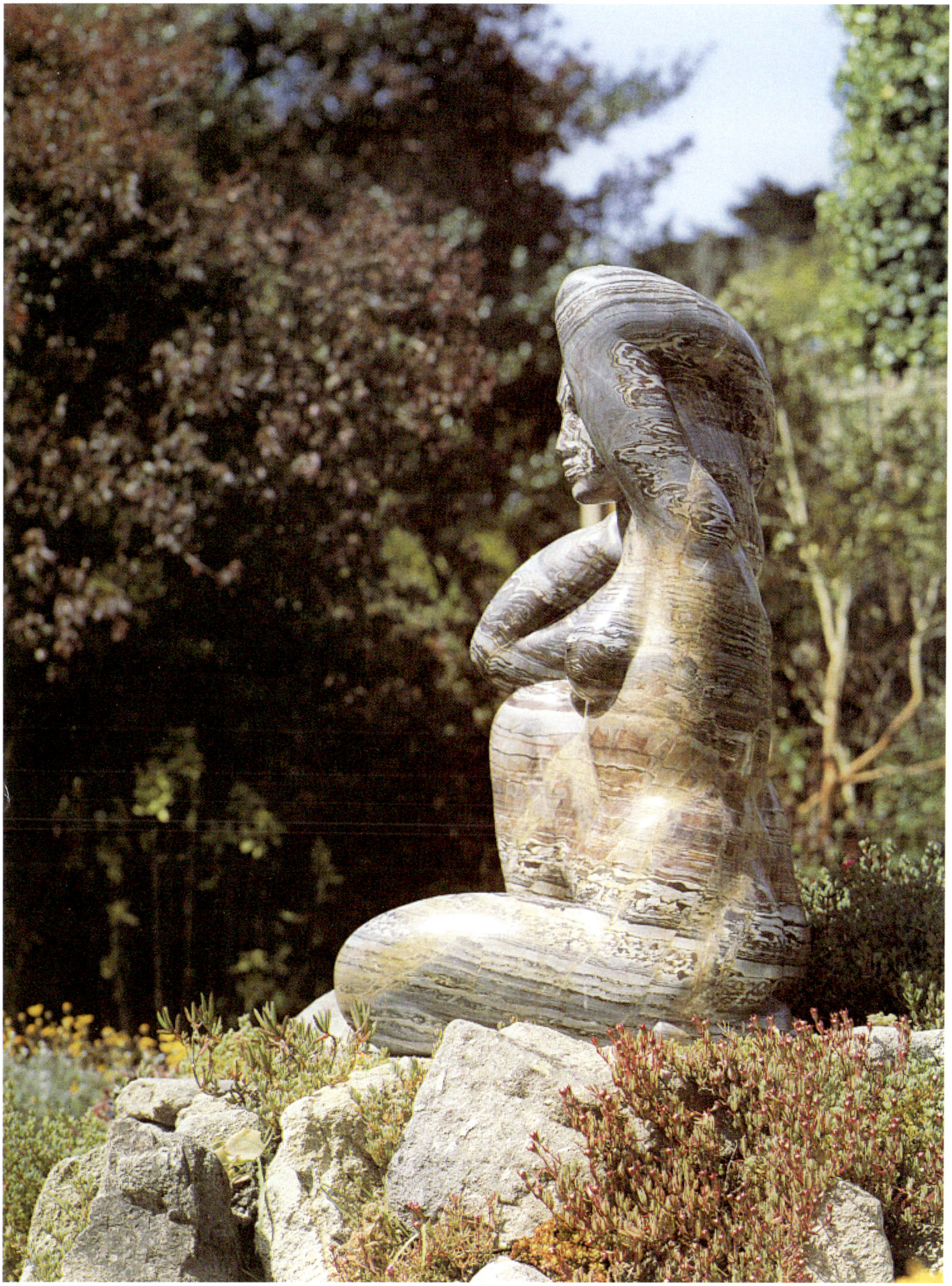

Gaia

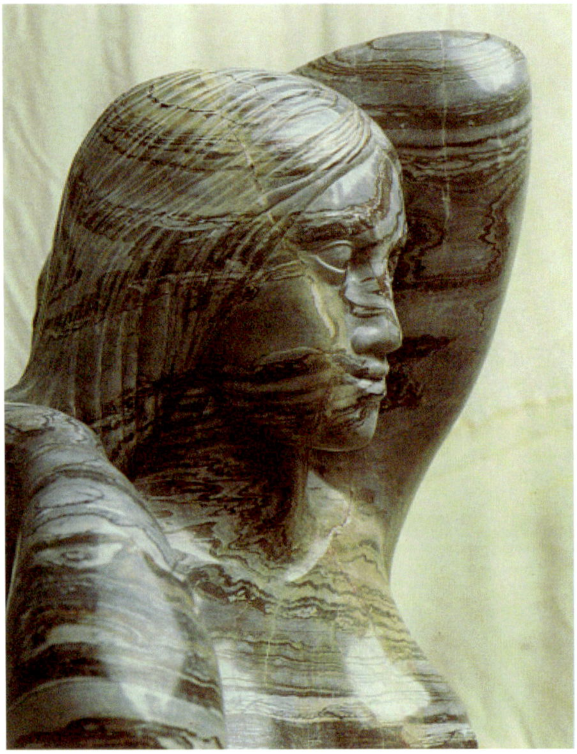

Gaia detail

what large object lay hidden beneath a shroud of dustsheets. We took the sheets off to reveal a magnificent marble carving of a kneeling girl. I saw and knew instantly that she should go in the centre of the Abbey Garden. I put aside all ideas of bronze. The power and presence of this carving captivated me totally and she instantly became the symbol in my mind for the reawakening of the garden . . . She would become the focus of tranquillity in the garden.

Tresco is a tiny island without motor cars so that the arrival of the marble girl was a major event which required considerable logistical planning. She is very heavy – about one and a half tons – and she arrived in a huge crate. We were faced with the problem of moving her from the tiny harbour to the chosen site in the garden, which inevitably was at the end of a series of twisting rock paths. Every form of ancient and modern technology was called into play . . . large cypress branches were cut from the island woods to make a huge tripod; this was secured to fifty-foot palm trees by blocks borrowed from fishermen; the estate engineer was in charge of making, placing and supervising the use of various levers and rollers and lifting tackle. The island stonemason had constructed a magnificent platform of granite in the circular garden and eventually, after hours of heaving and struggling, instruction and counter- instruction, theories that failed and some which didn't, she was finally settled in place.

It was decided that we should not give a name to her immediately, but wait and see and consider. It was some months before she became *Gaia*, but by then it was clear that this was not only a very great work of art but was indeed a symbol of rebirth, nature in its purest form, and that she was mother of the micro-universe that surrounded her.

So, finally, the block of marble that had been a birthday present, many years before, from George Harrison to David, had found its spectacular setting. The block of multi-coloured South African marble had stood in David's studio for a long time. Gilli and David had decided what to make but had given little thought to its final resting place. Gilli posed for what evolved into the figure of the earth goddess.

Dorrien Smith goes on to recall:

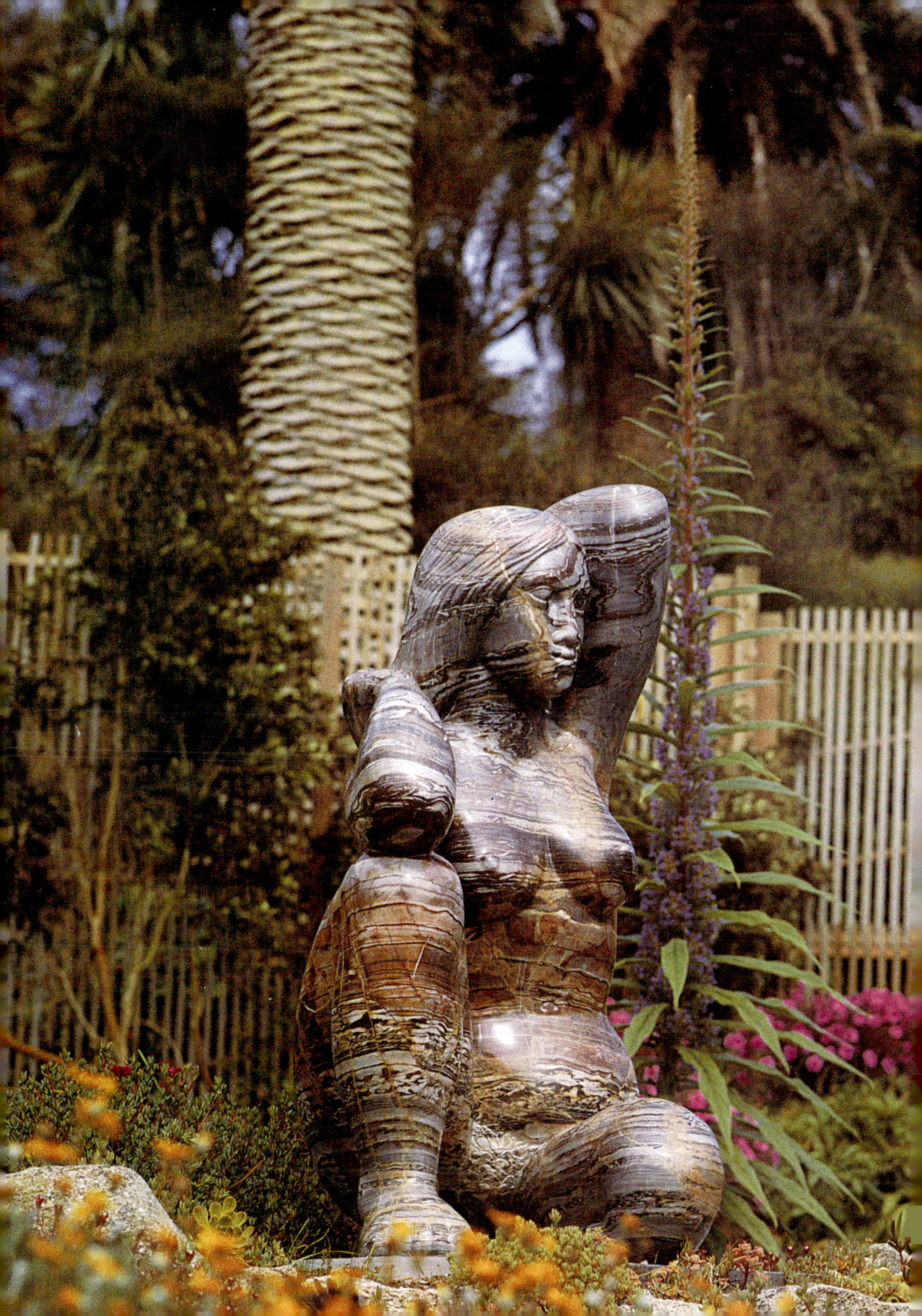

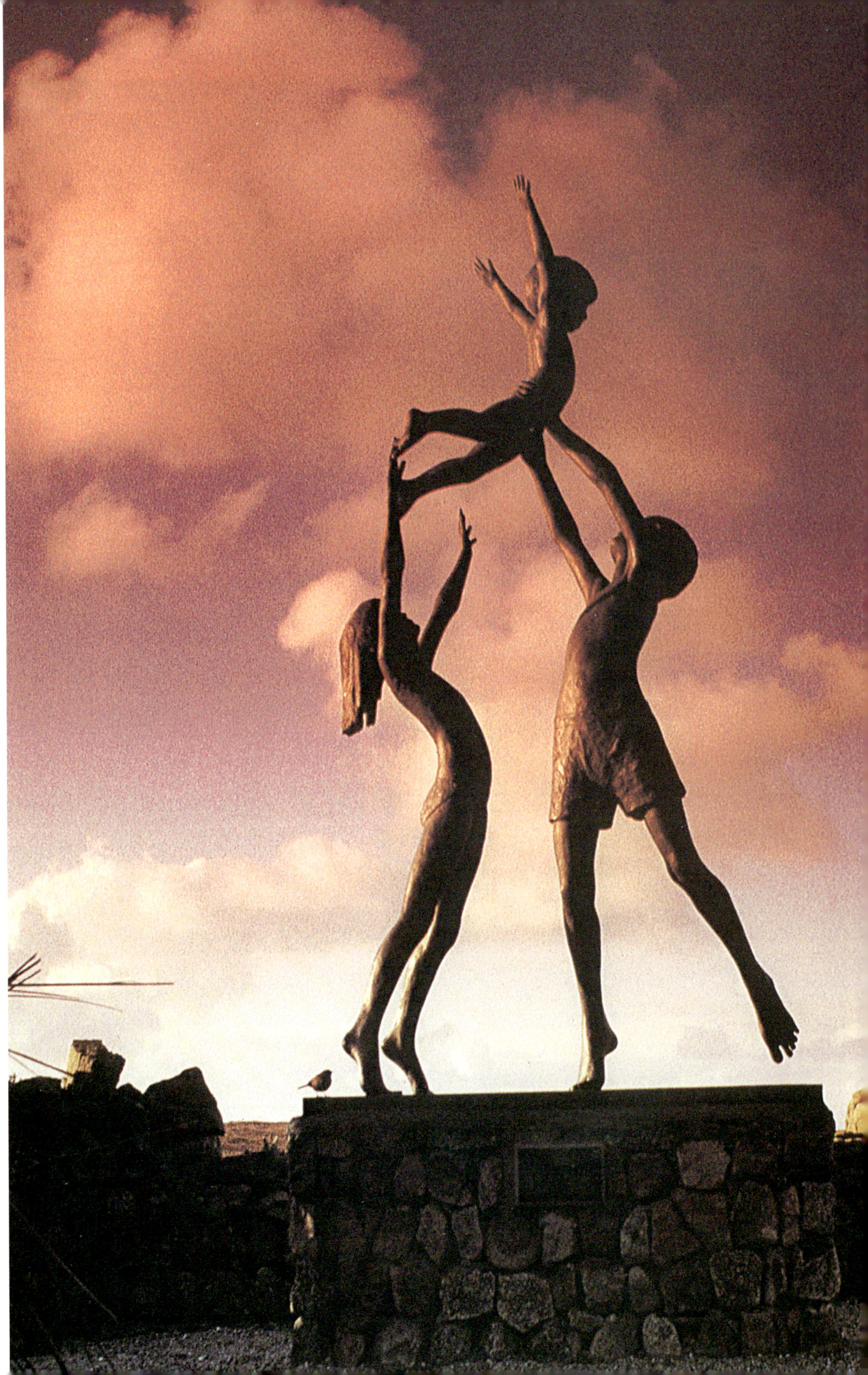

Such was the impact and excitement generated by *Gaia*'s arrival in the garden that it wasn't long before ideas were emerging for another totally contrasting work. There is one grand vista in particular in the garden . . . It was a very important site [as] it would become the first thing that visitors to the island would see as they emerged from the helicopter. From one side . . . it was seeking to be formal, but from the Heliport side it was important to try and capture an instant feeling for the spirit of the island. Tresco is most frequently referred to by adults as a children's paradise . . . It is a place where children can run free . . . they are playing, they are having fun and above all they are happy! . . . It took David's genius to translate this jumble of ideas and concepts into the *Tresco Children*. It carries all the messages we hoped it would. It is light and happy, it talks about the joy of living and the magic of the island. Thousands of people already love this sculpture; it makes them smile and conveys contentment, all in one statement.

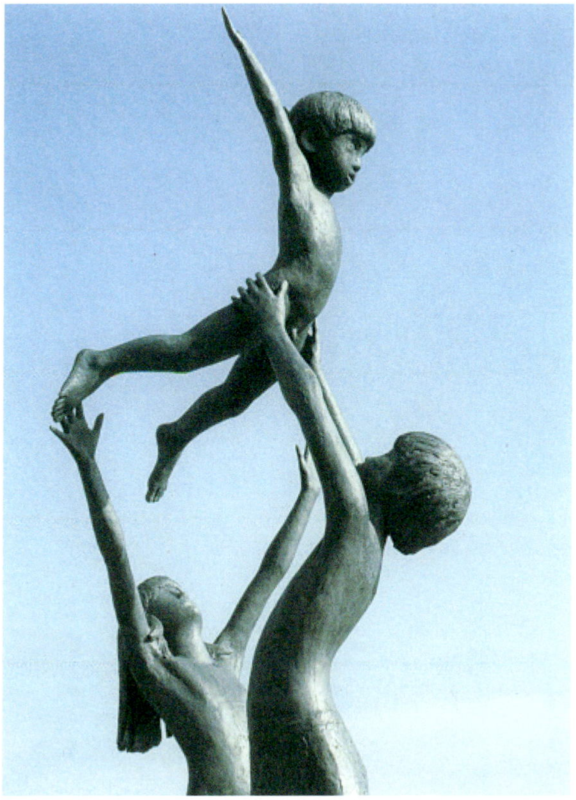

Tresco children

Tresco Children is one of David's most favourite pieces. A 120-inch bronze, it was designed to be seen from afar as well as near to, and was his attempt to express 'pure joy'. The models were the three children of Robert Dorrien Smith, who asked the Prince of Wales to honour him by unveiling the statue, as he was there on a visit with his family when it was installed. Prince Charles suggested his wife might enjoy the task. And so it was that Prince Charles, Princess Diana, the royal princes, William and Harry, Robert, his wife Emma, their three children and David walked to the statue's base to witness a most unusual unveiling ceremony. It was a private visit. No press were in attendance. Such was the informality of the occasion that Princess Diana was wearing jeans and a Michael Jackson souvenir leather jacket. David had rigged a sail up over the sculpture. When she asked David what she should do, he told her just to pull the string and the sail would come away. It was a windy day, and as the princess pulled the rope, the sail snagged and stayed caught somehow. Faced with a statue, eleven feet high and standing on a five-foot base, with a sail refusing to unfurl, Diana

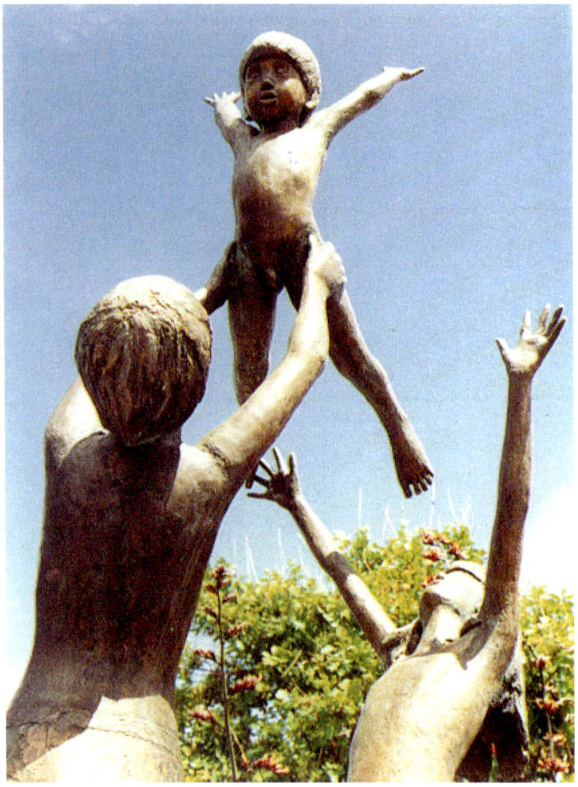

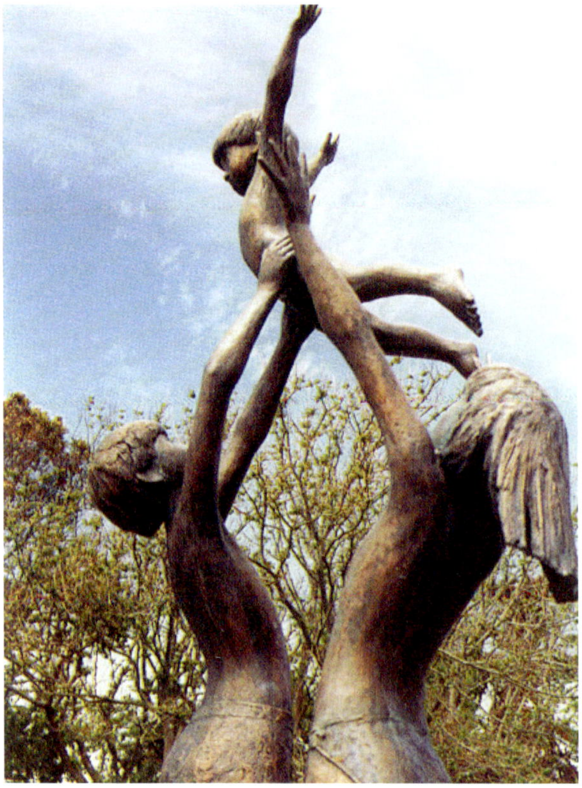

was at a loss. David pointed out that as she was actually performing the unveiling, she should be the one to clamber up and loosen the sail. Her response was instant. Asking that David 'give her a bunk-up', princess and sculptor climbed on to the pedestal and David, placing his hand under the seat of her jeans, hoisted her up to finish the ceremony. Eager to help, Prince Harry jumped up as well. Freeing the sail, the princess asked to be let down, but David, fearing for the little boy's safety, pointed out that her younger son was in the way. 'Well,' said Diana, 'I'm coming down anyway,' and so all three tumbled, rolling together in the sand beneath. Dusting herself down, Princess Diana confided it had been the first time she had ever really enjoyed an unveiling ceremony. Later, that same day, Prince Charles asked David to walk with him and show him *Gaia*. The prince told the Dorrien Smiths he had never seen a sculpture that blended into its setting like this one did. He asked David to consider making a sculpture like it for Highgrove, his residence in Gloucestershire. David agreed, but told him the stone would have to be similar rather than the same as the work had been made from a unique piece of marble.

By this time, David knew that his beloved Gilli had been diagnosed with terminal cancer. She was able to spend some of that last summer on the island, and when she died, in November 1990, her ashes were scattered near to David's remarkable contribution to the glories of Tresco.

18

IT WAS GILLI'S BEAUTY that had first captivated David all those years before. He tells an anecdote of a time when he was in Donald Kendall's office at the Pepsico headquarters, when *The Bear* was to be mounted in its spectacular setting on the front lawn. As they were discussing the arrangements, they saw Gilli walking away from them, towards another sculpture, a figure in the distance:

> *... and Donald Kendall and I couldn't believe that anyone could look so beautiful at such a distance, walking. Her movements were so extraordinary ... and she was just so incredibly beautiful ... her feet, they were just the most beautiful feet I've ever seen on a human being. Like the feet on the Charioteer of Delphi, they were like that. Yet she could appear quite ordinary, but she was incredibly calm. Like a statue. Like a peasant.*

Gilli was no stranger to artistic temperament. Her mother was a well-regarded writer, whose somewhat mystical novels achieved recognition in the post-war period. There were even rumours within the family of supernatural powers inherent in the bloodline. Benign witchcraft was not discounted as a family trait. And David recognised her exceptional skills:

> *She was always calm, and helped me by posing for me and by being there. In a way she sacrificed her own creativity to mine. She could have done anything. She did lots of so many things ... She was a potter. She used to make baskets. Once she knitted wonderful sweaters for me and all the children with images of our cat Lucy, its face on the front and the back of the cat on the back of the sweater. I can't tell you all the things she used to do and she was so good at. And her hands! There was a vibrancy – there's a line in 'Forever Young', a song by Bob Dylan, 'Let your hands be always busy.' She was a passionate gardener and there's a story I can scarcely dare to tell. One day she was on the lawn at Rushmere, standing looking at a tall tree. I said, 'What are you doing, Gilli?' and she was crying. She said, 'I'm saying goodbye to this tree.' The tree was destroyed the next day.* [In the great storm in October 1987 when millions of trees were destroyed and eighteen people were killed in England alone.] *She loved flowers, she loved plants, little tiny plants. She knew about trees and flowers. She just knew. She watched tiny*

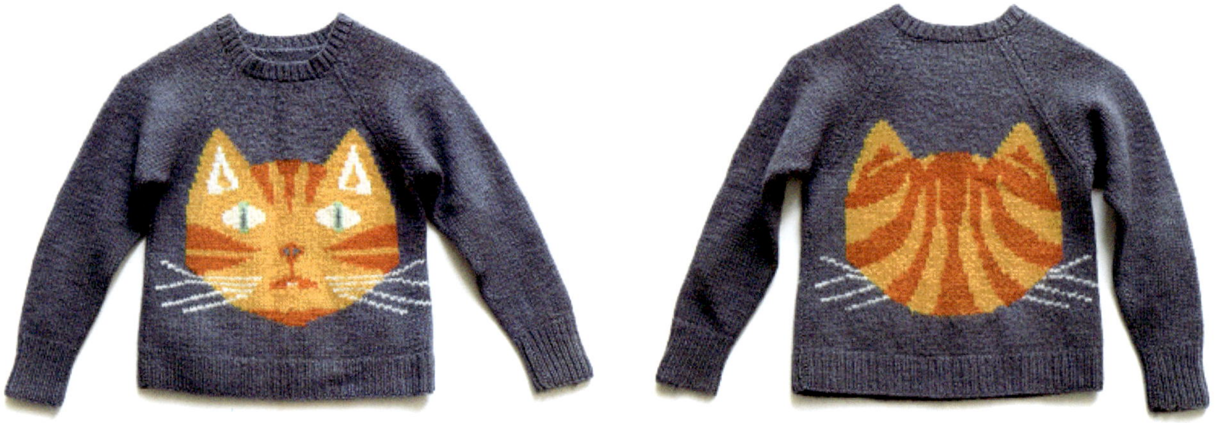

A jumper knitted by Gilli

weeds and plants. She said, 'They're all hoping to get bigger.' I can't tell you what it means. I can't really describe it . . .

Despite the complications, it became clear to David that he needed her. In the course of this book's writing, when asked whether it was, as the cliché goes, 'love at first sight', his reply was typically candid:

I don't know about that. Certainly she was the most beautiful woman I'd ever met but she didn't fall in love with me ever I don't think. But I'm so persuasive. I married her and I did bring up her children and she loved me, but I don't think she was ever in love with me as I was with her. I've said that she sacrificed her life to mine, but it's not quite true. She loved my work and she knew that she was helping in my career, and she was as passionately involved and interested in my sculpture as I was myself, so she didn't really sacrifice her life . . . but she did tailor it to my needs and my ways. She was a perfect person. She wasn't perfect, of course, none of us is perfect, and she had her fiery side and she had other sides. We know that everybody has, but for what it's worth she was the best wife a man could ever have and I was about the worst husband. In marrying me she got a bad deal. I wasn't a good enough man to be her husband and well I know it. It's no good saying that's false modesty because it's not.

David is also clear that his work and eventual success would never have evolved as it did without her unique qualities:

Ever since we were together, every time, Gilli helped me in so many ways. She freed me by doing all the mundane tasks, for all of our life together. She made the food, she did the housekeeping, she did the shopping: she did everything. When I wanted to eat, I told her I wanted to eat. I never kept to mealtimes. She didn't ever come into the studio and say, 'Lunch is ready.' She waited. And nobody but her ever came into the studio. She would never interrupt me when I was working, save when I asked her to . . . When she came into the studio, which was when I asked her, her taste was infallible. Once, Bill [Bill Amer] *and I were stuck. A big, big piece and we just couldn't get it right and Bill said, 'Time you asked Gilli, isn't it?' and I said, 'I suppose it is,' and so I asked Gilli to come and look. She calmly walked into the studio and she looked at the piece, and she said, 'Well, it'll be all right when you change that arm,' and I said, 'Change that arm? What do you mean, that's the best thing about it,' and she said nothing. Just stood there quietly, looking at us, and Bill said, 'She's right, mate, you know. There's something wrong with that arm.' Of course she was right and we changed the arm, radically. Support. She gave me total support . . .*

And it was not simply with David's art and well-being that Gilli's role was crucial:

She supported and protected me in every way that she could: from worry, from financial difficulties. She didn't like business any more than I did. Her dislike was almost too much at times. She was so uninterested in money that she left the boys with a bit of a hang-up about it. The worst thing the children could say about anybody when they were small was, 'Businessman.'

We were sitting at breakfast one day in our small house in Victoria Drive and Peter Matthews, who was one of the directors of Tooth's gallery – my gallery at the time – was there and he said to me, 'David, I promise you we could double your income from your work by finding you portrait commissions.' Before I could speak, Gilli said, 'I want you to understand that that's not what David wants. We don't want to be rich. We don't want to be famous. We don't want publicity. We just want to make sculpture,' and that was it. Loadstone of life! It was true. I've never been interested in money and Gilli shielded me from that world. I didn't have to think about it. I didn't have to say how much a head portrait was going to cost, or anything like that.

And Gilli could handle *that:*

She would handle it all in such a graceful way that they thought that it had come from me, but Gilli was doing it, probably for love of me, because she knew I didn't want that side of my life. I still dislike that side of my life still today. I don't like to talk about money and, as I say, the children were brought up to believe that business was the most terrible thing. It's not true but that's what they thought. [Gilli could also handle the paradox of David's considerable success.] *She was the counter-balance to my social side. I'm a very social person and I love parties. That's how I got many of my commissions. Being the star! Gilli was the opposite. She hated parties. She didn't come with me, she just stayed quietly, didn't come. She'd send me to them, but it wasn't her scene. Except once, when I was in St Moritz with all the grand people. Theo Rossi was the man. He said to me one day, 'My dear fellow, your wife should come out. She really should.' I said, 'Theo, she won't come. She doesn't like the social side of life.' He said he'd speak to her on the telephone. He said, 'Gillian, I want to tell you something. There's a red stag by my pool just outside my window in the snow and he's standing drinking there totally unafraid outside the window. Will you come?' She came.*

When she got there, Theo said, 'David you must excuse me but I'm going to totally annexe your wife. She's only come for a few days and it's so rare for me to meet a very beautiful women who's also very, very intelligent.' She stayed for two days and at last he persuaded her to go down into St Moritz with him.

The Palace Hotel has very grand shops, the finest jewellery, furs, everything and – Theo told me this afterwards, she never mentioned it to me – he said, 'Gillian I want

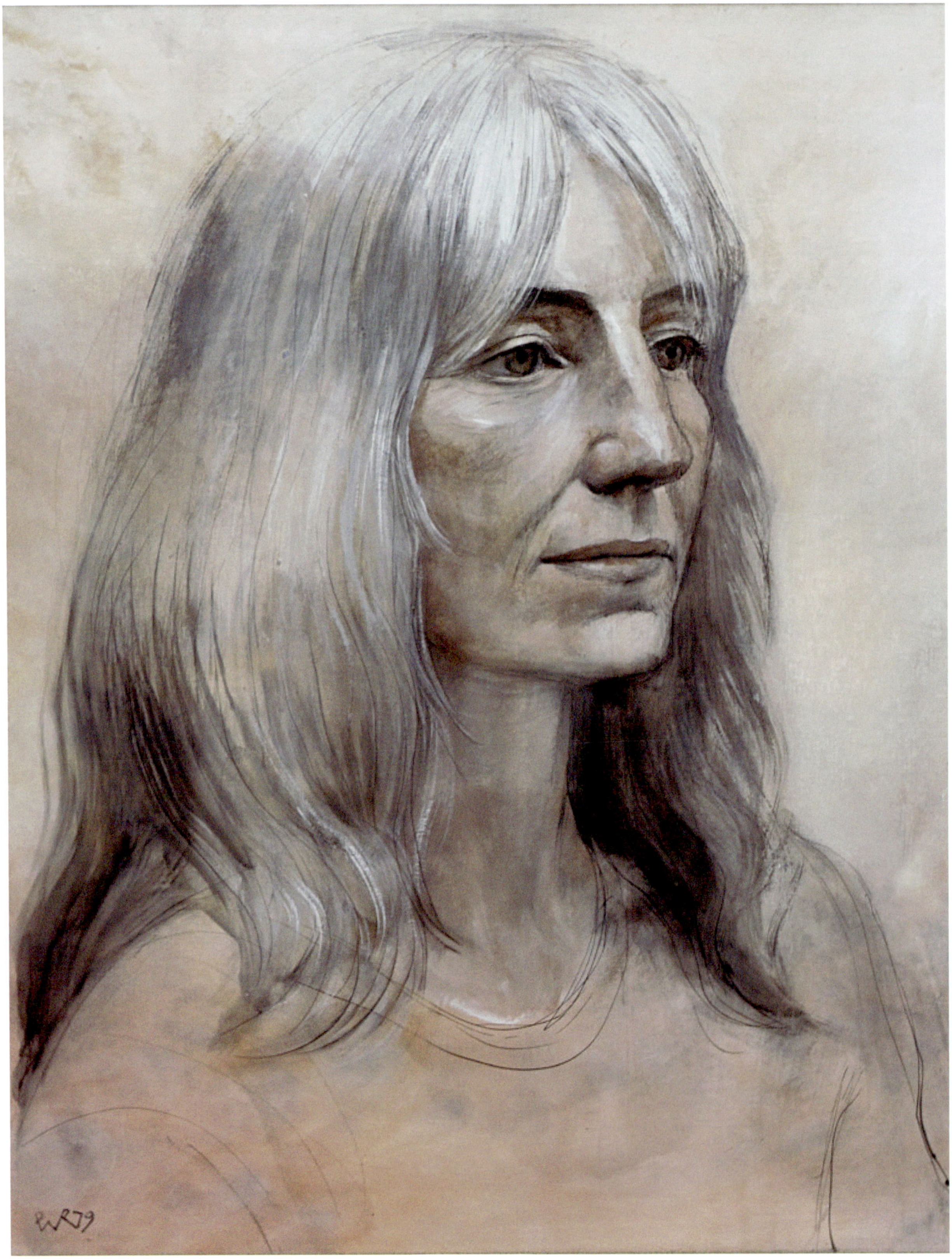

Gilli by Peter Rogers

to give you a present for the honour you've done me in coming here.' She said that wasn't necessary, but Theo insisted he wanted to give her something. They went into Harry Winstone's. 'What would you like?' and Gilli smiled and said, 'Theo, I don't like diamonds.' 'What about other gems?' Gilli told Theo she didn't really like jewels at all. 'Right,' he said, 'let me buy you a fur coat,' and you can imagine, but she said, 'I'd only spill honey on it.' So, in despair, Theo asked if there was anything that he could buy her and she said, 'Yes. I'd like some of those roses.' And she never even mentioned any of this exchange when she came back to the chalet. She just said to me, 'Look, what lovely roses. Theo bought them for me.'

It was the purchase of Rushmere that enabled Gilli's unique qualities to come more than ever to the fore. She didn't want to move there at all, initially. David was certain she was wrong, but she insisted the family home didn't need to get bigger, they didn't want to get a grand house. In the end, David's considerable persuasiveness won out, and once the deal was settled, Gilli worked her magic. David recalls:

She went off and measured the house and every staircase and she said there was a possibility of putting another staircase here and moving the linen cupboard there and then there'd be stairs up to a separate apartment which we could let, if we wanted or needed to do it. And the architect said it was impossible. Gilli told him to take a look and she was right of course, and for years, part of the house was separate. It was let, like an apartment, and, later on, when we got better off, we used to lend it to people. We lent it to Donovan, for instance, when he came back from Greece. He'd been on this boat and nobody would accept him in their houses and so he came and asked us (Don was very young), and he asked Gilli what he should do. People were always saying to Gilli what can I do? Can you help me? She was like an oracle.

Donovan, like many young musicians at the time, had fallen foul of the stringent laws on cannabis and his reputation preceded him to Rushmere. At the time, David was making a portrait head of Sir Alec Douglas-Home. The politician came in for a sitting and asked David what a policeman was doing by the gate of the house. David told him it was nothing to do with Sir Alec being there. It was to do with Donovan. Sir Alec retorted, 'Well, I'll see about that,' and suddenly the policeman wasn't there any more.

Gilli and David created a unique home in the large, rambling old house on Wimbledon Common. As well as Donovan, most of the singers David knew, his contacts fuelled by his growing friendship with the Beatles, would stay there, among them Jimi Hendrix and Joan Baez. It felt, especially with the children's growing involvement with music, a special place. It was at Rushmere that Edward assembled his iconic 'underground' rock group, the Ozric Tentacles (formed in 1984 and still playing all over the world) – David still remembers the 'row' they made – thus ensuring the house's creative atmosphere passed to a new generation.

Gilli's involvement with her children was total – 'She just applauded what they were doing. Whatever they did, she applauded.' There was, of course, a degree of unconventional behaviour. David remembers:

The children didn't go to school much at all. They went to [laughter] . . . My stepdaughter

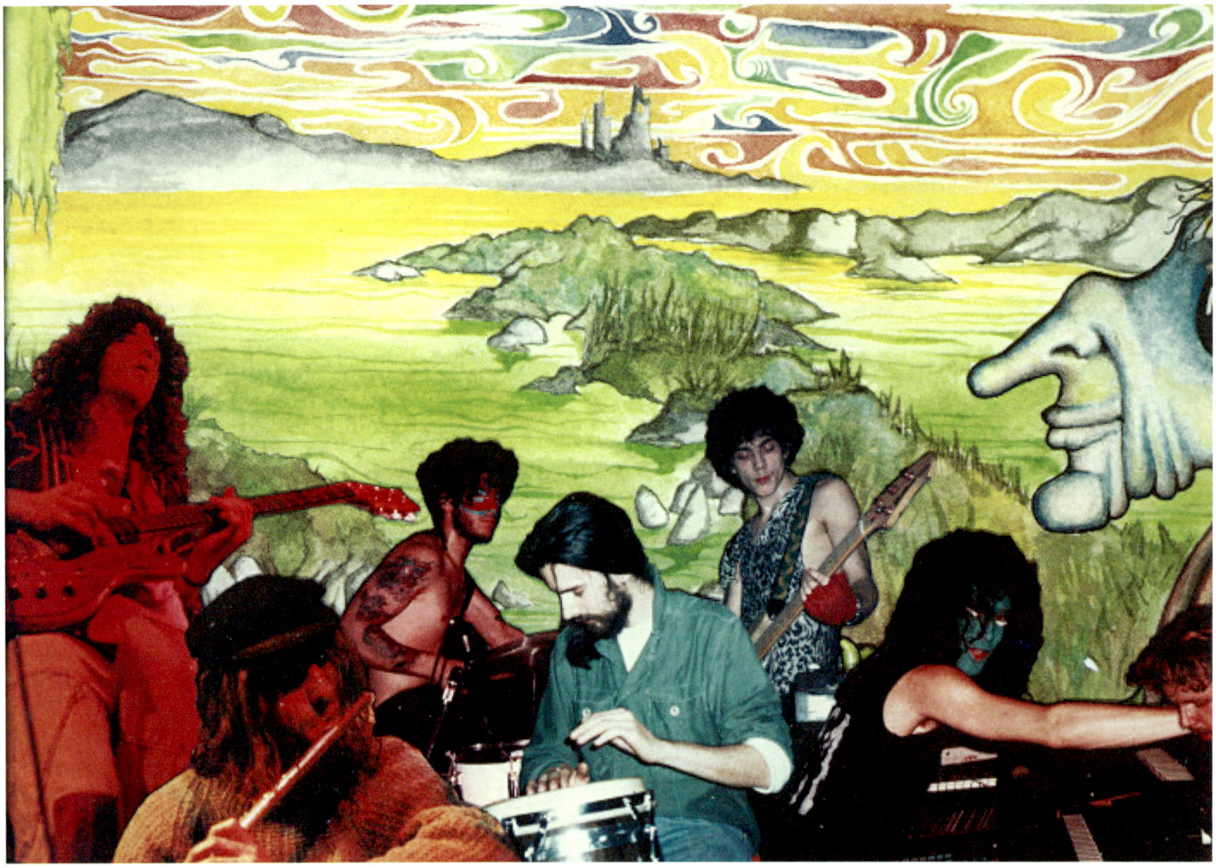

The Ozric Tentacles

Nicky posed for me for many of my sculptures, as did the other three. She was a very beautiful, empathetic model. She went to Putney High School and from there to Girton College, Cambridge, and got a second in English Literature. The only one who did any academic work! Johnny went to Abbotsholme because he liked one of the masters, but he walked out of Nottingham University.

Now Edward just didn't do any work at all. We thought he was not quite right in the head. A dunce, but then we said, 'Now come on, Eddie. What are you going to do?' and he said, 'I'm going to play guitar. That's all I do all the time.' He was at King's College, Wimbledon, and there was a piano teacher up the road, a very good one, and Edward did the octaves and all the things like that. Well, he went three times and then he told us he wasn't going there again and we said why and he said, 'He doesn't know about music,' and we went to see the man and he said Edward was totally unteachable and totally unmusical. I said to Edward, 'Why aren't you doing anything at school?' and he told me he only enjoyed the guitar and that's what he wanted to do with his life and so finally I said to the authorities at the school all he wanted to do was play the guitar, and they said, 'Well, we know that because that's all he does.' And I suppose he's played for about six hours a day ever since. That's all he does. Well, Edward has made his profession music. He's very gifted. He's just going off on a tour of Chile [2008] and is one of the most musical men I've ever met. He now lives in the Colorado Mountains.

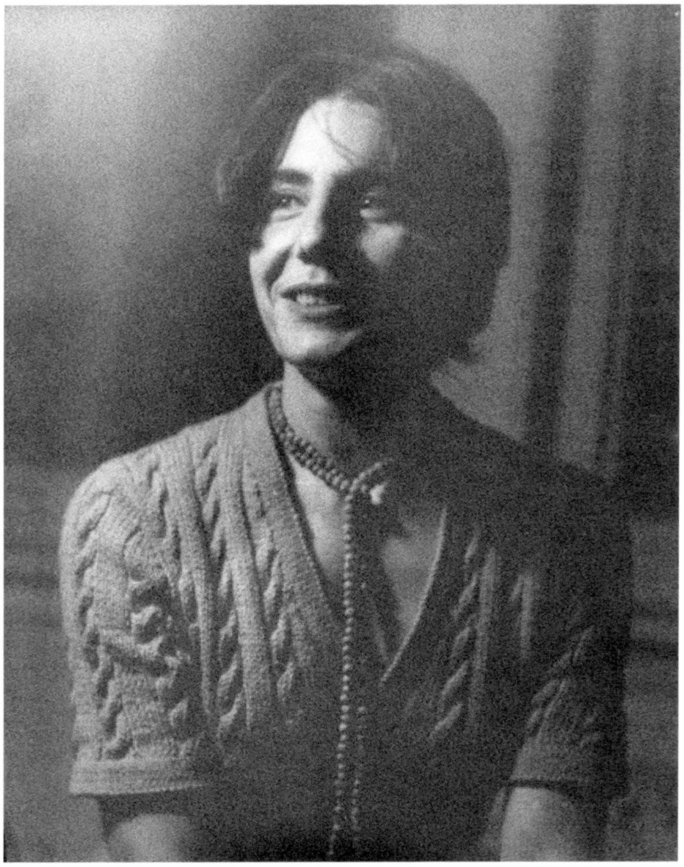

Gilli

Roly really was bright. The brightest of them all, I think. He seemed always supremely happy at home but all the reports from his kindergarten and school said he was disobedient. We told them he wasn't disobedient at home, but at school he just wouldn't do anything that they told him. Roly had a thing against authority. At one school they told me that he hummed all the time. I said but I've never heard him hum, he never hums. He got himself thrown out of Westminster. When I say he got himself thrown out, he sat on the roof of the headmaster's study drinking whisky and drumming his heels on the roof, just in order to be thrown out, which of course he was. He came back and I said, 'Well what's happened?' and he said it was a bloody awful school.

Perhaps Gilli's remarkable qualities can be best summed up in an anecdote about her and Roly, once more in David's own words:

She used to go for walks with Roly. They walked the length of the Thames. They started at the source up in the Cotswolds. Took them several days. She walked with Roly the whole length of the Thames, right out to the estuary at Gravesend, because Roly had said, 'What's a river?' A little boy – he was six, maybe seven. They walked and they stayed at pubs. Another time she walked again with Roly right round London. Now, that doesn't sound much, but actually it was right round the perimeter of London. It took them weeks but she did it because her beloved Roly had said, 'How big is London?' That's the sort of person she was.

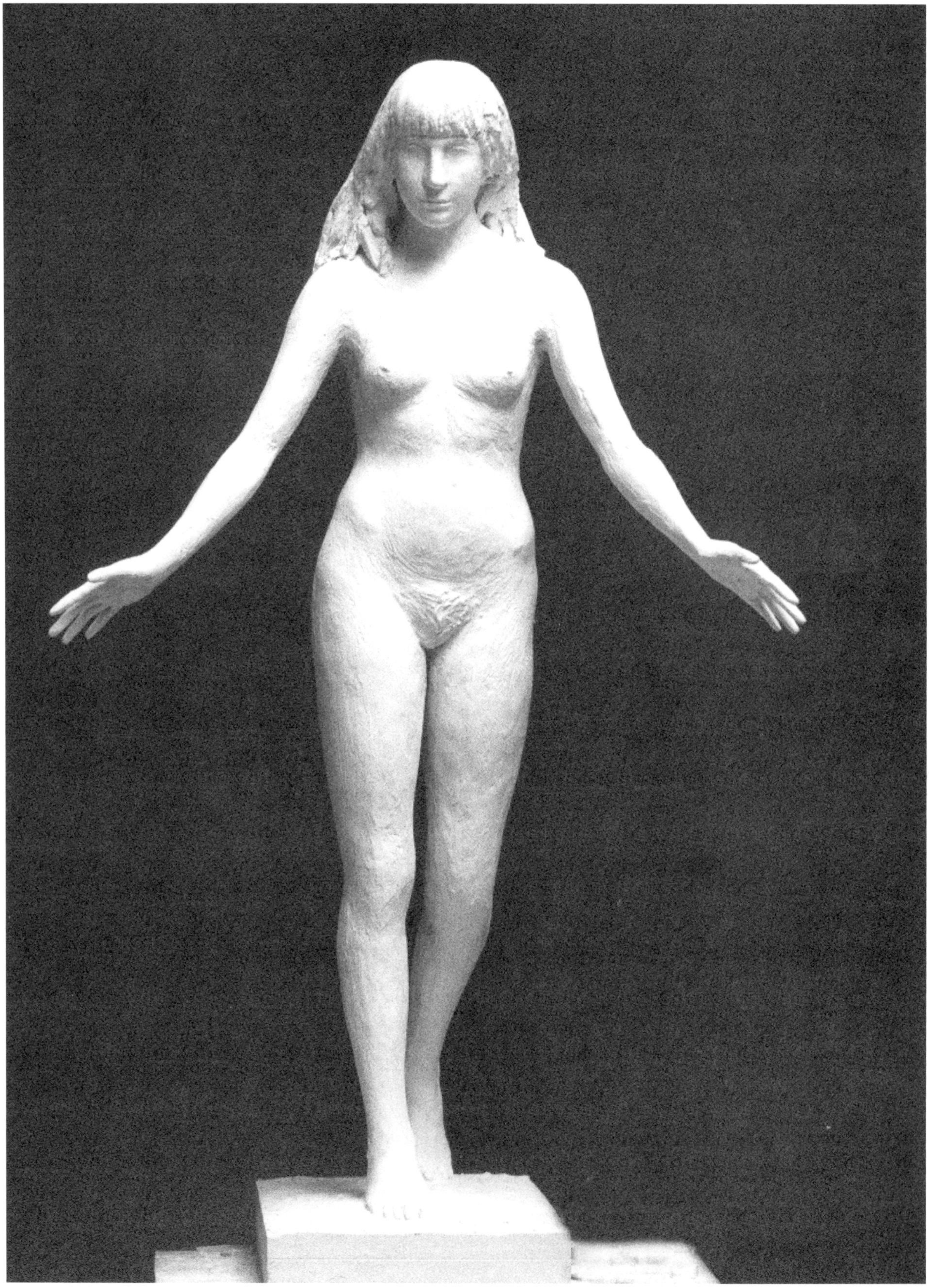

Gilli walking

19

THE SPRING OF 1993 saw the publication of a major monograph on David's work: *The Sculpture of David Wynne 1974–1992*, published by the prestigious London art publisher, Lund Humphries. With a Foreword by the Prince of Wales, the book was launched at the Carlton Tower in April. The launch party was attended by many of David's friends and patrons and celebrated in a spread in *Hello* magazine, with photographs of Viscount Linley, Sir Alec Guinness, Princesses Katya and Jean Galitzine, the Begum Agha Khan and Prince Hussein, among others. The guests of honour were Prince and Princess Michael of Kent. One of the photographs was of Mel Coleman and his fiancée Annabel Croft standing either side of a remarkable bronze which David had recently completed, *Gilli Walking*. At the end of the book was a series of short essays, some written by David's patrons and others by some of his 'subjects'. There were also one or two by critics.

Pamela Tudor-Craig, an eminent art historian, chose to write her contribution around David's remarkable sculpture of his wife:

. . . The day after her death he returned to his studio. In order that he might mourn constructively, the sculptor deliberately set himself the most difficult task he could devise. He modelled the figure directly in plaster, because it is the hardest medium to use. He chose the walking posture because it is the most subtle, and one that he had not attempted before. Her arms are open and outstretched. She used to walk like that when she was glad. Her beautiful feet tread without haste and without hesitation. She knows the way. As always happens when an artist is in touch with his deeper self, the sculpture carries more than a single meaning. David Wynne's bronzes have always been conceived in many dimensions, have told from every angle, and from every deflection of an angle. Here there are the added dimensions of time, of a lifetime and beyond a lifetime. The figure of Gilli walks towards him, as she came to his arms in the days of their courtship. Her back is modelled with an equal delicacy of loving remembrance; she walks away from him like Persephone entering the Underworld. Then, as all who have been bereaved discover, she walks beside him through the days of their separation. And finally there is the hint, and more than a hint, of the Gilli who will return to greet him when his time comes. The volume's dedication is simple. 'This book is dedicated to my beloved wife Gilli, without whose help and encouragement my sculpture would be much worse.'

Edward Burn also remembered Gilli in his essay. The law professor 'had been amazed that my old pupils wanted to mark my retirement by a bronze for the Law Library [at Christ Church, Oxford], and I was delighted that David had accepted their invitation.' He describes what happened next:

> . . . On that following Tuesday began a friendship which I treasure. I arrived by 9 a.m. at David's house overlooking Wimbledon Common. I rang the bell; the dog barked; and David opened the door. We had mugs of tea in the kitchen and I was led to the studio with its varied examples of David's genius. In the centre was a chair on a dais, looking like the chair for *Mastermind* candidates. I sat in it and wondered apprehensively what was going to happen. David made it so easy for both of us. We talked of this and that, and of him and her, and of words and the delights of Dr Johnson's *Dictionary* and Robert Graves's poetry. We compiled a First XI of English poets, with easy unanimity on the first nine. I was struck by David's insatiable curiosity and enthusiasm for everything in which he was interested: before he sculpted a dolphin or a racehorse, he swam with the one and rode the other. Meanwhile David was measuring my skull and recording the anatomical details on paper. I found the whole process strange and somewhat unnerving, delicately though it was done. As time passed, David started on the clay likeness, and I watched a work of outstanding craftsmanship develop into a perceptive work of art . . . . David was not, however, the only creator of the head. I met Gilli, their family of three generations and a pupil sculptor who worked in marble, all living in the large Georgian house. It was Gilli who was his best critic. He would ask her to come in and see how the head was getting on. She came in, gave a quick look and a gentle laconic reply. 'Make him smile. He does, you know. And the forehead is too high.' David thought for a moment. 'Yes, I see. You are quite right.' To avoid embarrassment to me, I was sent out of the studio while he used a sort of wire cheese-cutter, severed the forehead laterally, removed a slice of it and then joined up the remainder. Gilli was a very dear person and I got to know her well. We shared a love of gardens, and as I walked around hers with her, I came to realise what a superb partnership they were . . .

Following Gilli's death, David also completed the commission for Highgrove. *Goddess of the Wood* was carved from a large block of Rosso Orbico marble, forty-two inches high. The composition became simpler as the idea matured. Prince Charles had commissioned the carving for a specific place in a quiet woodland garden, within an oak grove. The figure was to be similar in feeling to *Gaia*. David had tried, over the years, to let his carvings perform like rocks,

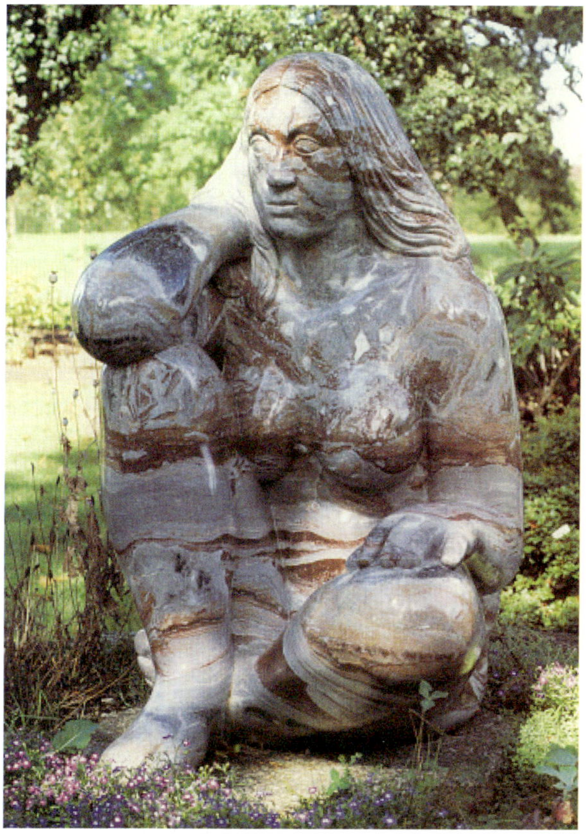

Goddess of the Wood

so that they would blend and flow with the natural world. They should, he thought, always seek to seem calm and still. He had always been struck by Rodin's advice, 'Contemplate your work at twilight.' Many hours of deep thought had gone into the creation of the work. The *News of the World* saw the sculpture perhaps predictably. On 4 August 1991, their correspondent, Clive Goodman, reported that:

> Prince Charles has bought Princess Di a huge statue that looks just like her. The twice-life-size marble girl was his surprise tenth-wedding-anniversary gift to thirty-year-old Di last Monday. And the first time she saw it was at a special unveiling ceremony in the woods at their Gloucestershire estate, Highgrove. A member of staff said: 'It's got longer hair than the Princess, but the face looks just like her . . . '

Even more press nonsense was to erupt over David's next royal commission. HRH The Queen Mother was to be ninety-one on 5 August 1991. To provide the public with a means of contributing towards a notable celebration of her long life, Prince Michael of Kent launched an appeal for one million pounds to create an ornate gate in Hyde Park. The Queen Mother Gates were to be sited at the entrance to South Carriage Drive, just off the lower end of Park Lane, across from Apsley House and Hyde Park Corner. It was an ambitious project. The scheme included adding several landscaped acres to Hyde Park, and reconstructing a part of the road system and the roundabout between Knightsbridge, Park Lane and Piccadilly. According to *Country Life* of 1 August 1991:

> Four artists and sculptors were invited by the Prince to submit designs for the gates. Giuseppe Lund was chosen to design them, and David Wynn [*sic*] the sculpture at their centre. Although the existing gates in the park are Edwardian and Victorian, it was decided not to follow their example but to create a more elegant, feminine design conveying a 'feeling of celebration'.

The gates do, indeed, mark a departure from the somewhat rigid lines of Victorian and Edwardian tradition by incorporating animals and flora, including the Glamis rose. 'The Queen Mother is reputedly "fully supportive of and thrilled with the scheme," says the Prince.' In an exclusive interview

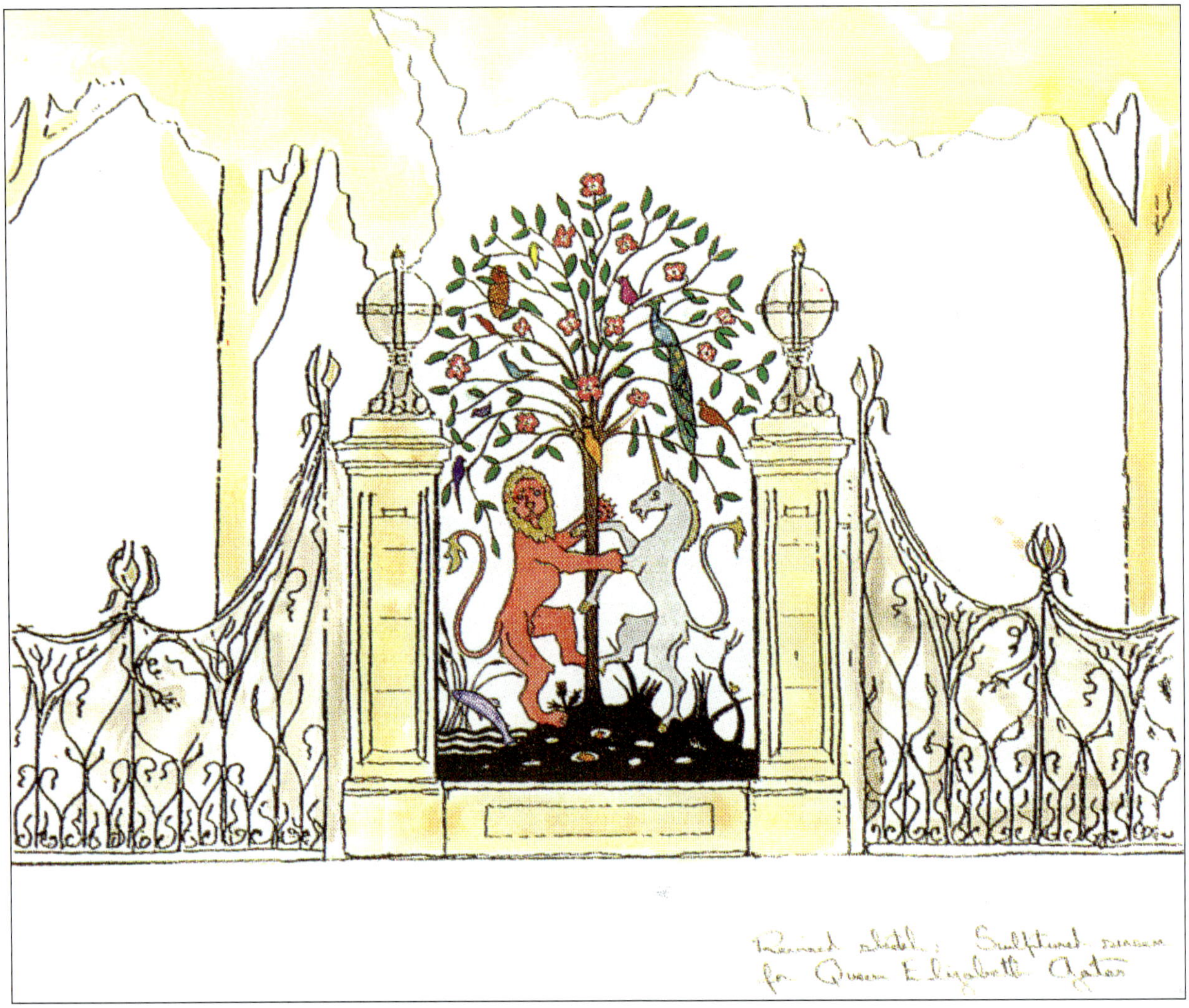

Preliminary drawing for the Queen Mother Gates

for *Hello*, published during the week of the launch of the appeal, the Prince told the magazine that he wanted them to be:

> exciting celebration gates, which would be of today. I didn't want them to be merely a pastiche of the many examples of Edwardian gates around the Park. I suggested that David Wynne take for his theme the royal supporters – the lion and the unicorn – and go to town on them . . . We have also included Glamis roses in the tree of life and a splendid Scotch salmon, because she is a great fisher-woman. We also thought it would be nice to have either a parrot or a peacock because, of course, she was the last Empress of India.

He also wanted to revive the idea of colour in public monuments. ' . . . the Queen Mother Gates will be brightly coloured. It was only when Prince Albert died that everything was painted black.' The launch was not without its problems. The *Daily Telegraph* of 24 July 1991 reported, under its headline 'Climbdown over lion in Queen Mother's gates':

> An ornate gate in Hyde Park to celebrate the life of the Queen Mother has been redesigned because the Royal family objected to the Lion of England clambering about 'in an undignified fashion' in the branches of a tree . . . Drawings of the central panel of the 100 ft. pair of iron gates, commissioned from the sculptor David Wynne, were printed and ready for circulation. However, Prince Michael of Kent . . . said the design was being changed at the last minute. He said: 'The central panel is having to be changed because of a decision taken within my family. The design showed the lion in the branches of the tree and it was felt that this perhaps took the heraldic theme too far. As a matter of fact lions do climb trees, and no one knows better than David Wynne, who has been to Botswana to see them. But it was felt that the lion should be put back on the ground, side by side with the unicorn.' Mr Wynne . . . has incorporated . . . a pheasant, which he thought would represent her reign as the Last Empress of India, until he was told by the Queen Mother that it is a Chinese game bird, not Indian. He said: 'The gates are for the Queen Mother and, of course, we would rather have them the way she wants them, so I was more than happy to alter my design.'

The Times of the same date went further:

> Commissioned to design a feature panel of ironwork in the centre of the gates, David Wynne, the sculptor, produced a light-hearted assembly of Queen Mother motifs, including assorted Scottish wildlife, the lion and the unicorn from the Scottish royal arms and a tree of Elizabeth of Glamis roses. While the unicorn pranced with heraldic correctness at the base of the tree, the lion was up among the branches like a cat after a sparrow. It was, Mr Wynne explained, a bit of fun. New drawings rushed out for yesterday's appeal launch showed the Scottish lion back on the ground and properly rampant after the Queen Mother, the Queen and the Prince of Wales had studied the original design and found it a little over the top . . . Guisseppe Lund, a Shropshire-based ironsmith who won the commission to produce the main gates, yesterday described his sensuously curved, intricate filigree design as 'feminine', and in dramatic contrast to the other gates into Hyde Park which are uniform in their Victorian and Edwardian severity. The gates will be coloured, partly by paint and partly by the use of oxidised bronze, titanium and stainless steel . . . Discreet approaches to industry have produced an unspecified sum towards the gates' construction, in return for sponsors' names being inscribed on the piece. Money is being raised by curious means. Individual donors are invited to buy a £1 stamp . . . and send it on a postcard to the appeal headquarters. The Royal Mail will donate the full amount of every stamp and carry the mail free . . .

Not everyone thought the design was appropriate. The *New Statesman* predictably considered the design 'appalling' and numerous letters appeared throughout the national press angrily suggesting the money be spent on hospitals and nursing homes. The public appeal also ran into trouble. The stamp scheme was not, despite the active

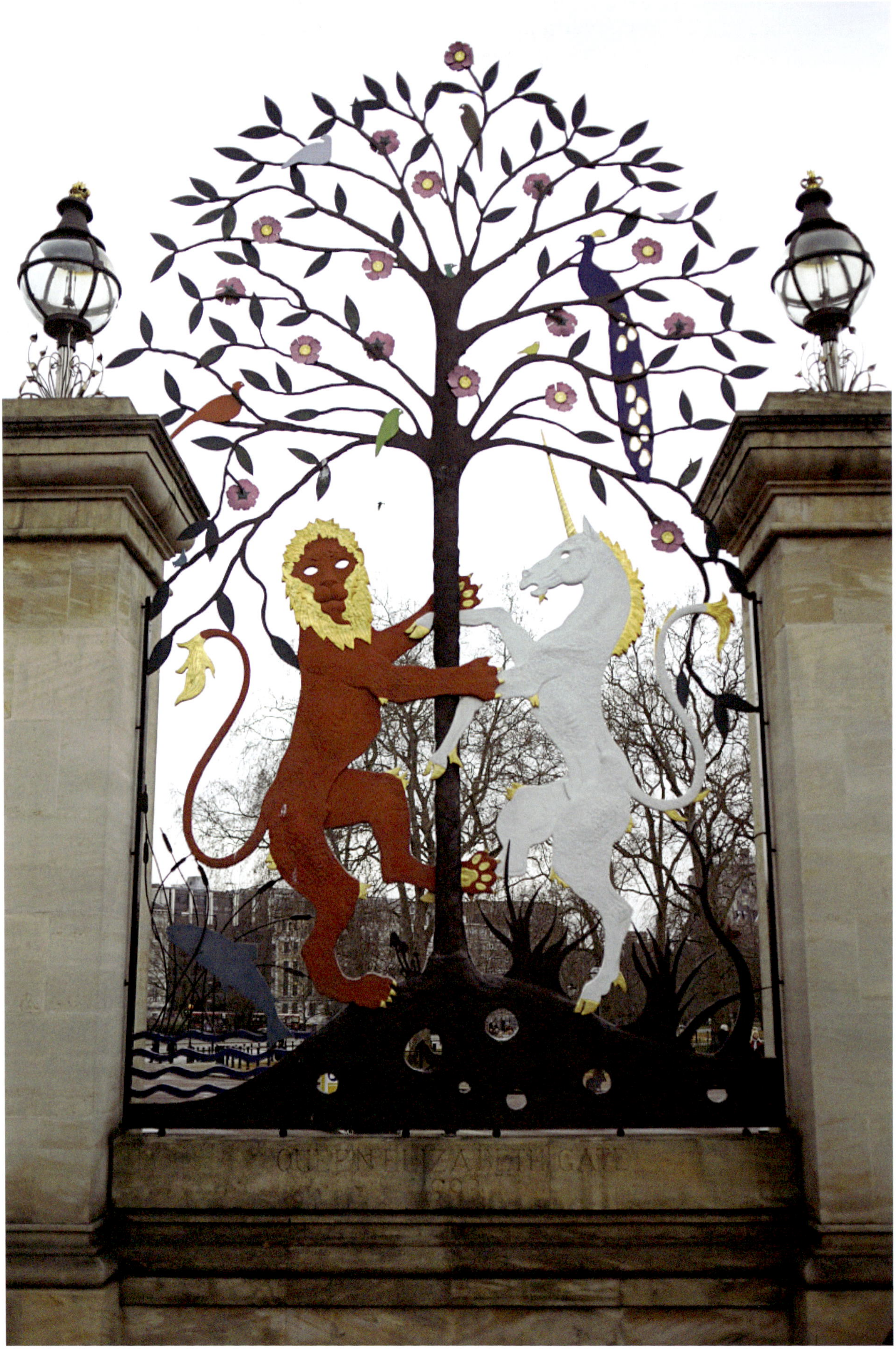

support of the tabloid press, a success. In February 1992, the *Sunday Times* printed a letter from Richard Briggs, chairman of the appeal, answering a front-page article from the previous Sunday's newspaper suggesting that the appeal for the gates was in difficulty. Admitting that the stamp promotion had failed, he went on to report: 'work has already started on the realignment of the approaches to the gate, while funds continue to come in from all over the country at a satisfactory rate'. The furore continued to run. The *Daily Express* on 7 July 1992 reported that the South African ambassador was:

> rattling a collecting tin and has already raised more than £4,000 . . . Unhappily the gates tribute . . . is not meeting the same response among British subjects. Due this year, the opening ceremony is postponed to Easter 1993. Prince Michael admits: 'The main difficulty is that we launched the appeal in the middle of a recession.' The Queen Mother's stated view is: 'Hurry up and build it.'

There were legal tussles, with lawyers from both sides, between the builders and Westminster Council about the rerouting of the cars which spun around the busy junction. In the end, all was resolved. An Act of Parliament would have been required to site the gates on their original spot and so, as a compromise, it was decided to reposition the gates several feet back, on park land. Legal and financial concerns finally assuaged, the *Evening Standard* of 9 October 1992 could report:

> Major work starts next week on the Queen Mother Gates project, now the appeal has topped £1 million, nearly two-thirds of its target. Workmen will begin quarrying stone for the supporting columns, tested for its durability, from a 400-year-old quarry at Chipping Norton, Gloucestershire. At the same time Chelsea sculptor David Wynne is to start work on the gates' central royal motif . . .

By 1 February 1993, *The Times* could print photographs of David 'with a clay relief sculpture of a lion and unicorn that will be cast in iron' [it was bronze] and Giusseppe Lund 'oxidising stainless-steel surfaces at his workshop in the New Forest'. The Londoner's Diary in the *Evening Standard* of 13 May 1993 reported that:

> workers toiling on the lavish gate currently being erected . . . have, I hear, become accustomed to the twice daily appearances of the Queen Mother's car, inside of which she can be seen leaping from one side to the other, the better to survey their progress. She has, it seems, suggested one improvement. 'The Queen Mother told me recently she should like to see a pigeon represented as a symbol of London,' says one of those involved with the gate's construction. This mild request is said to have induced a modicum of panic, partly because negotiations with the sculptor, David Wynne, of the gate's central section, have been delicate . . . Happily, Wynne assures me that no amendment is necessary. 'There already is a pigeon,' he explains. 'There are nine birds in all, including a peacock because the Queen Mother was the last Empress of India. I did receive a last-minute request from Prince Michael. He wants to paint one of the birds.'

By the 7 June, the *Daily Telegraph* could report that:

> Engineers lowered into place yesterday the most colourful sculpture London has seen for many a year . . . the centrepiece bronze sculpture of a red lion and a white unicorn on either side of an 18ft tree of life is by Mr David Wynne. Also depicted are a salmon, a thistle, a rabbit, a shrew and several birds, including a wren and a woodpecker. The sculpture produced a range of reactions from bystanders, from sighs of 'magnificent' to comments that it 'looks like the entrance to Disneyland'.

And finally, on 6 July 1993, just before the Queen Mother's ninety-third birthday and just after David's sixty-seventh, the controversial hundred-and-twenty-foot-long and twenty-one-foot-high monument was unveiled by the Queen. David now had more large public works of art sited within her nation's capital city than any other sculptor of his generation.

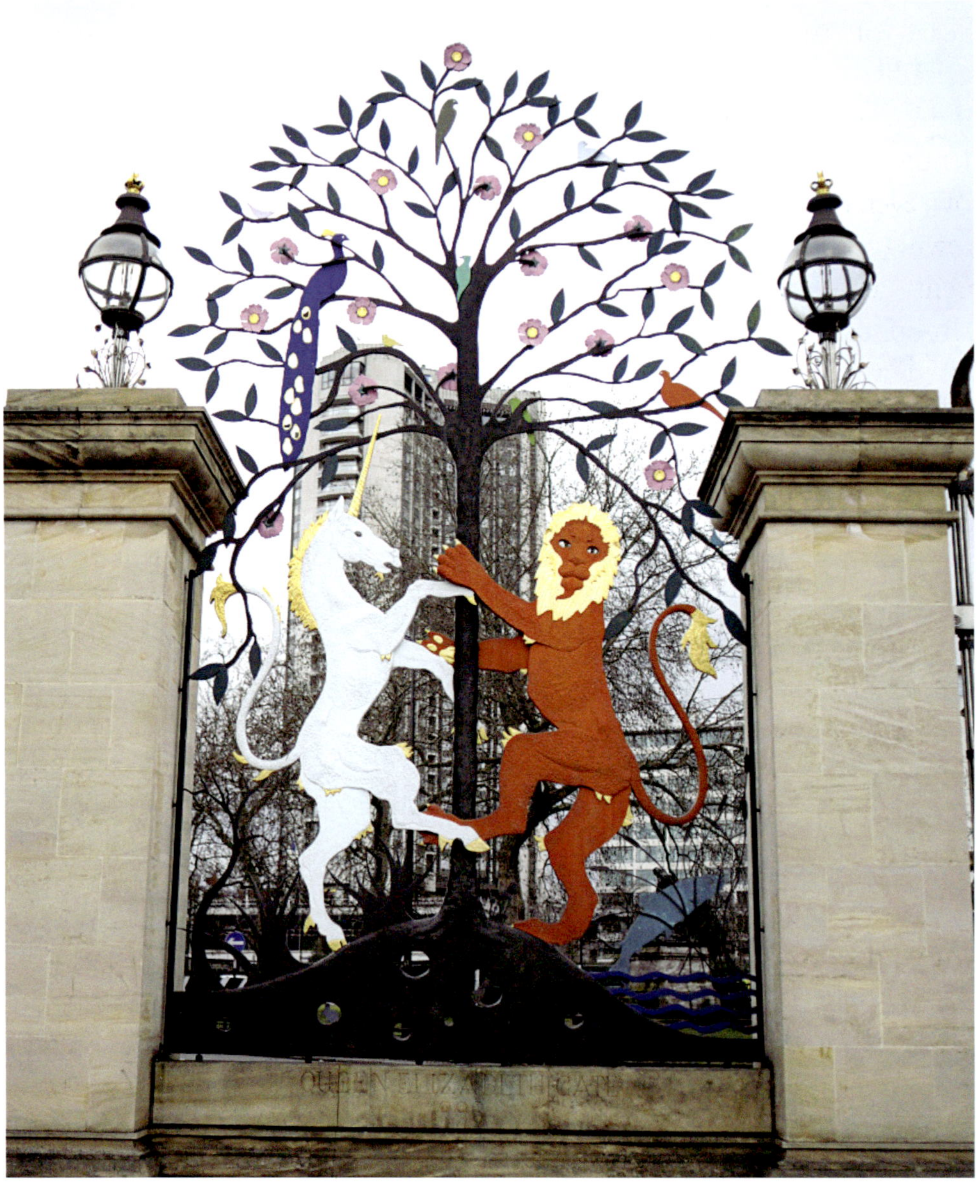

20

IN 1992, David decided to sell Rushmere. It seemed to him that with Gilli's death the heart of the whole remarkable enterprise had somehow been stilled. The childrenwere beginning to live independently and the vast house seemed too big now, even empty. He bought a much smaller town house, part of a residential development of a cluster of Victorian buildings in Fulham, near to Putney Bridge. He had a medium-sized studio created there, and though there had been talk of moving out of London altogether, he and Robin decided to build and share a large studio space together, where the big pieces could be made. They had the new studio built from scratch, in Northamptonshire where Robin and her husband Paddy lived.

David had met Candida Bond just before Rushmere was sold. Her father had asked him to sculpt a portrait head of his daughter, but after the customary first meeting between artist and sitter which David always insisted on, David suggested he sculpt a full figure and, to her father's surprise, the commission went ahead. Candida afterwards became David's assistant, moving into the new Fulham studio and developing, over the five years she stayed there, into an accomplished sculptor in her own right.

A year later, in 1993, his *Bologna Figures* were finished. Marchese Gian Luca Salina Amorini Bolognini was an Italian banker who with his wife had been the subject of the commission:

> . . . In order to commemorate the restoration of our family house in Bologna, David suggested a sculpture of my wife and myself. Obviously, he said, this group would have to be naked. After some hesitation we both agreed. Posing was an extraordinary experience. I learned the secrets of the creation of the human body, its complexity, the immense care taken in measuring, the sheer physical effort of producing from virtually nothing the spines and then the bodies themselves. In the end what matters is the harmony between the two bodies, the group, and the emotion that transpires. Then the movement. David . . . infuses movement into the sculpture, movement that emerged from the classical beauty of its form.

In 1994, David was awarded the OBE by the Queen. Stowe commissioned a portrait head of Lord Cheshire, VC. Plans were beginning to be made for a major retrospective, which opened at the Mall Galleries in 1997. It was called 'A Celebration of Life: David Wynne – 50 Years of Sculpture'. It was the largest exhibition of his work yet organised, with seventy-nine exhibits. As David told a TV crew who were shooting yet another documentary while the exhibition was being created, 'I wanted to see what my work over the last fifty years looked like. If it was any good.' Alongside the maquettes of his public sculpture, including *Boy with a Dolphin*, *Gaia* and *Tyne God*, were twenty-one African animal sculptures and portrait heads of the Beatles and Yehudi Menuhin. The earliest work on show was *Entry into Jerusalem*, made in 1954, and Pamela Tudor-Craig, in her Introduction to the exhibition's catalogue, highlighted David's most recent, *Awakening Lovers*, which he completed in 1996. Carved from a block of Carrara marble, the piece was destined to be bought by Chris de Burgh for his home in Ireland. The year 1996 also marked David's seventieth birthday. Tudor-Craig's Introduction considered David:

> . . . a master equally in marble or metal. [He] creates in both mediums, so in a sense he has two artistic personalities. In bronze he can convey the pounce of a leopard, the quiver of a horse, the fast volley of a tennis player, or the finger print of music. All that is swift and fleeting, scarce seen by casual eyes, he catches in molten metal. His bronze heads evoke the breathing essence of the sitters, from the very old to the newborn. Who else could capture the first hints of personality? He is, quite simply, the best portrait sculptor of his generation. In marble, on the other hand, he discovers the quiet plenitudes at the heart of mystery. In bronze he exults in the dance of life: in marble he reveals his own still depths; for this quicksilver man is a philosopher in stone.
>
> In a century when art has been used to express fragmentation, destruction and despair, David Wynne has stood for wholeness, sanity, compassion, and the celebration of all things lovely. Witness his most recent piece, *Awakening Lovers*. Does it not come from the country of the human heart?

In the following year came devastating news. David was in Africa when his son Edward telephoned to tell his father that his brother, Roly, had killed himself. He had thrown himself from a rooftop of a high-rise

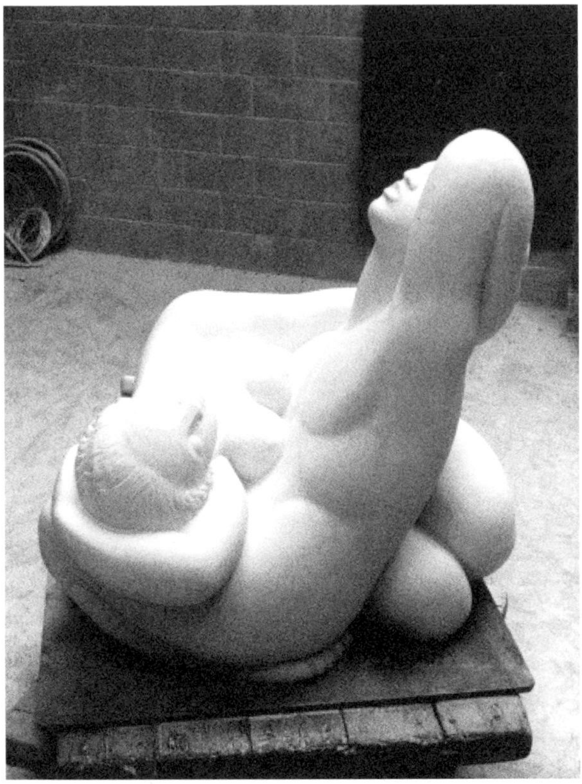

Awakening Lovers

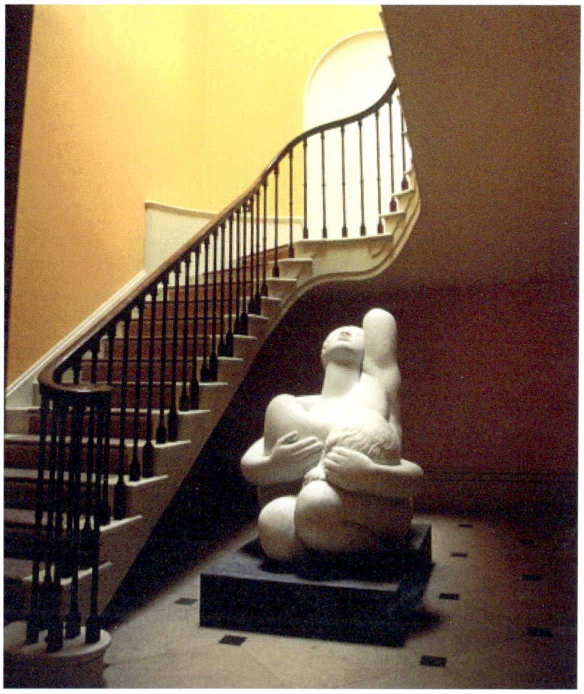

Awakening Lovers at Chris de Burgh's house

building when he was supposed to be in the care of a psychiatric hospital. Roly was the younger son of Gilli and David. Beautiful, talented and highly intelligent, his short life was fraught with incident. An abiding memory, which his father and siblings all attest to, is of Roly's hatred of authority. Having got himself expelled from Westminster, he maintained a rebellious disregard for rules of any kind, which often resulted in his being arrested. Usually it was for minor drug offences, though there was the odd aggressive incident. He once broke a police car's window in retaliation when his girlfriend was stopped and questioned. It was not unusual for David to be contacted in the early hours of the morning to be told that Roly had been restrained somewhere and could he be collected? The worst incident was when Roly was involved in a fatal car accident. He was hitchhiking, a girl passenger was killed and Roly suffered serious head injuries. Eventually, the boy was sectioned. He had attempted suicide before, once even lying down on a railway track to await an underground train, though the power was quickly suspended when it became clear what was going on.

David had visited Roly in the hospital just before he left for Africa. Roly had asked him to come and see him on his return; the boy had always liked hearing of his father's adventures. David was only going for ten days and his last memory is of seeing the boy 'walking away, looking fine'. Their relationship was profound. The model for his father's best-known sculpture, the young Roly had never objected to the arduous hours of posing he had to do, arms outstretched, as *Boy with a Dolphin* was created. Roly's musical skills were encouraged early by both his parents. Once, at a restaurant, he was handed a lute, perhaps the most difficult of stringed instruments, yet much to the amazement of the lute's owner, Roly mastered its technique in minutes. He was a gifted graphic artist, renowned for creating complex Gothic- and Celtic-scripted comic books or astrological charts.

Another vivid memory of David's is of Roly spending every evening of one year creating the most wonderful astrological card for his father to have at Christmas. But there was always a darker side. A horrific unhappiness. David remembers a conversation they had once had, when his son was young. Roly had clambered into bed with his father and asked David if he had ever felt that it wasn't worth being in the world at all. It was so awful. Had his father ever felt like that? David told him that he hadn't, but suggested, if he liked, that Roly tell him about it. The boy merely replied that it was all right. He

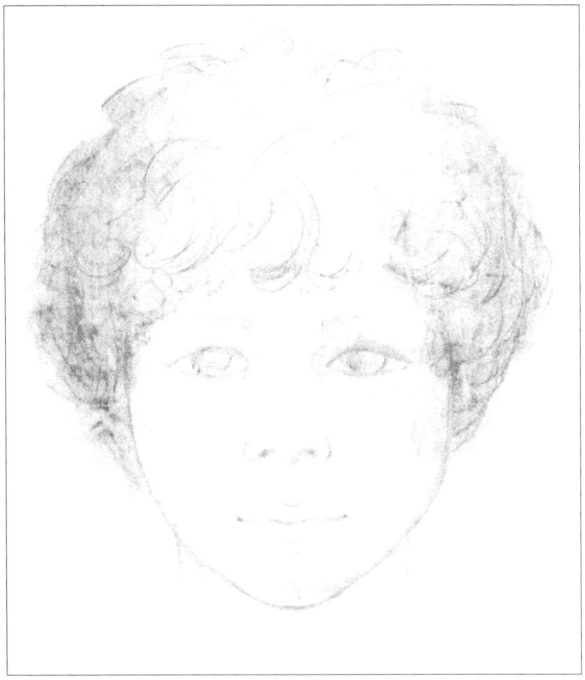

Roly drawings for the *Boy with a Dolphin*

had just thought his father might have felt like he did.

There is no comfort for any parent whose offspring dies before them. It is not how things are meant to be. David took what comfort he could – from his family, but also from those who knew his son. He remembers meeting a Romany friend of Roly's after his son's suicide. Roly had spent a great deal of his time with travellers, especially in Wales. The man approached David. ' "You're Roly's dad, ain't you?" and I said, "Yes," and he said, "Don't worry about Roly. He's an angel." ' David was to discover the exact same reaction from all the many other friends of Roly's. In his short life, he had garnered love, and in homage to that, an inscription was later added to the base of the iconic statue by the flowing Thames, where Roly's young body sways for ever above the surging dolphin.

Again, it was in his work that David found comfort. In November 2000, in the Lady Chapel at Ely Cathedral, the Prince of Wales unveiled David's life-size *Virgin Mary* statue. Carved from Portland stone, the statue had been painted, perhaps in response to the success of the Queen Mother Gates, in vibrant blue and gold. The ceremony was a light-hearted affair. Prince Charles had recently invested David with his OBE, making the wry comment that the sculptor would probably never wear his honour, but here it was anyway. At the unveiling, the prince had wanted to know, 'What have you got for us now!' David pointed up to the statue and Charles asked who had posed for it. David suggested that if he got it unveiled, he'd introduce the heir to the throne to the beautiful Dutch girl, Sanne, who had been the model. The statue's vivid sexuality inevitably caused some concern. There was much in the press about its 'carnal' pose. On a later visit to the

Virgin Mary, Ely

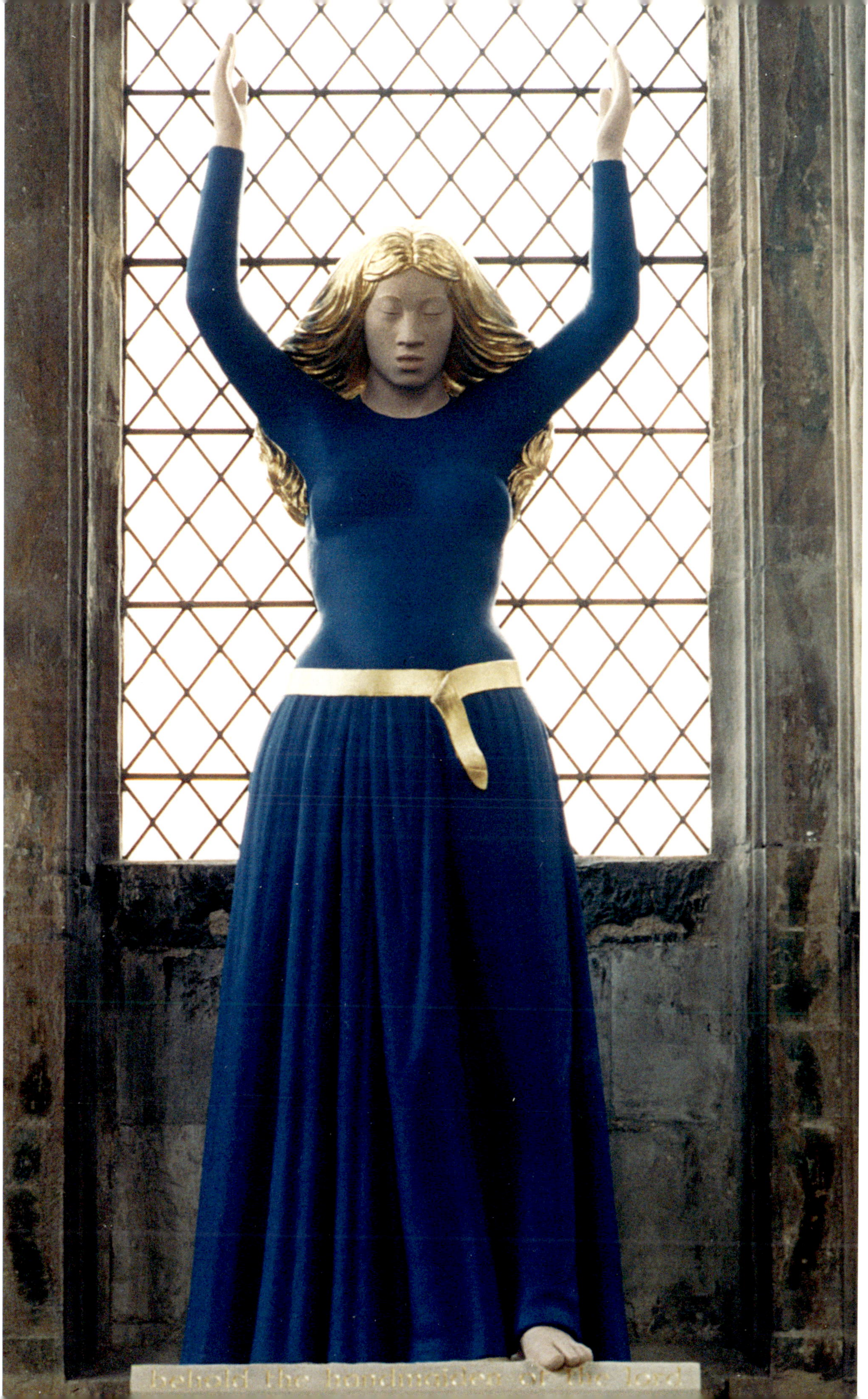
behold the handmaiden of the lord

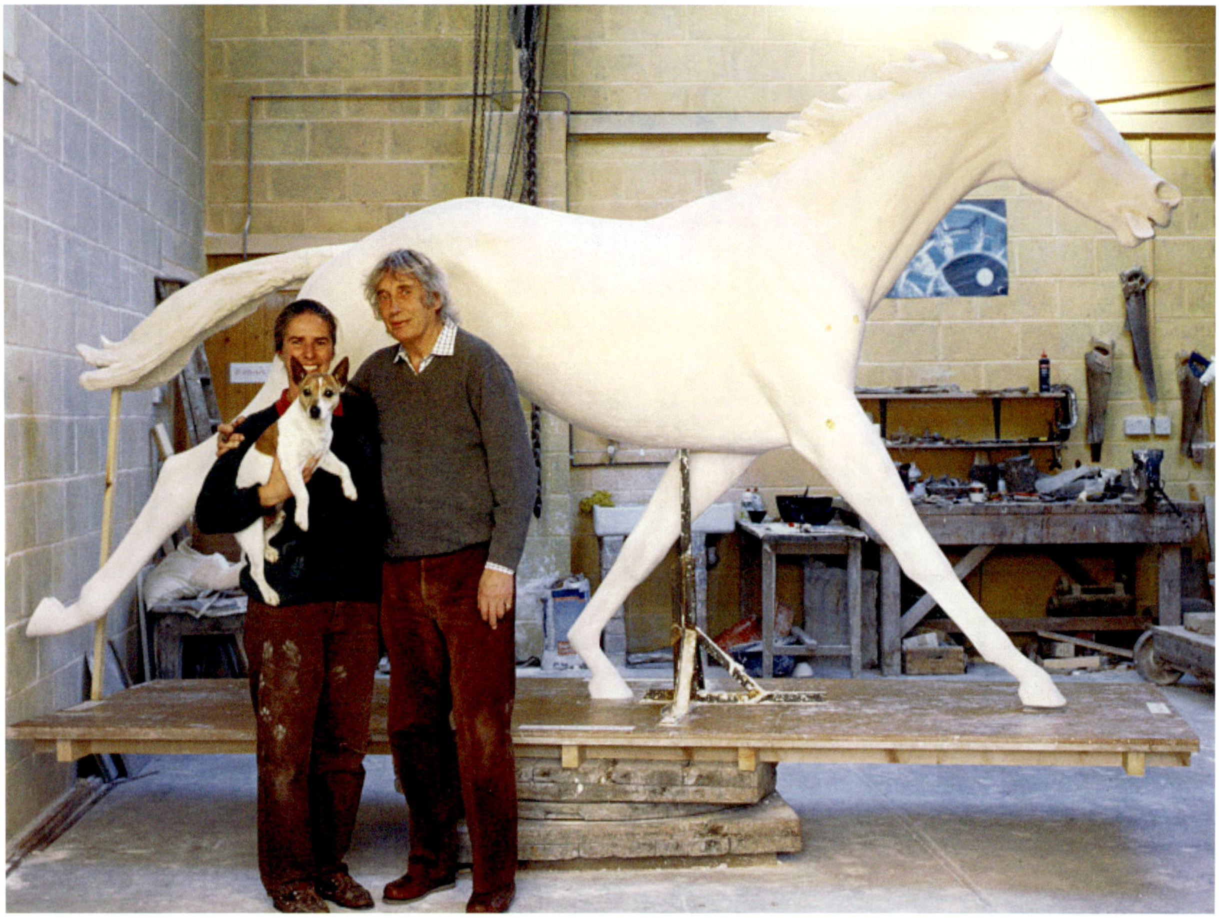

Shergar with David, Robin and the dog, Jos

cathedral, while David was talking to the Dean of Ely, a woman came up to the sculptor and asked if he had carved the statue. David said yes, and the woman told him she thought it disgusting. When the Dean asked her why, she said that, well, the Virgin was pregnant. 'Were she not,' replied the Dean,' I wouldn't have a job here!'

David's next commissions included the larger-than-life bronzes of the Aga Khan's racehorses, Shahrastani and Sinndar. He had earlier created a remarkable statue of another famous racehorse, Sharif Dancer. Sheikh Mohammed, the horse's owner, had seen David's sculpture of Shergar at the Aga Khan's chateau and had asked David if he would consider a commission from him. Shergar had been an exceptionally friendly and sweet animal, even allowing Robin to pull his forelegs out so that David could get a proper look at him. The Sheikh's stud was on the outskirts of Newmarket and, much to David's delight, Michael Stout was also this horse's trainer. But unlike Shergar, the horse was wilful, and though Robin and David were able carefully to measure and draw the animal, David persuaded the Sheikh that a sculpture a third of life-size, with the horse's groom portrayed, holding the bridle, would capture him best. The Sheikh was persuaded by David's point that in many of George Stubbs's paintings the human figure is used as a device to give scale to the horse. It also

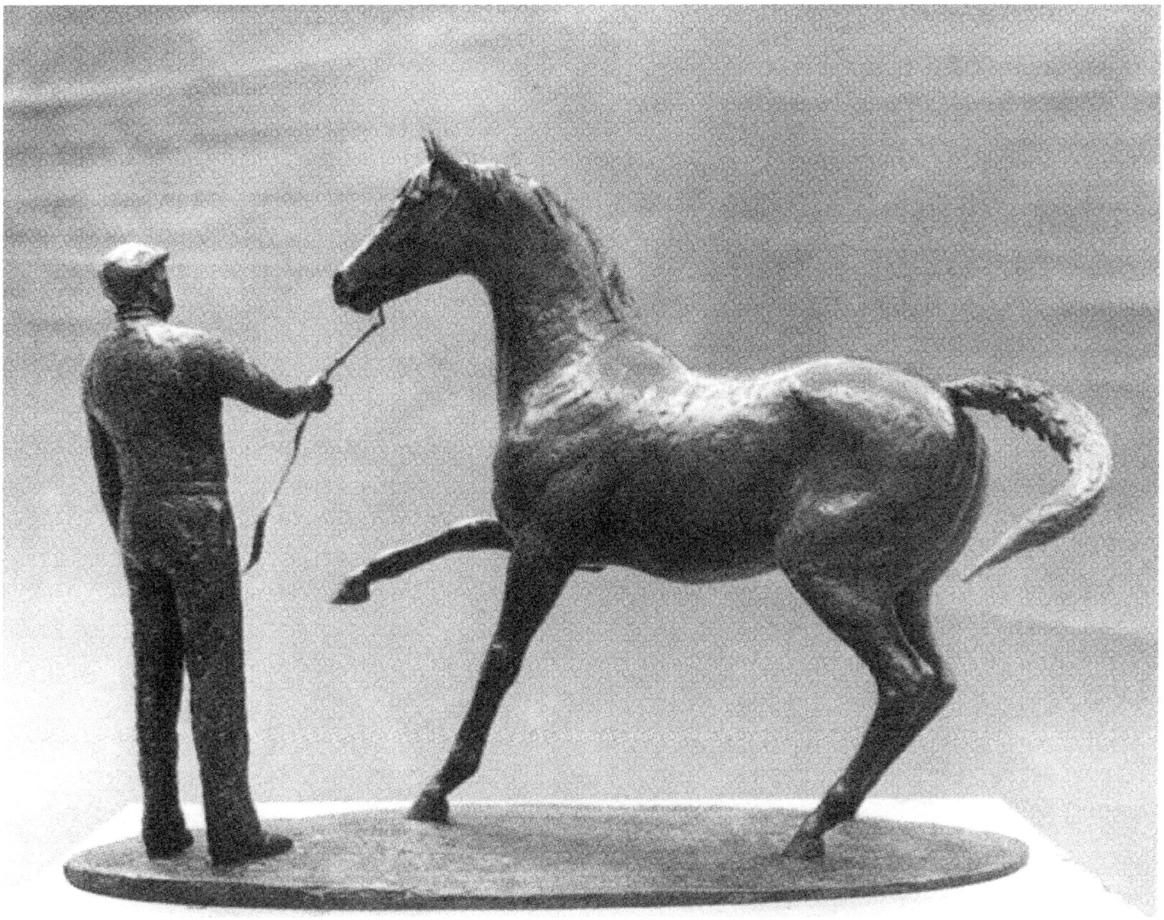

Sharif Dancer

meant, as Robin observed:

> . . . you had the quietness of the groom . . . to give a balance to the spirit and the life of the horse . . . That's why you wanted him standing there, somebody who was going to be calm and reassuring and a rock for this young adolescent kid on the block. The horse was incredibly lonely. Horses are social animals and he was in a paddock on his own. He got bored rigid. He wanted to play games. Just to balance his lively nature.

For the two other horses, Shahrastani and Sinndar, David insisted that, along with Robin, Andy Andrews went with him to Kentucky. Shahrastani was another remarkable animal. The horse had won the Derby. Two small sculptures were made in America, along with the inevitable copious drawings and measurings. The two large sculptures were finished in Northamptonshire and then taken over to Ireland, to be placed permanently on display at the Aga Khan's stud.

Chris de Burgh had already bought a considerable number of David's sculptures, and when the singer heard that David would be in Ireland, he invited him to hear him sing at Wexford. David protested he was too tired, but Tom, the manager of the hotel in which they were staying, insisted he drive them to the concert. Tom wanted to finish his Guinness before starting the journey across country, a journey which took hours.

Finally at the concert, Tom continually stumbled up from his seat for a refill. He continued drinking at dinner afterwards and would have driven them back had not Robin wrestled the car keys from the, by now, inebriated hotelier. Back at the hotel, David was told there had been a change of rooms. A wedding party had unexpectedly arrived, and David's things had been moved to another suite. After more Irish stout, the trio made their way to the top of the hotel. David discovered that his cufflinks, which he had put in a drawer in the first room, had been left behind. Back downstairs to retrieve them, David and Robin searched as Tom, deciding the room was too hot, went to open a window. Losing his balance, he toppled head first out of the window, which was on the first floor. Robin caught him by his ankles and yanked him back inside. 'Robin,' says Tom, 'you've saved my life. Come down to the bar and we'll have a drink.'

David first met Chris de Burgh when Chris was twelve years old. David and Gilli were staying at Bargy Castle, in Ireland, with the future world famous singer's family, and David remembers playing harmonica with Chris on guitar at the local pub, performing folk and blues together in typical hootenanny style. It was Gilli who suggested some years later that the young man come to stay at Rushmere to benefit from the very special atmosphere which had been created there. Here, under Gilli's constant eye, the Wynne children played their music while Donovan practised or George Harrison dropped by or David took a break from sculpting a portrait head of Joan Baez. It was no surprise therefore, as Chris began to develop a successful musical career, that his relationship with David evolved into a long and enduring friendship. The singer, like so many of David's other famous friends, has become an enthusiastic patron, purchasing many pieces for his Irish estate.

Patrons have always played a crucial role in the development of David's art and the sculptor seems always to have managed to stay close to them both emotionally, as a friend, and financially, in that the commissions have continued to flow throughout his long and sometimes troubled life. This symbiosis is neatly summed up by Alistair McAlpine, a patron for nearly half a century, in his Afterword to the catalogue of David's 'Celebration of Life' exhibition at the Mall Galleries in the spring of 1997:

> Thirty-three years ago I was captivated by David Wynne and his work and bought three pieces of sculpture that I could not really afford at the time.
>
> During the sixties I had a frenetic period of collecting and I learned about sculpture, in its many forms both ancient and modern. I visited David time and time again, often buying his work. As I look back on that first meeting with David Wynne, whether it was by intuition or by luck that I decided to buy his work, of one thing I am certain, I was right.

Subtitled '50 Years of Sculpture', the Mall exhibition was in effect a retrospective of David's career. Aged seventy-one, still battling at times with deep depression, bereft of his much loved wife and now living in less grand accommodation in Fulham, he continued to work, as the catalogue put it, 'prolifically'. Seventy-nine pieces were on show, ranging from his 1954 sculpture *Entry into Jerusalem* to his latest African sculpture *Stalking Leopard*, completed the year of the exhibition. Maquettes of some of his best-known work, including *Boy with a Dolphin* and *Grizzly Bear*, stood alongside portrait heads of Yehudi Menuhin, the Beatles, as well as Chris de Burgh. And *Sleeping Girl*, created in 1963, was near to *Sanne*, a statue of David's latest muse, and also just completed in 1997. A film crew shot footage of the large and comprehensive exhibition, where the epic *Tyne God* maquette nestled against an intimate statue of a heron, only seventeen inches high. Looking into the camera and asked what the exhibition was about, David simply answered, 'To see if I'm any good.'

Three years before, in 1994, David had been presented with his OBE, much to his delight, by one of his most distinguished patrons, the Prince of Wales. And seven years later, in May 2004, the *Daily Telegraph* actually began its review of David's latest exhibition with an allusion to David's ability to foster patronage:

> Like Jack Vettriano, Beryl Cook and David Shepherd, self-taught sculptor David Wynne is an artist whose popularity has never been matched by critical acclaim. But then, Wynne has never depended too much on the opinion of the critics. His list of patrons, from the Aga Khan to the British Royal Family, has kept him immune. And his work . . . is admired by millions.
>
> Wynne has not had to depend on art dealers either. But, to celebrate his seventy-eighth birthday, his first exhibition in a dealer's gallery for more than twenty years will open at Nevil Keating Tollemache in St James's on Wednesday . . .

The exhibition ran from the end of May

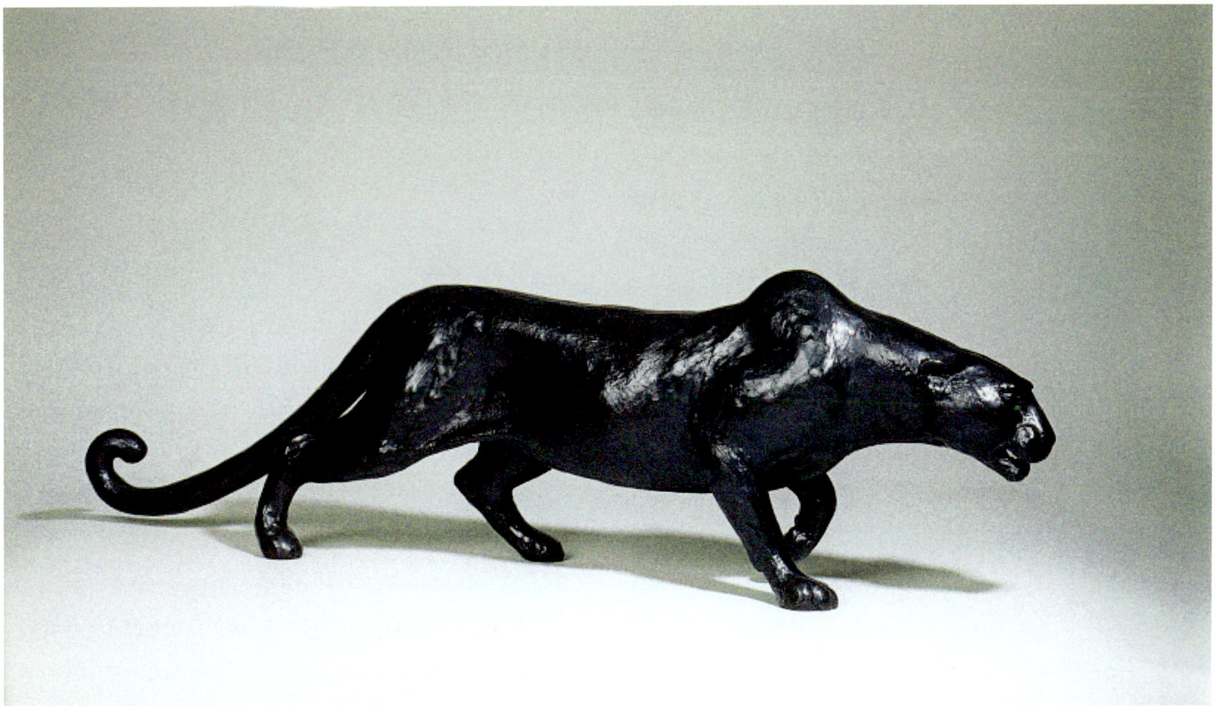

Stalking leopard

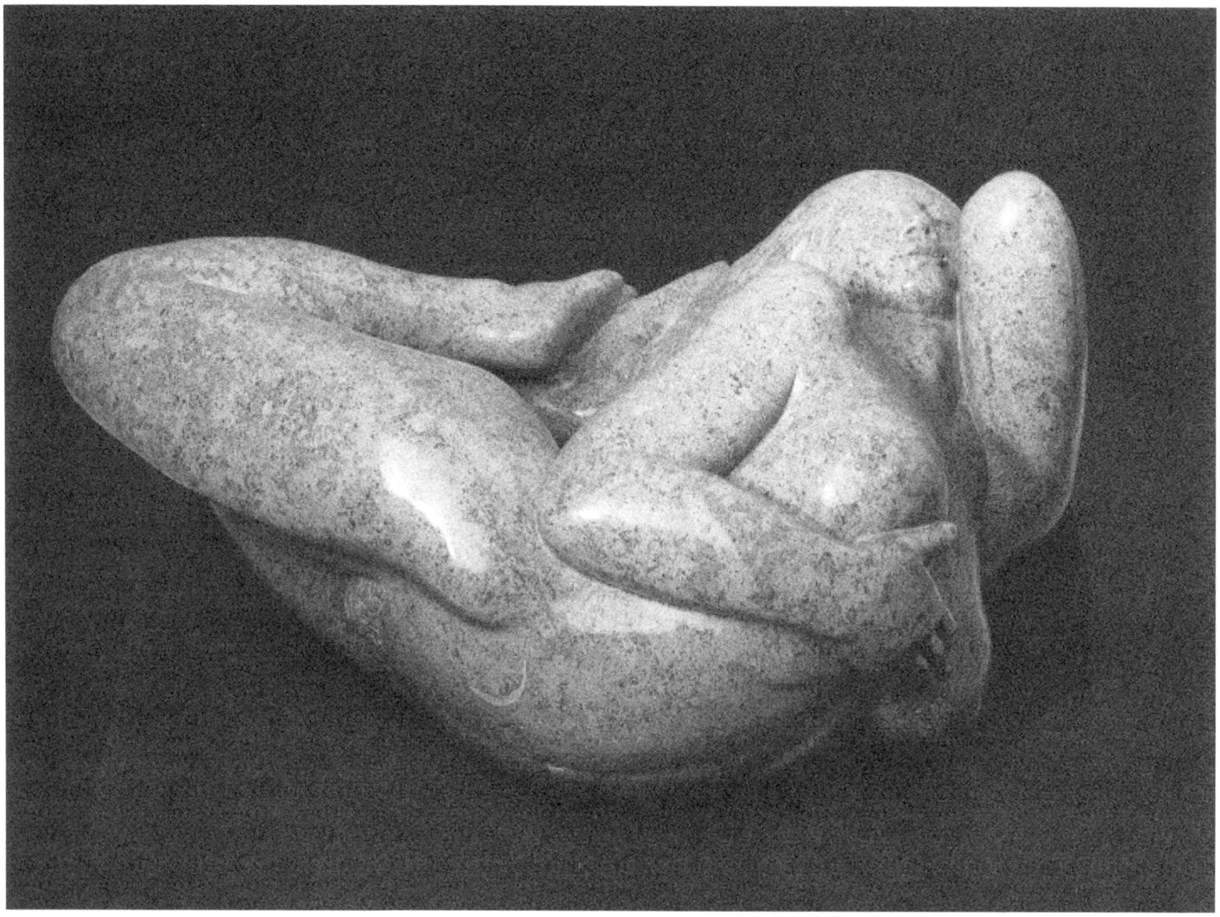

Sleeping Girl

to mid-June in the fashionable gallery, and forty-one sculptures were on show, thirty of which had been completed after the Mall exhibition only seven years before. A photograph of David standing by his unfinished forty-nine-inch-high carving in Norwegian rose marble, *Dawn Figure*, was the catalogue's frontispiece, an astonishing feat of endurance for a man of his years.

Again, his love of Africa was evident – with nineteen sculptures of leopards, lions and rhinos recording his seemingly indefatigable journeys to the continent – and two maquettes of recently completed private commissions were also shown. Both were major works: a bronze sculpture, *Melbourne Dancing Girls*, for an Australian collector and a ten-foot sculpture, *Pyramus and Thisbe*, for a new patron.

It was around this time that plans were formulated, again by David's friends and patrons, to create a lasting memorial to his work. In response to their proposal, Stowe, his old school, agreed to house a collection of more than a hundred pieces from David's creative output, bequeathed to the school in perpetuity, to be opened in time for his eighty-fourth birthday in 2010. The wheel, it seems, has come full circle. Most of David's maquettes and some other works he was not prepared to sell will now be housed permanently in the magnificent building, and will be accessible to the general public visiting the beautiful grounds which are managed by the National Trust. The David Wynne Foundation Trust, formed by David's friends, Sir David Scholey, Lord Lisle, Bill Shand Kidd and Robin Caiger Smith, his stepdaughter Nicola Reed and the school's headmaster Antony Wallensteiner, is behind the project.

And it was just after the plan had taken shape that I entered David's life. As a publisher, I had been sent a prospectus for a possible life of David, its text gathered together by, what seemed to me, a group who had assisted David in recording his memories into a tape-recorder. I was asked to see if a book was possible from the material. The prime movers in the endeavour were David's stepson Johnny, Robin Caiger Smith and David Inman, a fellow publisher, who suggested the initial approach to my smaller company. A mutual friend, whom David Inman had contacted, sent me the somewhat chaotic outline and asked did I know who David Wynne was?

Being a Londoner, I was of course a fan of *Boy with a Dolphin*, but I was also an avid listener to *Desert Island Discs* and I had never forgotten what I had always considered one of the most enjoyable of its programmes, David's second appearance as guest, with Sue Lawley as interviewer. Without much thought and, simply, intrigued, I met up with Inman to pursue possibilities. Gilli had first noticed Inman playing a flute at a school concert in Wimbledon and had told David to invite him to their house. He became involved with the remarkable atmosphere of 'the Rushmere Foundation'. He cautioned me that David, if we met, would be forthright, full of strong opinions, relentlessly, in the argot of the time, 'politically incorrect' and possibly 'difficult'.

In the casual way that publishers 'create' books, the two of us decided we would construct what essentially would be 'a coffee-table book'. I would edit the available text, fill in any of the gaps by talking with the sculptor, and write perhaps around 20,000 words, mostly as captions to the photographs of David and his work. There would be no long narrative; each prose piece would be related to an illustration, thus creating a melange of words and images to reflect the range and scope of Wynne's long life. It was agreed we three would meet at the sculptor's home and studio in Fulham and go for a meal in a nearby restaurant.

I had already done the text for three reasonably successful pop-up art books – on Van Gogh, Monet and Leonardo – and produced a celebratory account of the Royal Windsor Horse Show. I was nervous somewhat, but fairly sure I could do the job which was required for a book about a popular sculptor. I anticipated that I would be more a facilitator that an active participant.

It was on a Spring afternoon in 2006 that I first knocked on a heavy wooden door at the end of a gated cobbled close of what looked like a complex of converted workshops, near to the old Fulham pottery. The door was opened by a tall, startlingly handsome man with curly grey hair, offering a vigorous handshake and the words, 'I do like people who are punctual.' I followed him down a passage, lined with bookcases on which stood maquettes and smaller sculptures, some of which I was surprised I recognised, into a large bright room with skylights, more bookcases, paintings, plants and yet more sculptures.

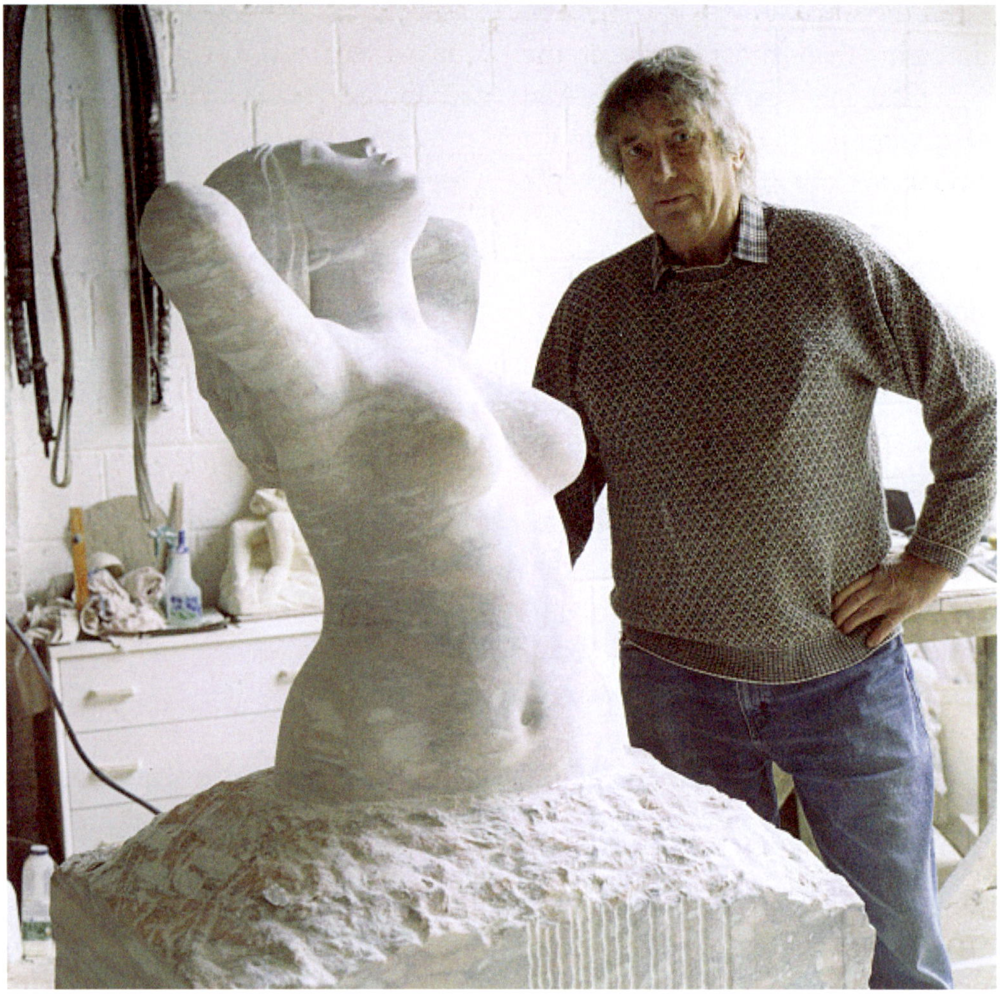

David with his unfinished carving in Norwegian rose marble, *Dawn Figure*

I noticed a bust of Virginia Wade, a ceramic by Picasso, a small, seemingly silver-plated head of the footballer Pelé on the large mantelpiece; a big oil painting which depicted Jesus hung high in a corner and to its left, in an alcove, glowed an exquisite green sculpture of a deity I took to be Buddha. On the other side of the fireplace I noticed two fine pencil drawings of a beautiful boy's head and across a wide opening, beyond which, behind a large table stacked with papers, there seemed to be an open-plan kitchen area, hung a remarkably well-executed portrait of a striking and equally beautiful woman with long grey hair. Wherever else I looked there were small, perfect statues of African animals. A circular iron staircase leading down to a dark basement was adjacent to a large red sofa, in front of the fireplace, where I was invited to sit and be given a glass of champagne. There was the unmistakable aroma of Havana cigars.

And so, for me, began a remarkable odyssey. By the end of the evening, past midnight, in a local bistro owned by a man called Felix to whom I was warmly introduced and who took an active part in the discussion, David had agreed to our idea. I was to meet with him the following week

having begun the work. I must also agree to attend his eightieth-birthday party at the Hurlingham Club in a few weeks' time. And of course my wife should come. I prepared a 'dummy' book for our first meeting – the equivalent, I thought, of a sculptor's maquette. I had divided a printer's blank bound book from an earlier project, which roughly met with the proportions for the book Inman and I had envisaged, into sections with appropriate headings, under which I had begun to edit the disparate text I had been given. It was clear from the start that David neither understood nor liked what I had done. I attempted to explain how I'd grouped the various bits of writing and suggested I leave the book with him, 'as homework' for him to fill in before our next meeting. He looked at me, but said nothing. We arranged to meet in two weeks' time.

He had not attempted to write anything when we next met. He had, he informed me, never liked 'homework'. I, on the other hand, had gone about trying to look at as many of David's public sculptures as I could. I visited the National Portrait Gallery, the renamed Carlton Tower, looked closely, for the first time, at the centrepiece of the Queen Mother Gates and went to the forecourt of the Mansion House. By chance in Wiltshire for a weekend, I had gone to Wells to gaze up at the *Risen Christ* and also visited the small Catholic church in Bradford-on-Avon where two of David's earliest commissions still stood either side of the main window. David, however, was more concerned at that second meeting with the sound system for his birthday party. He suggested I go with him in a taxi to Kensal Rise to collect it from a supplier who had let Johnny down and could not deliver. It was becoming clear to me that my involvement in writing this book was to be no simple matter.

It was that taxi ride which clinched my commitment to the project. 'I want the book,' he suddenly said to me, as we hurtled in a minicab around Shepherd's Bush, 'to be as enjoyable a read as Bill Bryson's are.' I knew then I had embarked on something which, even if I failed in the attempt, would give me the experience of knowing a remarkable man. At his Hurlingham party, surrounded by his family, world-famous rock stars, sporting legends, business tycoons, some outstandingly beautiful young women, a senior member of the royal family and legendary celebrities I recognised from certain fashionable magazines, I observed not only how much David seemed to be at the very centre of it all, but, as we all danced to an intimate performance by Donovan of his best-known songs, how much affection there was in the air. And I was the stranger, the newest recruit to David's special universe, where it seemed to me the constant celebration of love is manifest not only in his work but also in the way he lives his life.

Over the next few years I was to be intimately involved in the attempt to tell his story with his approval while being a witness both to remarkable further success in his professional life and to great personal tragedy. In a way, the final part of this book is as much a part of my story as it is of his.

We began a routine of regular visits together, with me either taking notes as David talked or recording his thoughts and memories into a small recording machine. I would transcribe the result of each visit in time for David's inspection and criticism at the next meeting. It was to be a long process, not made easier by the fact that David's memory could at times fail him. I found it strange that a man whose career had been so productive but who had disdained the commercial apparatus available to the successful artist – which he so obviously was – had retained so little in the way of documentation. At times his memory was exact. He always knew when I had made a mistake transcribing a sculpture's size or title. He remembered details of how each sculpture had been made and the problems which accompanied each installation or exhibition.

Around our tenth meeting, some three months into the routine we had established, he mentioned that Gilli had kept scrapbooks of the press coverage of his work. He seemed almost apologetic in showing them to me, stacked on the floor in his cellar. He had had no interest in collecting such things, he told me, but Gilli had insisted. The albums, with old press cuttings and photographs glued down, now brown with age, were a vital resource in establishing a sequence in David's rise to commercial success and in providing me with considerable insight into just what an extraordinary life David had lived. The albums stopped with Gilli's death.

During our first summer working together, David made a trip to his beloved Africa. We had written together by then perhaps the first third of his life. We were working on the period of his first international success with the New York exhibition and the enormous publicity which accompanied the Beatles' portrait heads. David returned from Africa and for a few weeks seemed fine, but it was becoming clear that he was entering a deep depression. I noticed that I irritated him if I transcribed something incorrectly or made a mistake. Eventually he mentioned that he felt unwell. Our work slowed down. Often we would have to stop discussing the topic which was concerning us and simply sit in silence. Once, to his embarrassment, he cried.

We began walking over Putney Bridge to eat together in one of the restaurants near the shopping centre. He was always courteous and alert, but I often felt that I might be contributing some additional stress to what was clearly an ordeal. Once or twice, especially if I saw him on a Saturday, we would watch sport on his television. He told me that getting absorbed in the action on the screen calmed him down. I lent him a copy of William Styron's book on that writer's own life-long struggle with depression, but I was never sure that he read it.

It lasted for four months. I turned up one evening and he told me he felt better. He had begun work that day on a small maquette of birds in flight. I asked him if anything had happened. He told me that he had walked one late afternoon along by the river and suddenly noticed some birds fly up and across, past the trees and over the water towards Barnes. As he stood and watched them he felt that something lifted within him – as if he had passed through the blackness. He told me this quietly, without emphasis, almost as if it was as ordinary an event as posting a letter.

Within weeks we were back into the routine. David had been told that the fountain he had made long ago for the Wimbledon Shopping Centre was being reconstructed after a campaign by an old lady who felt the statue should have been reinstated when the centre had been redeveloped. The local council had received a petition, accepted the cost of relocation, and invited David as guest of honour to the unveiling ceremony. He had to give, he told me, a 'bloody speech'.

A commission had come from the owner of a chain of food shops to create a large bird sculpture for his garden and David and Robin had started work on it. It was to be over four foot in height and positioned outside the man's country house, overlooking an extensive garden. The most convincing evidence that David was once more his proper self was his excitement at the chance to accompany Prince Michael on a trip to Russia. The prince had asked him to come with him to Moscow to attend a special gala concert in Red Square in celebration of the violin. Some of the world's most famous soloists were booked to perform in the vastness of the square, with a full symphony orchestra. The royal party would then travel to St Petersburg where the prince was to address a conference in the Russian Museum. David had never been to Russia and his excitement was clear. I saw him a few days before he went and while we were talking a man delivered a new pair of shoes. David told me he couldn't travel to Russia without good shoes. It turned out to be an extraordinary trip. Before the actual concert, the visitors were entertained in the Kremlin, shown rooms full of treasures rarely seen by guests and then driven by limousine under the walls of the fortress along a special road constructed solely for the Russian leaders to drive straight up into the central part of Red Square.

The plan to place a permanent exhibition of David's work at Stowe was also progressing well. Eventually to be housed in the Blue Drawing Room, in a spacious wing of the main school building, the collection comprises more than a hundred

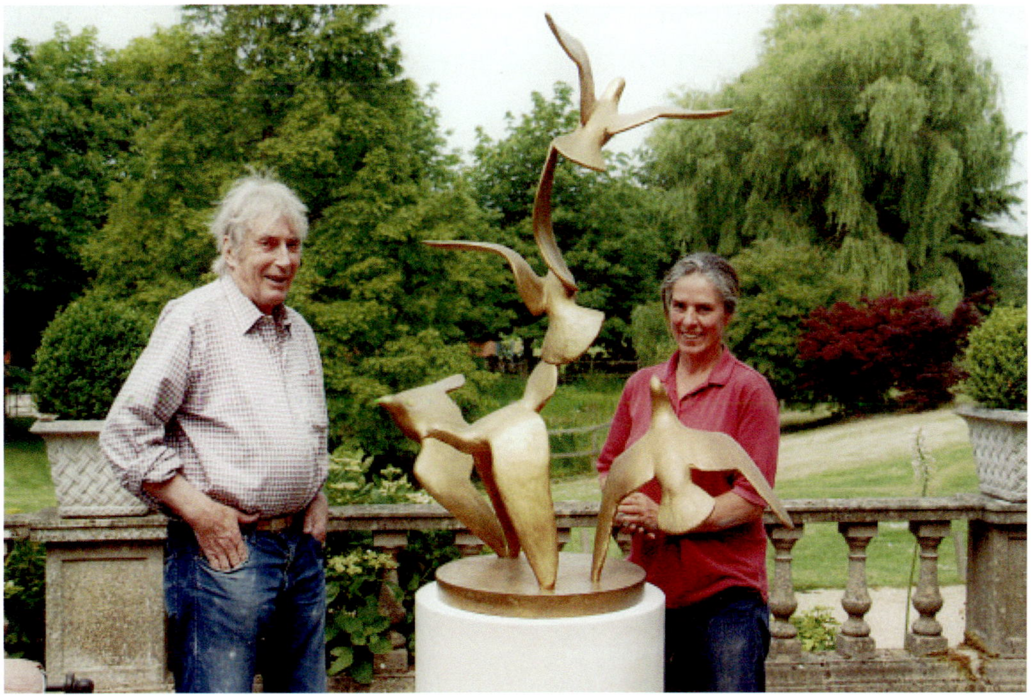

David and Robin with the large bird sculpture

exhibits covering the entire range of David's creative life. On permanent display will be the maquettes of most of his major works alongside many smaller sculptures of his beloved animals and birds, with a fine range of drawings, sketches and examples of the meticulous diagrammatic explorations he constructs on his drawing-board as each sculpture evolves. Careful measurements ensure each armature will work and fine lines carefully drawn show the outline of every piece.

Even with the recent development of what is thought to be mild Parkinson's disease, David's desire to work is constant. Irritated by a growing arthritic condition,

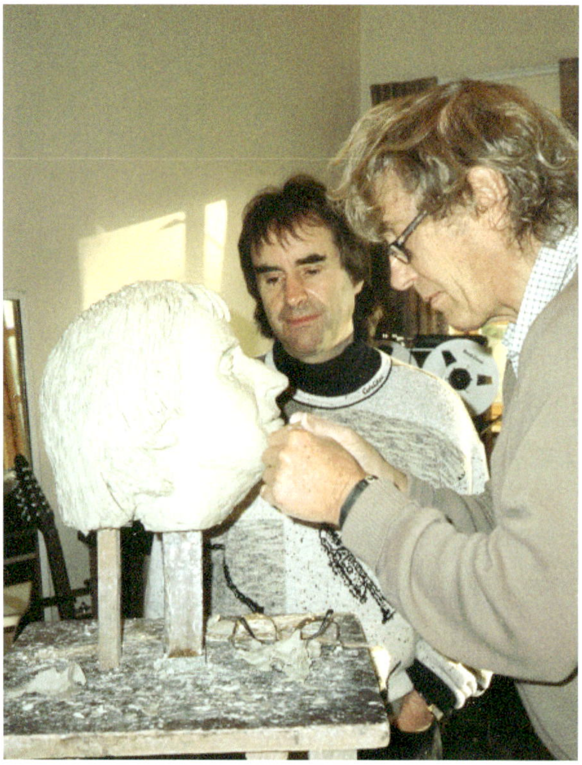

David sculpting Chris de Burgh

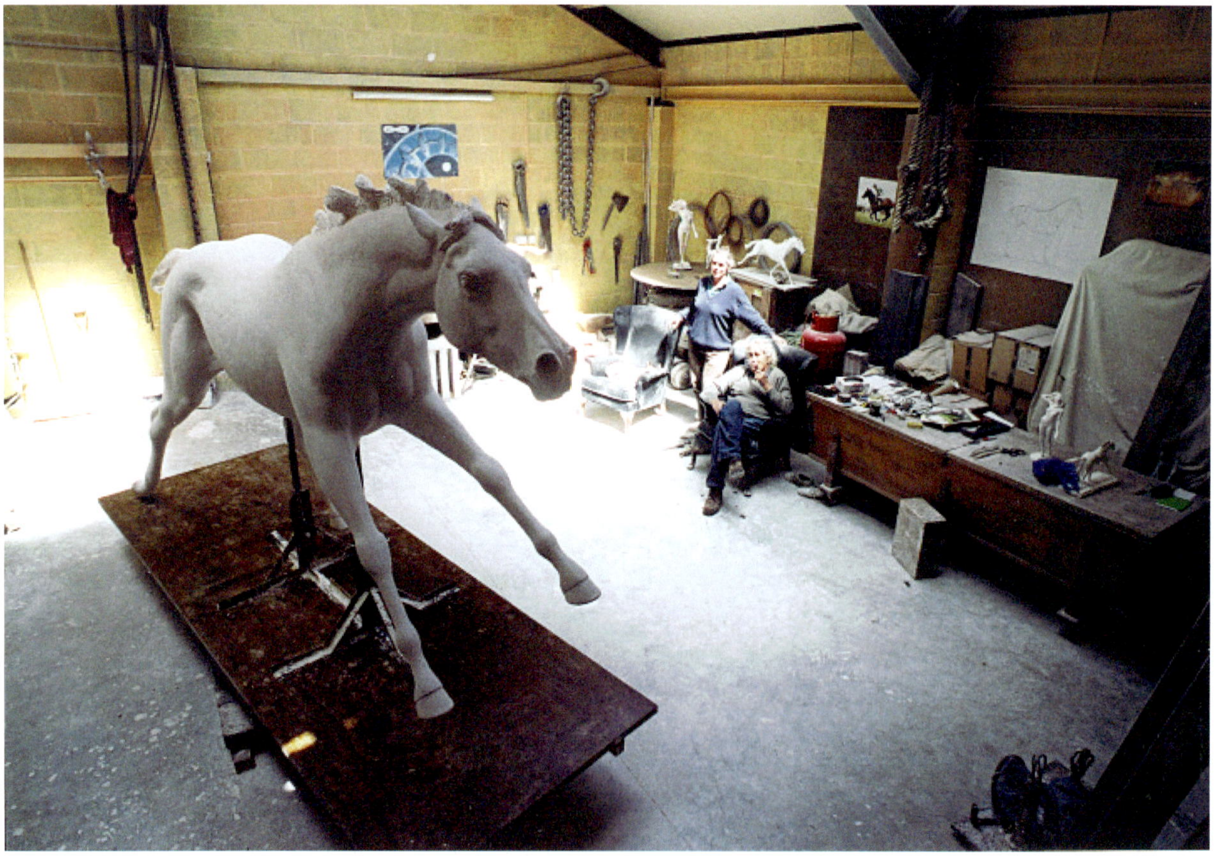

David and Robin in the studio with *Sinndar* plaster

his drive to create sculpture overcomes infirmity. At the end of our sessions on the book, he would often invite me into his studio to see what his current project was looking like. I never failed to marvel when, carefully removing the damp cloth, complaining bitterly about his creaking bones, he revealed a remarkable work in progress to my fascinated gaze – a figure on its way from armature to final glory. And when Trinity College placed *Girl with the Doves* in its grounds, marking the occasion with a grand dinner, David's professional journey seemed to me almost complete. One of his loveliest works will remain for ever in the place where his fateful choice of direction was made so many years ago.

In the midst of all these events, there came another devastating blow. I had arranged to see David late one September afternoon in 2007, but the bell wasn't answered. Concerned, as this was unusual, I pushed the bundle of writing I had brought for his approval through the letterbox and telephoned David Inman. I left a message hoping all was well. The next day, just as I was about to attend a book launch in Notting Hill, he phoned me back. Johnny had died in a motorcycle accident. Swerving to avoid a car, which had suddenly driven out in front of him on a Somerset road, David's 'dependable toad' had been killed instantly. It was a loss beyond measure.

I had witnessed their closeness. When I was with him, it was nearly always Johnny David telephoned when certain facts had to be checked or something needed to be done. And as David's telephone allowed for the speaker to be overheard, I had listened in on many conversations. There seemed to be no problem Johnny could not settle. He grew to be an expert woodworker and inventor. His ability to help David in the construction of difficult armatures was invaluable and always ingenious. Their closeness was profound. His loss left David desperate, but still he managed to work. Although he had his other children, Robin and a multitude of friends to ease the process of mourning, it did seem to me that a certain sparkle had been lost for ever.

But it was in his sculpture, the constant source of consolation, that he took refuge. The project he turned to was the creation of a large piece, *Horse and Dog*, which he completed with the help of Robin in 2008. A life-size sculpture of two animals frolicking, it was yet another work commissioned by a collector of David's art.

And what's left to say? David is once more engaged on an epic adventure. He is sculpting a life-size statue of the Beatles, commissioned to stand at Stowe. It will be completed by 2011 and, as I write, he is working on studies for the first maquette, George Harrison. The last time I saw him he showed me Harrison's electric guitar, lent to him by the singer's wife. John and Paul will be next. Ringo's drumkit will be carefully measured and the exact proportions will be honoured. No doubt, there will be one hell of party when the work is unveiled.

It is a cliché that life is circular (and it may well be that David will be setting out again on some new project in 2012), but this remarkable man, by serendipity, ferocious tenacity, huge charm and seductive bravado has come full circle. The timid Stowe schoolboy who loved animals will leave a masterpiece of sculpture in the grounds of his old school – a portrait of perhaps the greatest musical group of all time. As David so often tells me: 'It can't get better than this.'

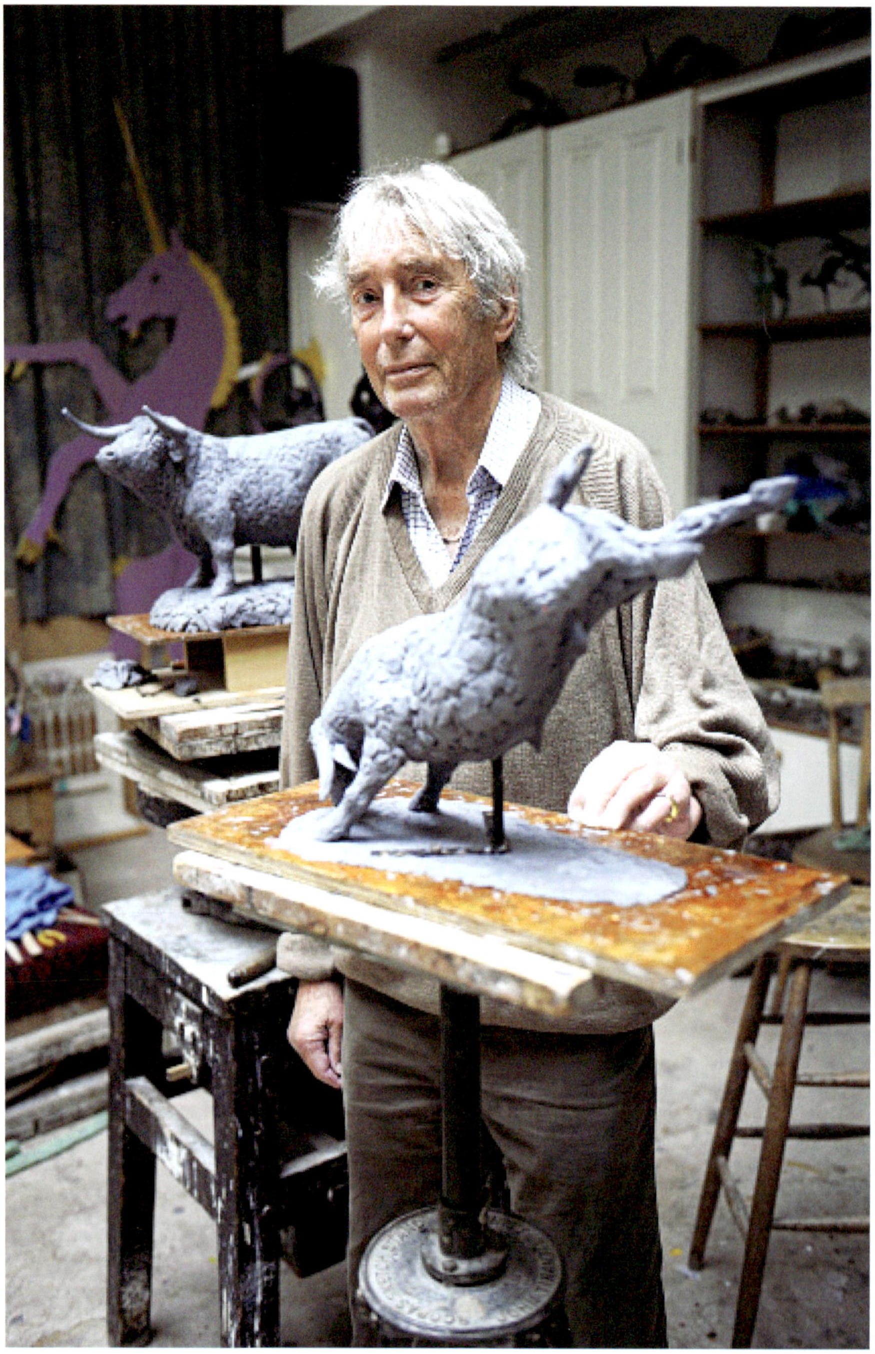

Envoi

Ever since I was a little boy I experienced feelings of wonder, love and even ecstasy sometimes when I watched a bird, an animal or a beautiful boy or girl – this is what I longed to share with people.

Measurements of SHAREEF DANCER : 9th August 1984 (

4 year old Bay ♂ by Northern Dancer, out of Sweet

Measurements of SHAHRISTANI 1986 (in red): Chantilly 31st

15·2¼ hds. + white 3 yrs.

by Nijinsky out of Shademah

Girth 64cm to ground 90cm

ridden by Wally S. with jockey Wally lad Geoff

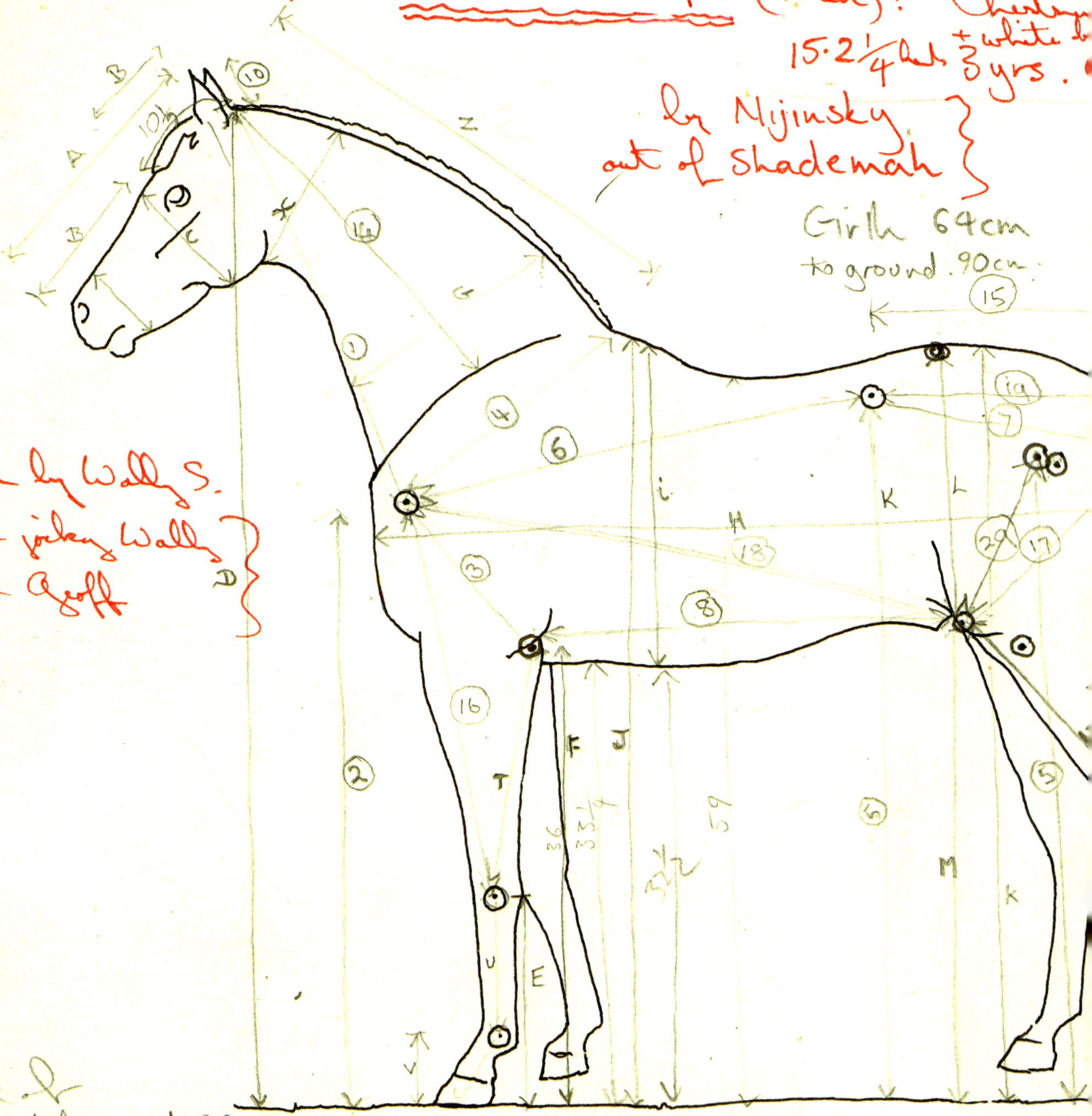

(28) Top of Hock pt to ground 23

(29) trocanta > stifle

(19) Hip to tail root 18

(20) Stifle > hock point 20

(21) " > " joint 22

(22) Stifle > ground 39½

(24) Hock joint " " 21

(25) Gt trocanta > ground

(26) Hip > ground ?

(27) Withers > back base 49

(9) – last rib to pelvi

(12) round Girth

(13) Tail tip to ground

(14) Poll to mid-shoul

(15) Hip to back of torso(

(16) Width (from side)

(17) Stifle to arm bo

(18) Shoulder to stifle